Auditioning on Camera

To win a screen role, an actor must learn to contend with an on-camera audition. Understanding how to make the crucial adjustments to one's craft that this kind of audition requires is vital to the career of any screen actor.

Auditioning on Camera sets out the key elements of a successful on-camera audition and explains how to put them into practice. Joseph Hacker draws on 35 years of acting experience to guide the reader through the screen auditioning process with an engaging and undaunting approach. Key elements examined include:

- textual analysis
- knowing where to look
- dealing with nerves
- on-camera interviews
- using the environment
- retaining the camera's focus.

The book also features point-by-point chapter summaries, as well as a glossary of acting and technical terms, and is a comprehensive and enlightening resource for screen actors of all levels.

Joseph Hacker is an associate professor of theatre practice at the University of Southern California. He is also an actor and producer with over 30 years' experience, having appeared in such seminal TV series as *24*, *Quantum Leap* and *The Twilight Zone*.

Auditioning on Camera

An Actor's Guide

Joseph Hacker

Routledge
Taylor & Francis Group

LONDON AND NEW YORK

First published 2012
by Routledge
2 Park Square, Milton Park, Abingdon, Oxon OX14 4RN

Simultaneously published in the USA and Canada
by Routledge
711 Third Avenue, New York, NY 10017

Routledge is an imprint of the Taylor & Francis Group, an informa business

British Library Cataloguing in Publication Data
A catalogue record for this book is available from the British Library

Library of Congress Cataloging in Publication Data
Hacker, Joseph.
    Auditioning on Camera : an actor's guide / Joseph Hacker.
    p. cm.
    Includes bibliographical references.
    1. Television acting. 2. Acting–Auditions. 3. Television broadcasting–
    Auditions. I. Title.
    PN1992.8.A3H33 2011
    791.4502'8–dc22
    2010052324

ISBN: 978–0–415–49099–3 (hbk)
ISBN: 978–0–415–58565–1 (pbk)
ISBN: 978–0–203–84617–9 (ebk)

Typeset in Univers Light
by Saxon Graphics Ltd, Derby

Printed and bound in Great Britain by
CPI Antony Rowe, Chippenham, Wiltshire

When I dare to be powerful
to use my strength in the service of my vision,
then it becomes less and less important
whether I am afraid.

... *Audre Lorde*
Feb 18, 1934–Nov 17, 1992

Contents

Exercises   x
Acknowledgements   xi
Preface   xiii

SECTION I
WHAT THE CAMERA REQUIRES

CHAPTER 1   Who you are shouts so loudly
            I can't hear what you're saying   1

            You and the camera 1

CHAPTER 2   "Just relax and be yourself" –
            a tototally worthless piece of advice 25

            Nerves and the camera 25

CHAPTER 3   When the camera is in the room,
            guess who's not there?   40

            On-camera interviews 40

CHAPTER 4 I asked him, "How do I get to where you are?" "Oh," he said, "that's impossible … but there are a million ways." 51

Agents, monologues and headshots 51

SECTION II
ON-CAMERA AUDITION STRATEGIES

CHAPTER 5 I knew you were perfect for the part the moment you walked into the room 65

Your on-camera entry 65

CHAPTER 6 Calm them by knowing what you want to do 83

How on-camera auditions go 83

On-camera audition strategies 87

Auditioning in pairs 104

Callbacks on camera 108

CHAPTER 7 "I really really really want to get this part but I'm not sure how I should play it" 114

The structure of drama and what it means to your acting choices 114

CHAPTER 8 He buys his ties in the city 137

Wardrobe strategies for on-camera auditions 137

CHAPTER 9 Your eyes/your thoughts 146

The importance of where your character looks 146

CHAPTER 10 The place/your thoughts 155

The place *is* the circumstance 155

SECTION III
SCENE PREPARATION FOR
ON-CAMERA AUDITIONS

CHAPTER 11 How to paint a nose   167

    Basic philosophy 167

CHAPTER 12 What needs to happen   177

    Analyzing the story/the scene 177

CHAPTER 13 Acting is doing. Meaningful acting
    is doing in an emotional context   183

    Creating the character:
    actions and circumstances 183

    Dealing with preconceptions 198

    Love scenes and further notes 204

CHAPTER 14 Somewhere, someone thinks it's funny 208

    Comedy: some guidelines 208

CHAPTER 15 Evil be now my good   225

    Auditioning for the villain 225

CHAPTER 16 Lights! Camera! … *then* Action   243

    Secrets to creating a winning
    "virtual" audition 243

CHAPTER 17 **Overall summary and a few choice perspectives** 256

    Final comment 256

    Bibliography   261
    Index   263

Exercises

CHAPTER 1   Twenty-Year Friend   11

Free Association Technique   17

CHAPTER 3   Practice Talking to the Camera in the
Second Person; i.e. Using the Word "You"   41

Body Expressiveness   43

Big as the Room   44

The Dynamics of Eye Contact   45

Look Back at Who is Looking at You:
The Camera   47

Put a Camera in Your Life   49

CHAPTER 5   Working with "Mental Verbs"   80

CHAPTER 13   Create a Character Portfolio   201

Speak Through What Attracts You   206

CHAPTER 14   Your Voice Needs to be Out "in Front"   219

Biggest Building in the World   222

CHAPTER 15   The Evil Shadow   232

Injury/Issue/Desire   239

Revenge   240

Acknowledgements

To my students: I have a thousand faces in mind, proud of you all, you know who you are … your energy, ambition and, yes, even occasional brilliance gratify my life as a teacher. I love what I do, and it is because of you. I am particularly grateful for the support of Edwin Porris and Julia McIlvaine, who took time to labor critically through my early drafts, and to my friend Joanna Kerns for her generous reflections on the topic.

To the faculty of the USC School of Theater, most notably Professors Sharon Carnicke, Angus Fletcher, Mary Joan Negro, Brian Parsons and Jack Rowe, whose invaluable advice and enthusiasm for my efforts encouraged me to persevere. To our former dean, Robert Scales, who took a chance on me. And to Dean Madeline Puzo who has had the vision to foster a faculty of rare energy, excellence, and devotion to our students in the performing arts.

To the editorial and production staff at Routledge: Talia Rodgers, Ben Piggott, Niall Slater and Stacey Carter; to Rob Brown at Saxon Graphics and Marie Lister; and to my sister Betsy Chimento who offered her considerable talents (and patience) in supporting this effort.

To my teachers: I cannot speak or write a word without the spirit of Peggy Feury, Bill Traylor, Stella Adler, Shawn Nelson, Bedich Batka, and my dear friend Horton Foote, Jr., teachers all, in their own way, legendary to me, who have inspired me over the years through their work and wisdom ... who not only extended their treasured friendship, but whose insights on the art and craft of acting are, in fact, the inspiration and measure of my work.

And above all, to my family ... my dear wife, Maurine, whose advice, patience and good counsel straightened my path; and to my children, Emily and Wells, whose looks of pride and encouragement ever guide me toward the light.

... My most heart-felt gratitude.

Preface

I have never read a preface in my life that didn't make me impatient to get on to the meat of the material. So I am going to keep this short.

For openers: You probably wouldn't be thumbing through this book unless something about auditioning is frustrating you, or you suspect there is something you need to know about auditioning on camera in order to advance your career.

Learning how to audition can be a bear. First off, you never get to see anyone else do it; you're always in the casting office alone. You sit out in the waiting room surrounded by other actors all of whom look pretty much like you ... and through the producer's door you can hear the dull murmur of an actor auditioning, often in a tone unlike what you have prepared. As you question your choices the door swings open and out comes the competition in a cloud of moist heat from inside the room. You try to read his face to get a sense of what is going on in there, but too late ... you're next. In you go.

Secondly, when you do *really* well and are therefore in contention, the casting people just stare at you in a peculiarly quizzical way and dismiss you with a far-off "thank you." (I refer you back to the last sentence of this book's dedication.) This is because casting the right actor is by far and away their most crucial decision. They are reluctant to lay claim to a possible choice too eagerly. (A lesson they probably learned the hard way.) The pressure to get it right is huge. Conversely, if they jump up and say "good job!" it's a good bet you're *not* getting the job, which can be very confusing. (They just want to get you to leave as politely as possible.) You drive home thinking you nailed it … but then they just stared at you. Or, you drive home thinking it didn't go very well … but they said you were terrific. You start fixing things that aren't broken, everything gets all out of balance, the whole process can spiral into a state of self-doubt and second-guessing.

And lastly, there is a world of difference between performing an audience-tested scene from one of modern literature's great works, which is what we rightly do in acting classes, and auditioning for a role in an original screenplay that has never seen the light of day. There is an uncertainty factor, an element of gamble in the latter situation since you never truly know whether your creative interpretation is going to work.

Over my 35 years as an actor I have auditioned for the camera literally thousands of times. When I look back on it all I realize that when things went well, the same things always happened. Not necessarily on purpose and not necessarily in the same order … but there they were. Whenever any one element was missing or hadn't unfolded as a natural and authentic response to the circumstances of the audition, somehow the encounter fumbled and success didn't materialize.

This book identifies those elements, puts them in a sequence, and offers ways to make them work.

In the opening meeting of my class, "Auditioning for the Camera" through the USC Theater Department where I have been teaching for over 15 years, I typically refer to this sequence of audition elements and then illustrate a crucial point by holding up a fold-out from *Sports Illustrated* magazine … the classic teaching tool, namely a pixellated sequence of photos breaking down a good golf swing instant by instant. You've all seen what I am talking about. Each side-by-side photo shows in small increments the sequence of positions a golfer goes through when he hits a ball well. And that is how I break down the process an actor faces when auditioning for the camera ... a sequence made up of specific events, event by event. That's the only way I know how to teach it, by breaking it down. But I emphasize with great theatricality that: You ... Can ... Not ... Hit ... A ... Golf ... Ball ... Like ... That! You have to swing the club. *Swing it!* You have to release yourself from the idea that you do this and then you do that and then that. You must let go of the sequence, trust your body, your training and your practice, and let 'er rip. Just so with auditioning: you have to be aware, know what it is you want to do, practice and see how it goes and how it feels; you have to make it your own in your own way and your own style ... and then you have to let it go and "swing the club."

YOU WON'T WORK IF YOU CAN'T "READ."

... Craig T. Nelson, actor

An actor doesn't go for very long in his career without realizing that the way an actor makes a living is by auditioning. The remuneration you receive when you finally do land a job is recompense for all the unrequited auditions that came before. These days an actor must master techniques tailored to the specific requirements of auditioning in front of a camera as opposed to those required for work on stage. As you pursue your career, you will witness in your workshop and scene study many actors who are terrific in class but they never get an agent, or if they do, they never land a role. The only answer to this contradiction must be because they are doing something in their on-camera auditions that isn't effective.

If you can get the job, you can do the job. The problem is getting the job.

An audition is not a suggestion. It is a full-out performance. Any director will tell you that 90% of directing is casting. As I said before, casting is the most crucial decision they face in putting a project together. If they select the right combination of actors there won't be a whole lot to talk about on the set. It is your audition that communicates to the director the full breadth of what you will bring to the role. It also confirms in your own mind that you and the director are "on the same page." Otherwise he wouldn't have cast you.

I hope to inspire you to realize that the audition is not a booby trap; rather it is the one unalloyed opportunity for you to show the powers that be how the part should be played.

Never lose sight of the fact that whenever you see a performance on the screen you admire, it's a good bet *it was performed **better** in the audition.* And when you finally do get cast in a part, you will see that what you achieved in the audition will compare very favorably to whatever you manifest the day of the shoot.

To get the job you will have to fit the physical and emotional circumstances of the script to the physical realities of the on-camera audition situation. You will most likely be auditioning in a strange office with a casting assistant operating the camera; you will likely be reading the scene without benefit of having read the entire script; and you will often be reading with a casting director who is both "acting" and watching you at the same time. There are no rehearsals and no re-takes. But even with these constraints, whether you read seated in a chair or move about in the room, you won't get the part unless you create a reality on camera that "makes it work."

Here's what will happen

Luck: preparedness in the face of opportunity

As your career unfolds you will see that success or progress most often comes from responding to an opportunity that comes from an unexpected direction. One thing leads to another. When you talk to actors whose careers you admire you will see that they each have a different story. There is no one way to make a career happen … But this is how it always goes:

> You will have some kind of a job or financial support that enables you to pursue your career. You are going to be studying acting. This is a must: you must be actively and persistently studying with a teacher you respect and with a group of fellow actors whose talent inspires your own. You will be involved in a theater group that produces plays regularly. And you will be making yourself available to act in student and low budget films.

Early or late, somewhere along the line you are going to get a meeting with an agent, a casting director or a producer. This is going to happen in one of four ways (in no particular order of likelihood):

- You are going to know somebody who knows somebody who, as a favor to them, will be willing to see you; or:
- You are going to have a chance encounter in a social gathering that leads to a meeting; or:
- You will be in a play or film that an agent sees who will, by virtue of your performance, be interested in meeting you; or:
- Either by way of the internet or by sending out a ton of 8   10s with a brief cover letter, some agent will see your picture and want to meet you.

So you are going to get this meeting … we'll need to talk about that.

The meeting goes well; the agent or manager arranges for you to meet others, or audition for others … we'll need to talk about that.

Those auditions, and sometimes those meetings, will very often take place on camera … and that is what this book is principally about.

A friend of mine who read the first draft of this book asked me, "Who is your audience: experienced or inexperienced actors?" My answer to him is both, since I wish I had known all this from the very beginning, but also I was a very experienced actor before many of the ideas in this book were evident to me.

Drawing principally from the lessons I learned the hard way as an actor through countless auditions, I have taught more than a thousand students in my years at USC. Truthfully, my greatest thrill is when my students come back after an on-camera audition and tell me it all went exactly as I said it would – just how we practiced – exactly as we discussed – and that what they learned from me worked. Here's what I teach them.

What the Camera Requires

CHAPTER 1

Who you are shouts so loudly I can't hear what you're saying

... Ralph Waldo Emerson

YOU AND THE CAMERA

The introduction of the video camera to the audition or interview process some 30 years ago frustrated me terribly. I had grown confident with the old-fashioned way of dealing with the casting people and/or the producers as they sat on a couch and watched what I had to offer. I liked that the warm bodies – the decision-makers – were right there in front of me. I could "read" them, their reactions to me, and adjust. But all that changed with the invention of the easy-to-use, instant exposure, autofocus, instant playback video-cam. Suddenly I was auditioning or interviewing in an empty room in front of some third-echelon casting assistant who was more worried about keeping his/her own job than helping me get mine; who was telling me to stand or sit in a certain place and not do anything that would screw up the camera work. It was altogether different ... very cold, very unresponsive, and most of all very quiet. Whoever was judging me might as well have been on another planet, watching my tape with a fast forward button in his/her hand. I didn't know what to do, or how to control the situation. I wanted it to be like it was before.

And in my resentment and frustration I got angry and burned a lot of bridges. Stupid. Slowly, through painful trial and error I learned what was required, how to prepare and what to anticipate. The following are observations and techniques that apply specifically to *on-camera interviews*.

The Camera

Spencer Tracy was once asked, what was the secret of acting. His answer was, "Don't let anybody ever catch you doing it."

Here is the most essential thing to realize about the camera: *It can pretty much read your mind!* I will allude to this many times for numerous reasons in this and coming chapters. The camera knows what is going on with you. It always does, it always will. It can see right through you. If you don't align yourself with your true state of being; if you try to pretend to be something that you aren't or avoid acknowledging what is true about yourself, the camera picks up on it. The camera is more sensitive to this than a live audience. It senses any disparity, if there is one, between your true state of being and that which you are presenting.

Especially in the beginning of your career, before you are a known entity, this basic fact about the camera comes into play big time when you go in to meet an agent or casting director who is just "trying to get to know you." These meetings are often videotaped. This type of meeting is called "a general" … meaning a general meeting. A "general" has no particular shape to it or objective other than to get a look at you and try to get a feel for who you are and what you're like on camera. You will run into this situation in "preliminary meetings" with casting directors for specific projects where there is no script and therefore no scene to perform. In this situation there is no way you can figure what "they" are looking for. Similarly, this type of interview comes up for commercials with no speaking lines, where the action is so simple anyone could do it …

where, for instance, you simply sip a cup of coffee or happily take a product off a shelf.

Under these circumstances you will be "interviewed" on camera. They'll ask you a question or two as a way of giving you a chance to present yourself. It is because of the unique power of the camera to know exactly what is going on with you that I have chosen the following two exercises/approaches as the subject of this book's first chapter. I call them **"Twenty-Year Friend"** and **"The Free Association Technique."** Their applications come actively into play in the above-mentioned circumstances.

We will deal with the nuts and bolts of on-camera technique soon enough. I know you're anxious to get to it. But these two approaches have so much to do with performing effectively for the camera that the other technical stuff won't matter until you "get" the essence of these two concepts first. You could call them square one in achieving success with your on-camera interviews and performances.

Twenty-Year Friend and The Free Association Technique

I will say it many times in many different ways: Your most essential job on-camera is:

To communicate your emotional relationship to whatever you are talking about through body language, gesture and tone of voice.

I want to make something clear. This does not mean you talk about your feelings. It means the viewer can perceive your feelings, not through what you say, but by how you say it ... your tone of voice, body language, and gestures. The camera is particularly good at this. Therefore, for example, if you ask me where I was raised, I might answer factually – flatly and remotely: "Cleveland." You learn very little about me this way. Or I can slump my shoulders, cast my gaze downward, smile slightly at the irony, then look at you as if seeking sympathy and answer, "Cleveland." Through this you learn a ton. There's a world of difference. And this latter is what the camera likes. *Who and what we are is communicated primarily through our body language, gestures and tone of voice.*

Numerous human behavior studies confirm this.

What else about the camera? In her insightful book *Acting in Commercials* (Back Stage Books, page 48) Joan See observes:

> *The camera wants you to express exactly what is going on with you. The more you share with it, the more it will take care of you.*

This is precisely why so many of our politicians seem so smarmy on TV; the camera magnifies the disconnection between their true nature and their public personae ... i.e. the way they think they should behave in public in their effort to control what we think about them. It is not attractive. In fact it puts us off. The same will be true for you on camera if you try the same thing.

Michael Caine encourages us to think of the camera as the perfect lover, who loves us completely just exactly as we are, and who indulges and craves our every thought, our every impulse; we can do no wrong (*Acting in Film*, Applause Books, page 3). What this means for your on-camera interviews is: If you are an actor who has an itch you are not scratching, the camera sees a person who has an itch they are refusing to scratch. If you are an actor who is bored but thinks you should be peppy, the camera sees a bored person trying to be peppy. On the other hand, if you are bored and you communicate your boredom, the camera finds you fascinating.

The camera sees exactly what is going on with you. There is no escape. Or there is utter freedom ... depending on how you want to look at it.

Twenty-Year Friend

So what to do? The answer is you must find a way to stop worrying about "saying the right thing" and start focusing on communicating your *emotional connection* to whatever it is you *are* saying.

If you think about it, this is actually how you behave with your best friends. When you are with them you have no particular agenda. You're not trying to control the direction of the conversation. Basically you compare notes about life. You talk about whatever comes to mind at the moment. You communicate your true feelings about it through body and gesture. You are as interested in them as you are in yourself. You ask about them. You react to what you perceive in them. You don't put on airs. There is no formality about it. You know you will be forgiven if you somehow say something "wrong." They are in your corner. They are on your side. They like you.

The camera wants you to behave the same way you do with your very best friends. So do the rest of us.

You need to start allowing yourself ... practicing ... the freedom of talking to strangers as if you have known them for 20 years. Start now. You will need this skill big time sooner than you think in these specific (and crucial) instances:

- Whenever you meet a person in the business, including big stars or famous producers.
- When you meet an agent for the first time ... right from the first instant you encounter each other.
- Whenever you are on camera for a "general."
- Whenever you are being interviewed on-camera for a part that has no script yet or requires something very simple, as often happens for commercials.
- Whenever you are paired up with another actor (with whom you have had little or no rehearsal time) to go in and do a scene where the characters have a specific relationship ... as if you were best

friends or newlyweds or work partners, etc. (We will talk about this important situation later.)

This skill is so important I tell my students they will not work until they master it. Or another way of looking at it is, when they finally do get work (or attract the interest of an agent or manager) part of the reason will be because they will have done the following: They will have allowed themselves to talk to casting directors, directors, agents, other actors, movie stars, bigwigs, even studio chieftains … all as co-workers, right from the first moment, just as with good friends they enjoy being with regularly; as people who are on their side; who work together; enjoy each other, and collaborate with each other; each confident that they contribute vitally to the whole; each being needed, each being valued, each good at what they do.

Be forewarned. I learned this lesson the hard way years ago. The second job I ever had called for me to play with Dean Martin. Dean Martin! I wasn't a big fan of his but it was … Dean Martin! I was introduced to him one minute and the next I was supposed to be his assistant in his law firm. I didn't play that first scene very well. I was intimidated and formal … because I didn't have control of "Twenty-Year Friend."

Look, I am not talking about doing a lot of cursing or expressing taboo subjects. But ask yourself: Why do you think the behavior you use with your best friends would not be winning with strangers? Your friends aren't crazy for liking you, are they? I am suggesting that you are not a crazy weirdo, your friends like you and they are not crazy for liking you … you should trust this. They like you for being who you are … so will an agent or a producer as well as the camera if you let yourself behave this way.

The first time this will likely come into play will be when some agent or manager calls you in because he saw your 8 × 10, or saw you in a local production, and would like to meet you. (See Chapter 4: "Agents, Monologues and Headshots.") What is misleading about these interviews, on-camera or otherwise, is they feel like formal social situations. You are in a strange place, you're meeting new people, you dress carefully, you want to make a good impression ... so you feel like you should be on what your parents would call your best behavior. "Appropriate." Everything they ever told you about making a good impression kicks in: grooming, manners, comportment. Our elders rightfully condition us as children to do this. We learn what it means; we learn how to do it; and we think it is the appropriate strategy for an acting interview. *Wrong*. Don't misunderstand me. This behavior is most definitely the best approach if you are applying for a job at a local bank or as a salesperson at a department store or in purely social situations. But in our business, as *actors*, this is not the best orientation to an interview. Because an audition or meeting with a casting director, or a conversation with a director is not a social situation ... it is work: you are at *work* as an actor. You must not go in hat-in-hand as if they are the cheeses and you are the lowly mouse looking for a morsel; or as if your version of sincere good manners and ardor are the key to being taken seriously. The interview situation requires you, the real you ... not the formal, mannerly you that is actually designed to control what people think about you. Believe it or not, the person you are is much more interesting and engaging than the person you think you should be.

A few years ago while addressing this issue with my students I exhorted the class: "Even if it is Warren Beatty, I am telling you, talk to him as if you've known him for 20 years!" Well, coincidentally, Warren Beatty and Annette Bening were guests at the cinema school across campus that weekend. One of my students went to the symposium and said to himself: "Okay, Hacker said to go talk to him like I knew him." And he did and they ended up having a 20-minute conversation. By the way, Matt started the conversation with the casual comment, "Nice sport coat!" I can tell you if Matt had gone up and genuflected and humbly said, "Oh, Mr. Beatty, I am so honored to meet you, etc.," that conversation would have been over in ten seconds. Guaranteed.

I remember a Brian Epstein interview on public television, recalling when he first met the Beatles; he said he didn't decide to be their manager in the beginning because he recognized some major talent in them; the fact was he just liked them. He thought they were funny.

Another one of my students, whose father was a big mucky-muck financier, reported that she decided to try out my Twenty-Year Friend approach on some of her father's biggest international potentates. Her father had asked her to play host to them while he finished up some calls. Later the word came back: "That was the most confident, impressive, self-assured young woman they had ever met."

Years ago toward the beginning of my career I went in to meet with Mike Fenton, a well-known casting director who was meeting actors to fill one of the smaller parts in a feature called *Damnation Alley* (1977, directed by Jack Smight). As I walked in all pumped up bright and smiley I saw him slumped at his desk, clearly weary, girding himself for yet another interviewee. The impression he made in that microsecond was very strong. I don't know what possessed me but I dropped my façade, stopped in my tracks and said something like: "Man, it must wear you out to deal with all the peppy people who come charging through this door." We talked a little bit about that. Within three minutes he reached for the phone and said to the director: "Jack, I got a guy up here I want you to meet." Yes, I got the job. Looking back on it that was one of the first clues I got about the importance of Twenty-Year Friend. I cannot tell you how many of my students come back saying Twenty-Year Friend is one of the most important contributors to their success.

Okay, enough of the testimonials: how do we deal with this issue? What follows is an approach that my students find both effective and enlightening.

The guide is: Treat all people the same. Learn to talk to strangers as if you have been friends for 20 years. Almost every student I talk to reflexively bolts at this idea. It seems dangerous. "They will run from us in abject terror because they will think we are crazy weirdos!" or presumptuous or disrespectful. But if you follow this guide you will be surprised by how positively people will react to you. I know this might seem counter-intuitive but I've got a million anecdotes to verify this.

Exercise: Twenty-Year Friend

Write out precisely and thoroughly, as if you were a novelist with yourself as the subject, how you behave (what you *do*, your gestures, posture, eye contact, facial expressions, tone, subject matter, how you begin, how you end, and, very importantly, your assumptions, etc.) when you talk to a friend you have known for a long time. In two columns, for as many pages as it takes, compare and contrast this to how you behave in all these categories with strangers. This is your "best friends" list.

Read your "best friends" list carefully. Pick a category and incorporate it into your conversations with strangers. Use your "best friends" list as your guide. Practice this. Each of us has to find our own path. Basically, it seems to me, this is a process of being willing to compare notes about life as it is unfolding that very day at that very moment, commenting on what's really going on with you, and being interested in what is really going on with them. It is not a process of rehashing or exploring the past, nor is it a process of explaining yourself, since your best friends have already long ago been through all this with you and you with them. They accept you and like you for exactly how you are. You know they are on your side and you know you are on theirs. Make this assumption with strangers. It will pay dividends.

As for myself, what works is to start the exchange commenting on whatever is or has been truly on my mind no further back than within the last ten minutes. I call this my "ten minute" rule. I trust what is really going on with me, just as I do with my best friends.

If you are having trouble, try working with the following:

- Stand next to a stranger without talking; imagine that the two of you are friends. See what that feels like.
- Do not begin your encounters with a question. *Make a statement about yourself and what is really going through your mind at that moment.*
- Declarative sentences like:
    "I just got these new shoes. My feet feel great!"
    "I wonder why they always put green olives in glass bottles but put black olives in cans."
    "If I have to stand in another line today I think I'll explode."
    "I saw the greatest concert last night."

- It is commonly easier for an actor to imagine an "outer" reality is true rather than an "inner" one. By this I mean, for example, it is usually easier for you to make believe that I am your brother than it is for you to make believe that you are my brother (or sister). Get it? Therefore: *try talking to a stranger as if they have known **you** for 20 years rather than the reverse.*
- Choose situations (a checkout line, sitting in a new class, waiting for a bus, etc.) where you are both on equal footing. Waiters, policemen, librarians have a role to play … the exercise with them will not serve you. Elevators are no good, generally, because the stranger feels trapped.

Remember: your friends *like* you. From now on this is how you will talk to directors, casting directors, agents and other actors when you meet them … as if you have known them for 20 years. Even Warren Beatty.

Important note:

This is the easiest exercise in the world not to do, or to shine it on in a half-hearted attempt. It is not something you will learn over the weekend. It is like being trustworthy or polite or thoughtful or disciplined … you have to remind yourself each day and continue to encourage it in yourself.

My students call me, all excited and nervous, when they have a meeting with an agent. I settle them down and we go back to this important precept. Nothing is always true, but it is a good bet that this orientation to these professional encounters will set you on the right track. Try to imagine the first time you go in to meet with an agent or director. He is going to call you into his office and you are going to sit down and there will be some exchanges between the two of you, small talk, which will go on for a few minutes, maybe longer. What do you think is happening during this seemingly innocuous portion of the interview? Everything! This is where "Twenty-Year Friend" comes into play. (This is, by the way, where I apply my "ten minute" rule … offering up spontaneously a declarative comment about something that has happened to me no longer ago than in the last ten minutes. I get this going before we even have a chance to settle into our seats.) Then after the two of you talk for a while the agent is either going to advance the relationship by suggesting he see some film on you, or meet his partner, or come back next week for a monologue … like that. Or: He is going to shut down the meeting by saying something like: "Well, thank you for coming in. Just to let you know, what we are doing now is getting a sense of who is out there. We are not signing anyone at the moment, but in the spring we are thinking we might expand our client list. I will call you then. Goodbye." So you see this initial interlude is very important. "Twenty-Year Friend" is a capacity you need to encourage in yourself.

Free Association Technique

When I first started out I was very active. Many of my auditions were for commercials, many for TV roles; a couple were for film roles. I went on lots of general meetings. I ran into the question "Tell me about yourself" or "What have you been up to?" over and over again.

Especially in commercials, but also in general on-camera interviews for casting directors or agents, "They" would turn the camera on, ask me to "slate my name," which means to say my name directly to camera, and then ask me a question – "to present myself" was the way they put it. And very often these questions had nothing whatsoever to do with the product or the part I was reading for. They seemed so random and off the point. I didn't know why they were asking me such dumb questions or what they had to do with anything. I didn't know what they were looking for or what they wanted from me. And most of all I didn't know what to do. Like you, I ached in my heart to do well. I wanted to do right. I wanted to give a nifty answer. I wanted to have at least some sense of control over how things went. I knew I was a much cooler guy than I was presenting. I tried relaxation exercises. I tried not caring. I tried memorizing what I would say. I practiced in the car before I went in. I tried being the way I was at the prom that night years ago. I even tried alcohol. But no matter what I tried, nothing worked. I always drove home hating myself for the dumb nervous phony fumbling way I presented myself. Finally, after about a thousand of these, I gave up. I said to myself "Screw it! I'm just going to answer with whatever comes into my head." I started booking like mad.

The next section of this chapter deals with what I discovered.

> *WHO YOU ARE SHOUTS SO LOUDLY*
> *I CAN'T HEAR WHAT YOU'RE SAYING.*
>
> … Ralph Waldo Emerson

It is hard to interview someone. It takes thought and energy and caring. Most of the casting people you meet will be short on all three.

It is a mistake to depend upon the good energy and *simpatico* of a casting director for the success of your interview. This is not to say you can't look forward to serendipitous rapport with casting directors. These satisfying exchanges will definitely happen. But you must

always come to your auditions prepared to create a winning interview/
audition event single-handedly.

In life there are numerous reasons for asking another person a
question. One of them is to find out the answer. One of them.

Especially in an on-camera interview, the purpose of the agent's or
casting director's question *isn't* to find out the answer. The motive for
the question has nothing to do with garnering *facts* about you. The
purpose is to give you an opportunity to respond. Distinguishing the
difference between an answer and a response is comparable to
identifying the difference between the content of a remark and
substance of a remark. ("I know she said 'Hello,' but what did she
mean by it?!")

> *Again: The function of an actor in an on-camera*
> *interview is to communicate their emotional relationship,*
> *through body language, gesture and tone of voice,*
> *to whatever they are talking about.*

We see it all the time in class: It is very common for a viewer to totally
forget what a person said in an on-camera interview (the factual
content of his/her response), while at the same time the viewer
maintains a vivid and specific impression of the on-camera person
(likable, interesting, relaxed, a fish out of water, nervous, whatever.)
The most memorable and winning moments in our on-camera
interviews are the specific flashes of verbal and physical behavior that
communicate emotional points of view. Put another way, the camera
likes the same quirks that our best friends like about us. Public-
speaking experts analyze that the impact or impression a person
makes on an audience is composed of 55 percent body language, 38
percent verbal tone and range of expressiveness, and only 7 percent
verbal content (*Silent Messages*, Albert Mehrabian, 1981). In light of
this, re-read the Emerson quote at the top of this section.

The camera zeros in on your *behavior* – body language, gesture and
verbal tone. The content of what you are saying … the facts

themselves ... are unimportant. *Not one conclusion will be drawn from them about you.* It is your behavior as you communicate your response that is crucial.

In addition, because the casting people are taping dozens of candidates, and because later they will be making their selections from the tape while holding a fast-forward button in the palm of their hand ... it is best for you to be communicating your connection to these emotional relationships as early in the session as you possibly can.

One more time: *Your aim in a casting session is not to be entertaining, funny, lovable, interesting, or anything like that. Especially, it is not to be factual. Your aim, rather, is to actively communicate your emotional points of view expressed through your tone of voice and body language.*

So, what to do?

> *WRITERS BLOCK IS CAUSED BY*
> *THE DESIRE TO BE BRILLIANT.*
>> ...Stephen Cannell, writer/producer,
>> *LA Times*, Sunday, June 1, 1997

Let's start with the following observation. Let's say you were asked: "What did you do for Thanksgiving?" If you pay close attention to your thought process, in your mind you will flash on the image of, say, your grandmother's mashed potatoes, or the smiling face of your cousin Jimmy ... but you will respond with a rational and understandable verbal translation of what that image means to you in relation to the question. You will probably answer verbally with something like: "I went to my grandmother's." And in "real life" this is as it should be. This is how sane and rational people communicate with one another in everyday life.

But the interview process is not everyday life. So, let's take another example. Let's say you're asked, "Where are you from?" Your answer would probably be the name of your hometown. But, again, in reality, *in the process of thinking of the literal answer*, a very specific image comes into your mind … the doorknob of your house, a certain maple tree, the chipped paint on a basketball hoop, the shouting mouth of your mother. Now, rather than leaping to respond with the name of your hometown, examine the specific image. Widen the view if need be. You will see that the picture that came into your head is actually your point of view of an event – a moment – in your life.

Exercise: Free Association Technique

So that you can explore the phenomenon I am talking about, get someone to ask you the following questions without you previewing them. See what happens.

- Which way do you think you feel jet-lag more, traveling east or traveling west?
- What is the difference between supper and dinner?
- Would you rather visit the North Pole or the South Pole?
- Tell me about the smallest fish you ever caught?
- Did you have a good time at your high school prom?
- When was the last time you ever got stood up?
- Where were you raised?
- What have you been up to lately?
- Tell me about yourself.

See what I mean? As you think what the factual answer would be, an image comes into your mind.

The principle is this: the event/image is not random. The snapshot image that pops into your head has a very specific personal connection to some aspect of either the question or its answer. And, further, it has a strong, though perhaps unapparent, emotional component for you … specific and emotional. This is fertile ground. Since the aim of the interview is to communicate your *emotional* points of view, this event/image offers a potent starting point for your response. "Slow down," I tell my students. Don't be so anxious to chatter. Take a few seconds. Think what the literal answer to the question would be. And as you are doing this, pay attention to the first image that comes to mind. Trust the first one. Even if it seems totally innocuous or does not immediately seem relevant to the question you have been asked: Trust it. Make this event/image the subject of your response. See where it takes you.

What seems to work best is to focus only on whatever image or action is contained in this very narrow sliver of time. Talk about only that which is contained within the frame of the "snapshot." Remember, your aim is to communicate, through tone and gesture, your emotional relationship to the specific image or action that came to you and what you and/or the others are doing. Keep the time frame as narrow as possible. In other words, resist the temptation to tell the story behind the event, or explain what came to mind. Simply focus on talking about whatever it is. You are going to say, "But that's a non-sequitur, it doesn't make sense. They will think I'm crazy." Bear with me. You *are* going to answer "factually" but not until the end of your response. Using the Thanksgiving example: you will talk about the mashed potatoes, or your cousin Jimmy, without explaining it. (We are looking for a response that lasts about 30 seconds, give or take.) And then *end* your response with something like, "Anyway, I went to my Grandma's. We had a really great time." Bring it all back together that way.

Tendencies to avoid:

- Use the right tense. The event happened in the past, so use the past tense.
- Avoid sentences like: "The first thing I see is … " or: "When you ask me that I think about thus and such … "
- Talk about your subject without a lot of qualifiers. Just talk about it!

"Focusing on describing the details of the image or action" and "Communicating emotional points of view" seem to be contradictory aims. The latter seems to require some verbiage about "what and why" which is excluded by the former. This is exactly correct. There's only one way you can solve this dilemma. The answer lies in communicating your emotional point of view through your tone of voice and your physical behavior. This is precisely what the camera craves to see.

This process is not restricted to past events. It also includes any "random" thoughts or ideas sparked by what you may have been asked. These can come to you often in response to typically wide-open questions such as: "Tell me about yourself" or "What have you been up to?" Questions like these might have you responding to something you read in the paper that morning, or what you were thinking as you came through the door just moments before, or the look on your friend's face that morning at breakfast. I guarantee you that listing your résumé or your biographical statistics won't contain the emotional connection the camera craves to witness.

Actually, a good thing can happen when you embark on a response before you understand its meaning. You have to discover its relevance as you talk. (Trust the principle: the event/image *is* relevant to the question, but its relevance may not be immediately apparent on a *rational* basis.) This takes courage. But there is a payoff. True seeking and actual becoming are among the most compelling things to witness in an on-screen close-up. So, not knowing "where this all goes" or "what this has to do with anything" gives you a perfect chance to shine.

Communication of emotional relationships is often most memorable when they are associated with very specific physical details. Emotional responses and specific physical details seem to go hand in hand. Invest in these details. Pay attention to the really "dumb" ones, the ones you instinctively feel the impulse to pass over or to apologize for mentioning. They will yield the best results by far. Consider no detail be too insignificant to explore.

Here is what I am asking of you: I am asking you to put everything aside, everything that you thought or imagined would be happening, and take time out to explore and express with an open heart and generous spirit, the details of some long forgotten moment, totally innocuous, some "never in a million years" thought or event, that comes to mind. Can you do that? Respond. Share. Open up. Give. Communicate … Try it.

In fact this is the starting point for all stand-up comedy or poetry; anything creative for that matter. It is exactly what all your teachers have been referring to when they have been saying over and over to "Be specific, be specific, be specific!" In fact, you will see that it is very much like you do with your best friends, anyway. They don't think you're nuts.

An added benefit of narrowing your focus to a specific detail is that it will suddenly become very easy to talk. You'll see; because you won't be mentally preoccupied with composing language to convey complicated events.

Don't try to be brilliant. It will just bottle you up.

> *THE FUNNY THING ABOUT SCREEN WRITERS IS,*
> *THEY NEVER KNOW WHAT THEIR STORIES ARE ABOUT.*
>
> … Irving Thalberg, 1899–1936,
> "Boy Wonder" movie producer

Do not let yourself be sidetracked by seeking to account for the psychological meaning of the image. Trust me, we are going to come to our own conclusions no matter what you say. The "meaning" of your response may occur to you, or it may not. This is not a Freudian exercise. Identifying the "meaning" is not the object. It is actually the booby prize. If a "meaning" occurs to you, include it if you like but don't dwell on it. If no "meaning" occurs to you, do not apologize. There is no need to. (After all, what does the actual answer to "What did you do for Thanksgiving?" have to do with acting in a movie or TV commercial in the first place?!)

The impact you make will have little to do with the rationale of your response. Your impact will have only to do with your behavior – gestures, facial expressions, and tone of voice – as you convey, say, your sense of enjoyment, or frustration, or bewilderment as you respond. Besides you will tie your response back to the question, which requires no more than a single sentence at closing.

The interview format is not designed to identify the "good" people, or the "reasonable" people. It simply is looking for memorable flashes of human behavior.

You are playing it safe if you "set up" the circumstance for us, or if you try to explain everything. This need to explain ourselves or our circumstances is rooted in the perception that if we make ourselves understood we will be liked or accepted or forgiven. But, in fact, it is very boring to listen to. ("Next!")

Therefore, avoid the temptation to create a narrative or a context so that it all "makes sense." Let the interviewer figure that out … that's what makes it fun for him. Interpreting your response will keep him interested. It will keep him involved. His conclusions may be different from yours, but they would be anyway … and it is exactly what Thalberg meant by the above quote.

You have to practice.

Here's a good example. Not long ago in class I asked a student: "Tell me about the last time you phoned someone long distance." This was her exact response:

"I reached out to pick up the starfish. I'll never forget how blue it was. But the water was so clear, like I was flying, I didn't realize how deep below me it was. It was shimmering on the edge of the coral wall. I signaled Carley but she didn't see me. I started down. My lungs felt like they would burst. But I kept diving down. Pumping with my fins. To where I could just barely reach and flick it with my knife. It let go of the wall in a cloud of purple dust and actually seemed to float right into my hand. Like it was meant to be … I had it. When I broke the

surface and gulped in a lung full of air, I thought to myself "My God, I'm alive!" I was in Hawaii. I felt so proud for finally getting myself there. Later that night, at the motel, I splurged and called my mother … she lives in Dayton … to tell her about the diving … and the starfish … and how blue it was."

When she started talking, this student did not know where this response was going. The event had actually happened long ago. She hadn't thought about Hawaii for years. She didn't have the slightest idea what her blue starfish had to do with my question about telephones. But boy did she ever shine as the images unfolded and the connections revealed themselves to her.

Notice she responded first (talking about diving down for the starfish) … *then* she answered (by connecting it to the phone call to her mother). *First respond, then answer.*

Take a look at the guidelines compiled on the next page and see how closely this student's response follows them.

Yes, this approach doesn't work sometimes. No, it doesn't work for everybody. Yes, it feels very risky. But all the other approaches become "raps" about ourselves. We all know how sick of ourselves we can get when we hear ourselves giving the same pat answers over and over. Try to imagine the situation of the casting director who hears these practiced renditions day after day. It's a disaster.

And also, we want to walk away from our auditions feeling we didn't betray ourselves. We want to feel that whatever comes, at least we were true and we were authentic. At least we didn't fail at pretending to be something we weren't. Because, believe me, that's the absolute worst.

The Importance of Authenticity

Read this: The following is an excerpt from the *LA Times*, Calendar section, Sunday, May 2, 2004, page E25. Fox News Network's producer, Roger Ailes, was featured.

"A large broadcasting company once hired Ailes … to evaluate talk-show hosts on its local TV station. Ailes devised a trick to help him decide whether the hosts were any good. He would watch the shows in his hotel room with the sound turned off, closely scrutinizing each host's gestures, facial expressions and body language when interacting with guests. 'If there was nothing happening on the screen in the way the host looked or moved that made me interested enough to stand up and turn the sound up, then I knew that the host was not a great television performer,' Ailes later wrote."

Further:

"Ailes, who signed such hosts as Chris Matthews, Charles Grodin and Geraldo Rivera, said, 'If I have any ability, it's probably to find talented people and set up a structure that they can work in. I look for authenticity in people and then develop a show from there.'"

Authenticity. That's want we want. It's better than anything you can cook up.

Summary

For your on-camera interviews:

- The auditors and the camera want the real you. Treat all people the same.
- The camera is only interested in what is really going on with you. Who and what we are is communicated primarily through our body language, gestures and tone of voice.

When asked a question to present yourself:

- As you consider the factual answer to the question, trust the first image that comes to you.
- Be specific. Focus on an isolated moment in time. Do not rush ahead.

- Avoid trying to set up the story.

    Do not try to create a narrative or explain the circumstances.

    Do not explain relationships.

- Try starting with an action sentence.

    "I reached out to touch ..."

    "She looked at me and I ..."

    "I turned when I heard the sound ..."

- Use body language, hand gestures, tone of voice to let your emotional connection to your response come through.
- Let it take you where it wants to go.
- Do not try to "make sense." Leave all this for the listeners to do. It keeps them fascinated.

    Don't explain anyone's motives.

    Don't impart your theories or conclusions.

    Don't relate the logic of why you are telling what you're telling.

- Keep the length of your response to about 30 seconds.
- Wrap it up at the end with a simple sentence that "answers" the question factually.
- Then, "Look back at who is looking at you" (meaning the camera).

CHAPTER 2

"Just relax and be yourself" – a totally worthless piece of advice

NERVES AND THE CAMERA

The point of Chapter 1 is to encourage you to realize that, especially on camera, whatever is truly on your mind is more interesting than anything you can cook up. And, that the way you behave with your good friends is the most appealing manner you can manifest.

I want to continue to talk about on-camera interviews, as opposed to on-camera scene work, because that is what's most likely to come first when you start your professional career. To address this effectively we have to talk about nerves.

Don't kid yourself: You are going to be nervous.

As I said before: the camera senses any disparity between your true state of being and that which you are presenting. If you are nervous and try to hide it, the camera will see a nervous person trying to cover up the fact that they are nervous. The camera will sense that something isn't right, that something is "a little off." No matter how clever your words, the viewer won't hear them. They will be too preoccupied by watching something far more fascinating: you trying to cover your nerves. (You know what I'm talking about; we've all been there.)

We are going to build on the following idea:

> *The camera wants to know what is really going on with you; the more you share with it the more it will take care of you.*

To be effective on camera we actors need to find a way to express or include our nervousness when nerves are present. Otherwise the camera won't "like" us.

I want to make some observations about nervousness – stage fright – by first observing how some very seasoned performers deal with their nerves. Then I will suggest some perspectives and strategies for dealing with nerves. These approaches will help you do well in both your on-camera general interviews and your on-camera auditions and scene work – and in life, for that matter.

Two examples

In my "Auditioning for the Camera" classes I begin the discussion concerning nerves and ways to deal with them by showing several video clips. The first is a clip from ABC's *20/20* of Kirk Douglas, the world famous actor now in advanced years, being interviewed by Barbara Walters. Ms Walters begins by informing the audience that her guest, "the famous Kirk Douglas," has recently survived a stroke – "the toughest role of his career" – which is to be the topic of the interview. She turns to him to begin the interview but is taken aback when he unexpectedly reaches out, touches her on the arm, and interrupts her, saying: "Barbara, before you begin … " "Oh!" she says with surprise. He continues: "I'm nervous. I am nervous because since my accident when I get excited I can't speak. So, please don't excite me, Barbara." He has a smile and a twinkle in his eye. She answers by graciously saying: "Well, I won't excite you if you promise not to excite me." "We will see," he says. "We will see." It is a warm, spontaneous, and humorous exchange.

I turn off the monitor and ask my class if they felt Kirk Douglas appeared to be weak or out of control, or was in any way diminished by the fact that he acknowledged his nervousness. The class overwhelmingly answers, "No." They uniformly agree they loved him; he was adorable. In fact, by the end of the interview, if you were to ask any viewer their impression of Mr Douglas during the interview, it is very likely that none of them would even recall that he stopped the show to call attention to the fact that he was nervous.

The next clip I show is from a videotape of Richard Pryor, on stage in front of a live audience. It is from his 1981 one-man stand-up performance called *Live on Sunset Strip*. You can still rent it on DVD. It's genius. Highly anticipated, it was Mr Pryor's first public appearance following an accident that left him badly burned. But it doesn't get started very well. From the moment he comes on stage his presence seems awkward and a bit stutter-step; until he stops the show and says: "Can I get some water? There was supposed to be a stool with some water." A man in the first row way at one end of the stage offers up a glass. "I have to walk way over here? What is this, April Fool's or something?" As the man hands him the glass of water, Richard Pryor comments, "Whoa, brother, you're nervous-er than me." As he walks back to center stage he spots the stool with the water he had been promised. "Was that here all along!?" Clearly it had been. The audience laughs knowingly. Then he drinks deeply, pauses and says, "All I needed was some water to calm down, re-lax. Because I know you all want me to do well. And I want so much to do well for you. But let's just relax, calm down, and let whatever happens happen." The audience erupts into loud and loving applause.

And certainly my students notice, just as with Kirk Douglas, they themselves do not have any negative reaction whatsoever to what Richard Pryor did … the live audience in fact loved him for it … stopping the show and making fun of himself for being nervous.

They *stopped the show* to acknowledge their nervousness! I saw it again on the televised 2008 Country Music Awards. One of the country-and-western stars came out to announce the next nominee and he said with a self-deprecating laugh that he was nervous; he didn't want to bungle the intro but he was afraid he would because he felt an extra pressure to get things right since he used to date the recipient. We didn't mind a bit, in fact it was endearing. When Bill O'Reilly, the television commentator, interviewed Rosie O'Donnell concerning her views on gun control, she interjected her opening thoughts with: "Let me tell you, this is the best weight loss program I have ever been on. I have had diarrhea for a week worrying about this interview."

Now why do I show these clips? Because all of these very experienced and savvy performers did four things that I want you to experiment with and integrate into your on-camera auditions or meetings. Four things:

- They told the truth about being nervous. They acknowledged they were nervous.
- They identified specifically how their nerves were manifesting themselves.
- They had a sense of humor about their situation.
- They were performing for a cause larger than themselves.

If you are like most of my students, I suspect you can't wait until you reach a point where you don't get nervous any more. I wouldn't be surprised if you were very critical towards yourself because you get so nervous you can't think straight. You likely think if you were a good actor you wouldn't get nervous. I bet you think pros like Kirk Douglas or Richard Pryor don't get nervous. I bet you think if you could just relax you would be so much better. And I bet the last thing in the world you do when you are nervous is to admit that you are. I bet you think it would make you appear to be weak, or out of control, or somehow un-cool. It would ruin everything. No one would respect you.

Here is the painful truth. Everyone gets nervous. This is not going to change. Your nerves or self-awareness while performing may diminish over time, but it is also a sure thing it will pop back up at some future inopportune time. Humans are primates; primates are social creatures; for us primates, belonging to "the group" is a paramount concern. We feel threatened when we feel we are being judged by the group or by a superior. Everyone does. It never completely goes away. Ask Kirk or Richard.

> *"I WAS AFRAID, BECAUSE I WAS NAKED, AND I HID MYSELF."*
> *"WHO TOLD THEE THAT THOU WAST NAKED? HAST THOU*
> *EATEN OF THE TREE, WHEREOF I COMMANDED THEE THAT*
> *THOU SHOULDST NOT EAT?"*
>
> ... Genesis

The ancients understood exactly what a painful curse this is. That's what the fig leaf represents: our nakedness, our sense of separation from our surroundings, our shame, our anxiety, our self-awareness, our nerves. According to the seminal mythology of our culture, stage fright is the perfect punishment for mankind's disobedience to God.

> *"Just relax and be yourself"* –
> *a totally worthless piece of advice.*

If it were possible to "just relax" there would be no such thing as stage fright. And, paradoxically, "being yourself" is not something you can *do*. Still, you are going to get this admonition all through your career, even from some very experienced and well meaning directors and casting people. They are trying to be helpful. It's just that they don't know how to help.

Develop a Personal Strategy

The essential ingredient of any winning audition/performance/ interview lies in the presence and expressiveness of our body as it is connected to our thoughts and emotions. Nerves and self-consciousness keep us from "being in the moment/being in the room." The experienced performer knows it always costs something to acknowledge nervousness, but it is the only way to free yourself. They know that the more you try to hide nerves, the more they control you. Seasoned performers also know that there is no escape … the camera always sees what is really going on. They make a winning move by adapting the following 4 strategies. See if you can tailor their strategies to fit your own personal style.

The pros acknowledge what is true about their state of being

It always feels dangerous to take this step. Do it anyway. The pros know that you don't die of it and the benefits are great.

Nerves are about wanting to win, to have things unfold without a hitch; to go perfectly. Paradoxically, the willingness to acknowledge the imperfection of the moment is the most winning move.

The truth will set you free.

- Acknowledge to yourself the truth about your circumstances.
- List out loud to yourself the specific grisly details included in the negative outcome you are forecasting for yourself.

You will have to take a moment and identify how it is and why it is that you are nervous. Be specific. Be truthful. You won't be able to be in command of your nerves if you try to use a gimmick or a cover-up to escape. It won't work. The truth always costs something. The dumb, embarrassing, stupid, idiotic truth is always hard to acknowledge. It is uncomfortable to confront. The willingness to pay the price and acknowledge your nervous expression is what people admire about performers and effective public speakers. "I don't know how you do that, you're so brave, you seem so confident."

The pros verbalize specifically *how their nerves are manifesting themselves*

Ask yourself, "Specifically, how do I know I am nervous?" By this I mean identifying your pulse rate, perspiration, thirst, shaky knees, clammy hands, muscular tension, tired brain, racing thoughts, yawning, having to pee, etc. Be specific about what physical manifestations are signaling that you at that moment are nervous.

Identify how your nervousness is expressing itself. List, specifically and out loud to yourself, the physical sensations that comprise your "being nervous."

Consciously call attention to your nervous manifestations and intensify those expressions, e.g. stiffen your neck muscles; try to raise your heart rate; take extra deep breaths, twitch more emphatically.

> *Acknowledge the syndrome,*
> *the syndrome diminishes.*

I asked a student the other day how he knew he was nervous. He said because his ears were warm. I mean, you've gotta love that. "My knees are shaking." "My pulse is up." "I can feel a little drop of perspiration dribbling right down the back of my neck." Specific. Kirk Douglas identified that he *couldn't speak clearly*. Richard Pryor identified that he was *thirsty*. Rosie O'Donnell acknowledged her specific nervous manifestation. *Take pride in being very accurate*, very specific. It is the cornerstone in our truth-seeking as performers. And find the humor in it.

One of the basic tenets of effective public speaking is to establish right off the bat something in common between you, the speaker, and the audience. Nothing is more human than being nervous. I read somewhere that over 90 percent of the whole human race is afraid of public speaking. (By the way, the same survey revealed that less than 50 percent are afraid of dying!) If you are specific about it, acknowledging your nerves is a human touch that will establish a connection between you and your audience. It will endear you to them if you share, with humor, the very special way your nature is expressing itself that day.

Sometimes you will encounter a casting person who will say in one way or another, "Oh, don't be nervous. There's nothing to be nervous about." Don't let this put you off. Be patient with them. There are fools in every walk of life.

The pros enjoy a sense of humor or irony about their nerves. They appreciate it about themselves

This is very important. You don't need to be a stand-up comic. What you *do* need to do is genuinely appreciate how bizarre nerves are and be willing to acknowledge it. A human being sits in the chair and is fine, then walks ten feet over to the camera or the podium and suddenly the surface of his eyeball changes! Come on, that's funny! You've got to find some humor or irony in that.

> *Few qualities are more appealing than*
> *self-deprecating humor.*

Watch the invited guests on talk shows. Watch what the pros do. They join the human race ... meaning they acknowledge that this time the laugh's on them. Admittedly some have writers, but it doesn't take a writer. The principle is the same: with an extemporaneous remark, acknowledge with humor the truth about your situation as it actually is at that moment. If you watch you will see seemingly very confident performers come out and, in one way or another, if they need to, find a way to say: "The joke's on me." I spoke at a funeral years ago at which Sean Penn was also asked to speak. He was married to Madonna at the time. He opened his remarks by commenting that he hadn't felt this nervous since the previous night when he saw his wife in underwear.

Accept and appreciate your nervousness. It is real and reasonable. Look for an opportunity to express the humor or irony in it.

The pros identify a good cause (other than themselves) to be nervous on behalf of

> *WHEN I DARE TO BE POWERFUL, TO USE MY STRENGTH IN THE SERVICE OF MY VISION, THEN IT BECOMES LESS AND LESS IMPORTANT WHETHER I AM AFRAID.*
>
> … Audre Lorde
> Feb 18, 1934–Nov 17, 1992

I assign this quote to be the anthem of all actors' work, the declared theme of this whole book. When you are afraid but go forward anyway, then you are the definition of bravery. There is no more winning quality.

Identify a good reason for being there … beyond yourself and your own glory. Be there on behalf of someone or some issue or situation that is worth being nervous on behalf of. You won't mind being nervous nearly so much if it's for a good cause. You will see it actually makes you a hero.

Tactics for dealing with nerves for your on-camera auditions

Now I want to take the above observations and work them a little bit so they can be applied effectively to both your on-camera auditions and general meetings. To accomplish this we need to embrace three tools or "tactics".

1st tactic: Comment with humor on the reality of the moment

You say, "I can see how all of the above might be helpful for public speaking, but I can't stop the show (or the scene) and acknowledge my nerves." No, you can't. But you *can* acknowledge them as you enter the audition room. You *can* comment with self-deprecating humor on the fact that you are nervous and how you know it – i.e. the physical manifestations of your nerves – as you walk in. For example: "I sure must be nervous because my heart's pounding a mile a minute." Or: "Don't ask me to shake hands because I'm so nervous about this meeting my hands are soaking wet."

> *Always find a way to acknowledge with humor*
> *your nervous expression as you enter.*

Let me take a moment to describe further what I mean by: "Comment with humor on the reality of the moment." First of all, this comment, which you will say out loud, must be *unplanned and unrehearsed.* It is totally "off the cuff." This is critical, because otherwise it just becomes an act, a gimmick, which is what you are trying to avoid in the first place.

As you enter the audition room, as you pass through the threshold of the door, you will comment with humor on whatever specific truth about the situation hits you at that very moment. It could concern your nerves, or it could be something like: "It's warm in here." Or: "This carpet feels spongy." Or: "I like that painting." Or: "There's more of you in here than I thought." Or: "Boy, my heart's pounding a mile a minute." Or: "You all look like you've had a long day." Or: "There was this really weird man outside." … whatever is *truly actually true at the moment.* Don't think. Just say it. "Wow, nice view." You have to have the guts to say what's true. (Just like you do with your very best friends.) Just say it! Remember, it is for you not them.

Experiment with this. Find your own way, your own style. I am recommending that you always include a comment like this upon entry, and further, if your nerves are rampant, use this comment to acknowledge your nerves with humor.

Commenting like this is a powerful tool for a number of reasons. It makes you look like a pro, confident enough in the situation to make a relaxed comment. If you ever have a chance to sit on the other side of the casting desk and watch a parade of actors auditioning one by one, you'll see what I mean. This comment not only gives you a chance to make fun of your nerves if need be, it knocks the perfection out of the equation so that you can get your body in the room and react to what is truly there as opposed to what you thought should be there or wanted to be there. It also loosens the auditors up and actually serves to initiate an exchange between you and them that puts you on even ground.

One further note: The entry feels social, but it is not. It is a crucial part of your audition, which we will discuss further in Chapter 5, "Your On-Camera Entry." If they ask you, "How are you?" do not answer merely "Fine." Answer with a comment on the physical expression of your nerves. "My hands are as clammy as a dish rag, but other than that I'm terrific."

I like to comment to my students that "they," the auditors, don't know what we actors do or how we do it; to them we are like witches, a little mysterious and magical. They kind of expect us to be weird or eccentric. Or at least they accept it as part of the package if we are. (Have you ever talked to an engineer about acting? They will look at you as if you come from a different solar system!) The point I am trying to make is that the casting folks really don't judge us by how we execute our audition just so long as we make our magic. And we cannot make magic if, because of our nerves, we don't "get our bodies into the room." You have to know yourself; you have to be in tune with your body. It is okay to take a moment and stretch like a competitive swimmer or a dancer before you sit down in front of them. It is okay to shake out your hands or take a deep breath as you comment with humor about how your nerves are expressing themselves at that moment. Warning: *You will crash and burn if you make a gimmick out of this.* But you will find that if you consciously call attention to your nervous manifestations and the intensity of those expressions ... e.g. stiffen your neck muscles; raise your heart rate; take even deeper breaths; twitch more emphatically, in an honest and spontaneous expression of whatever is truly going on with you at that moment … your nerves' hold over you will diminish. Trust this.

2nd tactic: Identify why your character might be nervous in just the same way you are

The second tool involves another important concept. After you have a number of auditions under your belt you will come to recognize a pattern: that you are rarely, if ever, asked to read a scene that is not pivotal. Think about it. The scene is invariably going to involve your character in a crucial situation … a situation where the character himself is also likely to be nervous.

> *IF I'M NOT NERVOUS FOR AN AUDITION*
> *I KNOW SOMETHING IS WRONG.*
>> … Anthony Quinn, Oscar-winning actor

Identify why your character might be nervous in just the same way you are. Always explore this possibility and make this part of your preparation process.

While you are reading over the sides, strategize how, in the event that you, the actor, are nervous at the time of the audition, you might choose to make the character nervous in the same way. Create a rationale to draw on, if need be, so that your nerves will fit with the character's situation. For example, conceptualize the scene so that it might include – if you need it to – that:

"She/he is so beautiful she/he makes you nervous," or
"The police might think you did it," or
"You don't know what you are going to do," or
"You have never confronted anyone like this." or
"Whatever it is, you have to do it quickly," or
"In the past you always got this wrong and this time you absolutely must get it right."
Etc.

See what I mean?

The cruel irony is that the more you want to do well, the more nervous you are likely to be, and the more nervous you are, the more poorly you will perform. That is exactly what is likely to happen if you concoct your character's situation such that he/she can't possibly be nervous. You've got to work it the other way around. You'll see. Give your character permission to be nervous (if that's what happens) by virtue of your interpretation of the character's situation. It will lighten the load. It will allow you to focus on what the character is *doing* rather than feeling. It will get you back to doing what is the essence of the scene, rather than being preoccupied with trying to deny your nerves or steer your emotions.

I heard Jack Nicklaus, the famous golf champion, recall on television his first Master's win. It was his first big championship win. He was in his early twenties. He said that he hit a great approach to the final green, but he knew he had to sink the putt to win the tournament. He related that as he walked toward the green he was so nervous he could hardly stand up. Then he added that as he stood over the crucial putt he could feel that he was still very nervous, so he took about 10 percent off his stroke, and sunk it. See, he didn't go lie down somewhere and try to calm his nerves. He accepted them and incorporated them into his performance. We actors need to learn to do the same thing.

3rd tactic: Step back and identify why the scene's worth doing

Make your work be about something beyond yourself and how good an actor you are. In terms of your scene work, the character will be in a situation. That situation will be connected to an overall theme embodied in the story. Identify how the theme describes a component of the human condition and why it is of value to the world, why it needs to be explored and expressed … either heroically or comically … but definitely valiantly and bravely … By you.

A final thought

You know, whenever I give a speech or plan for a meeting … if I find myself preparing the speech word for word it never goes well. As I practice I have to focus on what it is I want to communicate and why, as opposed to how I am going to say it. Of course I say it over and over again. But when I gravitate to the words, as if only those specific ones will do, it is a red flag that I am on the wrong track. Experience has shown me time and again that things won't go as planned. My nervousness in front of the audience will invariably cause me to forget a word or a specific turn of phrase. If I have focused my preparation on the words having to be just so, I will start mentally scrambling to remember how I said it while rehearsing at home. I will become more and more focused on how I said it before rather than on *what* I want to say right now … and the whole thing falls apart. It becomes a self-conscious memory exercise rather than an effort to define at the moment what I want to communicate. In other words it loses its life, which is the most important and communicative part. I do better when I focus my preparation on the ideas, the points I want to make and the emotional impetus for why the audience needs to know what I have to say. I do better when I practice making those points a number of different ways … then trust that I have found a way to say it and I will again. Yes I might fumble a little, but if I keep my sense of humor, I am alive in front of my audience and that is ultimately what any audience, including the camera, responds to.

A fact

If you are nervous because you know you are unprepared or out of shape artistically, or intellectually, or physically … then none of the above will help you. You've got to stand for something. Quit kidding yourself and quit wasting people's time.

Summary

To be effective on camera we actors need to find a way to express or include our nerves when they are present. Otherwise the camera won't "like" us.

- Accept and appreciate your nervousness. It is real and reasonable. Look for the humor or irony in it.
- Appreciate how your nerves are expressing themselves. Identify the physical sensations that comprise your "being nervous."
- Ask yourself: How might my character be nervous in just the way I am? For what reason? Allow your nerves to fit the character's situation.
- Upon entering the room, comment with "humor" on the reality of the moment.
- Before you settle, if need be, consciously call public attention to your nervous manifestations and the intensity of those expressions, e.g. stiffen your neck muscles; take a deeper breath; take a moment to stretch; twitch more emphatically. Do this with humor.

Which brings us to the next chapter.

CHAPTER 3

When the camera is in the room, guess who's not there?

ON-CAMERA INTERVIEWS

Your on-camera interviews (underline *interview*, not a scene) will be very much enhanced when you are capable of doing the following:

- Be able to talk to the camera as if it were a person
- Encourage your body's expressiveness on-camera through posture and gesture
- Understand the dynamics of eye contact
- Encourage the act of actually thinking on camera
- Have a way to end your responses
- Establish your true relationship with the camera.

We are going to discuss these six issues and suggest some techniques to master them.

Learn to talk to the camera as if it were a person

When the camera is in the room, guess who's not there? The decision-maker!

In order to make contact with the decision-maker, who will be viewing your interview later on a playback monitor, you need to make contact with the camera. Therefore, you need to learn to talk to the camera as if it were a good friend. That's what the camera likes.

Exercise: Practice talking to the camera in the second person; i.e. using the word "you"

This exercise yields great results. It will help you establish a natural working connection with the camera. It will get you over the strangeness of being in front of this weird, often intimidating, machine. Keep practicing this until you sense that you are actually talking *with* the camera, having a conversation with it. Strange? We actors do this all the time when we rehearse on our own … we talk to the lamp or to the doorknob, don't we, as if it were the other character in the scene? We strive to make contact with the door knob … same with the camera. It should feel as if you are talking to a friend. Cold flat facts won't work. The camera should know how you feel about what you are saying by how you say it. Just like with a friend. Demand this of yourself. Work on the following:

- Describe the camera to itself using the word "you."

   For example: "You're weird. You only have one eye. Your legs are skinny. You have these strange looking wires sticking out of the side of you. I like that knobby thing you have off to the side, though." Etc.

- Look at the camera for a moment. What person in your life does the camera remind you of?

   For example: "You make me so uncomfortable! You remind me of my mother, because she is always judging me, just like you are now. You never say what you are thinking even though I can tell you are having very specific responses to me. I hate that." Etc.

- If all cameras are the same camera, recall for the camera the first time the camera photographed you.

For example: "Remember that time down at the lake when you were photographing me? Dad had you in his hands – you remember – and I was in my little pink dress. Remember? Mom was calling from the raft that we should swim out, remember? And I didn't want to because I wanted to stay in my dress. Remember? Sure … And dad was laughing – you remember – because I was making such funny faces?" Etc.

- And others:

    Complain to the camera how it intrudes on your life.

    Compliment the camera as to how it enriches your life.

    Entice the camera to come with you on your next adventure, inviting it along so that it would want to go with you.

    Confide in the camera as to what you think it thinks of you.

Encourage expressiveness through posture and gesture

As human beings we place enormous importance on meeting or experiencing people "in person." Why? What's the payoff? The answer is: there is an informational transaction that occurs through the presence and expression of the individual's body. We have all experienced how powerful this can be. It is especially important on camera. Take a look at the most recent presidential campaign: Obama versus McCain. Picture them in your mind, just how they moved and carried themselves. Whatever your politics, we each instinctively drew conclusions about the nature and differences between the candidates based on these crucial factors.

The expressiveness of *your* body is the defining feature of your "personal" presentations, live or on-camera. When you take your place in front of the camera or at a casting director's desk, strive to bring your body with you.

Exercise: Body expressiveness

Videotape yourself as you have a friend interview you from off-camera. Direct your responses directly to camera, not the interviewer.

As you sit (or stand) in front of the camera, strive to feel that your posture and/or physical attitude are as if you were at home, or some other safe supportive place. (On the comfortable porch of a vacation cabin, perhaps?) Try to lose any sense of formality. Seek a comfortable repose. Let yourself slouch a little. The aim here is to explore a variety of comfortable postures … whichever postures make you feel at home. Perhaps pull your knees up under you; or try sitting three-quarters to the camera. Remember this is not a "corporate" interview. We want to know the "real" you.

Make sure as you talk that you do not allow yourself to get "frozen" in a given position, which can happen almost involuntarily especially if you are feeling "on stage." Shift positions occasionally. You will see that this occasional slight shifting to a new comfortable position will invigorate your connection to what you are saying.

Encourage yourself to be physically expressive. Use your hands when talking. It will enhance the emotional component in what you are communicating by encouraging a greater physical involvement in whatever you are trying to express.

> Note: With regard to using your hands, remember we are looking for authenticity. If I tell you to take an aspirin, don't take the whole bottle.

Play back the tape with the sound turned off. Evaluate the effect of your gestures and physical expressiveness. Do they communicate your emotional connection to what you were talking about?

Observe the expressiveness of your non-verbal reaction to each question, even before you start to answer. Notice your non-verbal behavior whenever you pause to think.

Quiet your fidgeting. Some of us tend to get very fidgety when we sit nervously in front of the camera. Our foot "jazzes" up and down, our crossed leg wags back and forth.

Exercise: Big as the room

To quiet such behavior, imagine, as you sit there, that you are as big as the room. I don't mean that you puff yourself up physically, but rather that you imagine your energy, your chi, your aura, extends out from every surface of your body – out from the sides of your arms, your chest, and your back – to the extremities of the room; all the way from the top of your head and shoulders to the ceiling, all the way out from the flanks of your body to each of the four walls, and down from your bottom and thighs to the floor. You will find that you can easily maintain this mental adjustment as you carry on a conversation. This adjustment will calm your body and will allow you to focus on incorporating the more effective physical expressions we discussed above.

The dynamics of eye contact

"Who do I look at? You or the camera!? Where do I look? Where should my eyes be looking?!" These are classic confusions for the novice. Here is the answer:

> *Treat the camera as if it were the most important*
> *person in the room, as if it were the person*
> *you were most intent on reaching.*

Remember: this is for an interview, not a scene.

You are going to walk into a room and there is going to be a camera there and a person operating the camera and perhaps some other people will be there too. They are going to talk to you. They are perhaps going to give you some simple instructions, and/or have a conversation with you. Your best move when talking with them is to include the camera as if it were the most important person in the room.

I liken this to the following situation: As if you were in a corporate boardroom standing at the end of a long shiny table with all the vice presidents seated along the length of either side, and with the CEO seated at the far end. Treat the camera as if it were the CEO. In this example, if a vice president asked you a question, you would look at him/her and begin to answer, but the vector of your intention would be to communicate your response to the CEO, and that's where your eyes would go once you got started. Your eye movement/response includes everyone in the room, but the main body of your response is directed directly to the CEO … in this case, the camera.

Exercise: The dynamics of eye contact

As you videotape yourself being interviewed, experiment with the dynamics of eye contact. At the outset of an exchange, especially with a director or person of influence, it may feel natural to want to make eye contact briefly with the actual person who is interviewing you. This will work as long as you then turn the body of your response to camera. Experiment with this. Find the right rhythm. It is as if there are two people listening and the camera is the one who is the most interested.

Again: if you make genuine contact with the camera, you will make contact with whoever is watching the monitor … the decision-maker.

Thinking on camera

There is nothing more fascinating on this planet than the face of a human being who is thinking … actually thinking. The most pronounced difference between acting on camera and acting on the stage is that on camera the audience can watch you think. They can, in effect, read your mind.

On camera, you may take your time, you may *think* before you respond. Don't you dare fake it, but if you are actually thinking, the viewer will find it fascinating.

Most people I observe feel reflexively compelled when they are first on camera to talk a mile-a-minute. They assume that since it's all so quiet and empty in front of the camera it's their job to fill the space with the sound of their own talking. They jabber away hardly taking a breath. That is, until I ask them a question that takes some concerted thought to answer. (For instance: What is it like to be asleep and not dreaming?) Believe me, as the person on camera ponders how to describe this, the viewers wait in rapt attention for their response.

Do not feel you have to hurry. Take your time. *It's okay to think!* We will find it as interesting as anything you have to say.

How to end your responses

Do not confuse the following with performing a scene, in which you will not make eye contact with the camera once the scene begins. But in the situations where you want to contact the decision-maker, such as when you are:

- being interviewed on camera, and are responding to a question directly to camera so that "We can get to know you"
- performing a monologue to camera
- doing a commercial in which you speak directly to camera
- serving as an on-camera announcer

– in these cases, end your response by simply looking back (actively) at who is looking at you, that is: the camera.

Let me explain. In life when you're talking to someone, it's human to look into someone's eyes to see whether the other person is getting what you're saying. Are you reaching them? When you talk to the camera, your intention has to be for the camera to "get it."

Notice TV news reporters. When they're done commenting or reporting, they simply look back at us, the viewer … actively … directly into camera. As if they were looking at us. They don't gaze. They don't go into a trance or freeze their faces in a deadpan expression. Their attention does not focus on their own faces. Rather, they look outward to the camera, actively, as if it were the person they are talking to. Plus, they don't comment on what they said with a facial gesture, looking heavenward or shrugging their shoulders philosophically.

But the camera is cold and unresponsive. It's not like a human whose response will be perceptible to you when you finish. Therefore, you have to create the connection. You must look into the lens *actively* but without "pushing."

Exercise: Look back at who is looking at you: the camera

To attain this "active looking," seek to explore without judgment, "molecule by molecule," the nature of the darkness in the center of the lens. Actively explore the nature of the darkness. Experiment with this. Moving your eyes' focus from spot to spot within the little dark circle in the middle of the lens will not record as movement to the viewer. It will make you look alive, as opposed to assuming a deadpan gaze.

To get a feel for what I am talking about: Look at an object in the room. Look at it! Don't push, rather seek to gather and accept judgment its nature. Look to find out what's there. Then look inward as if into your own head. Then back outward at the object. It's the looking *outward* that works. Looking outward – to the lens, to whom you're talking – is what I am talking about; as if you were

> looking into the eyes of a person you just said something to and are awaiting, without challenge, their response.

On camera you will never have to do this for more than a few seconds because this will signal to the viewer or camera-person in a very human way that it's now their turn to contribute to the exchange, or ask another question or say thank you and turn off the camera.

Again: When you're finished with your response – just like in life – look back at who is looking at you: the camera. Hold this active looking until "they" ask you another question, or in some other way respond to you, or until they turn off the camera.

Never comment facially on your own response or performance.

Never comment negatively on your work. No looking heavenward, or wincing, or shrugging apologetically. Someone once said: "Never complain and never explain." This is good advice for an on-camera interview. (You are talking as if to a best friend, remember.) And, after all, if you don't think much of your response at the moment, how is the viewer supposed to take it?

When the interview is over: *leave happily.*

And by that I don't necessarily mean peppy, rather just somewhere north of "five" ... if we're gauging one to ten with "one" being a total disaster and "ten" being orgasmic.

Establish your relationship with the camera

Another exercise that brings greater benefit than you might think is to put a camera in your life. Let me suggest that all cameras are the same camera in the same way as a friend who shows up in different clothes each day is still the same person.

Exercise: Put a camera in your life

Get a camera, any camera (but *not* the one that might be part of your computer monitor!) – a $7 disposable, a 35 mm reflex, an old 16 mm movie camera, a home video camera … it doesn't matter – and put it somewhere in your living space at home with the lens cap off. Don't make a shrine out of it; just put a camera as if absently on a counter or a dresser-top or a shelf where it can see you … no big deal … so that it can watch you live. See what it is like to actually live on camera. It is different from performing. (And you need to know the difference … so you will stop performing.) Every once in a while, a couple of times a day, for a second or two each time, glance at the lens. Make eye contact with it. Acknowledge it. It's just between the two of you. And notice to yourself your relationship to it. Do you like it? Do you hate it? What? Does it impose on you? Does it intrude? Does it make you self-aware? Do you relish its attention? Is it lonely? Is it stern? Does it need a friend, perhaps? Does it make your life better? It doesn't matter "what." The value is to become aware of the actual relationship you have with the camera. Let that be just as it is. It will grow or change with time.

Do this. It will pay bigger dividends than you might expect. In my own experience, this exercise led me to understand that the camera was actually lonely … always sitting on the sidelines observing, never participating, never given a chance to respond or offer a thought. It must sit mutely and suffer without defense all the opinions people have about it. I came to realize the camera wants to be included, shared with, appreciated.

You will find, as have many of my students – with all the variables that can take you by surprise in an on-camera interview or audition – the *one* constant, the *one* thing you can count on when you come through the audition door is that little round darkness in the center of the lens. Make brief eye contact with it, just for an instant, just between the two of you, you and the camera, just like at home … you will find something reliable there, an anchor, a constant you can trust.

Summary

If you are likely to be interviewed on-camera, set your mind for it.

- It is your *behavior* that wins them, not your facts. It's not the content of what you say, but rather how you express your emotional connection to the content, that's important.
- Talk to them as if they have been your friend for years. Share your observations about the small dumb details or thoughts of your life … just like with your friends.
- To communicate with the decision-makers, include and communicate with your friend the camera.
- Don't fake it. The camera is interested in one thing: What is truly going on with you.
- Trust the principles of the "Free association technique."
- When it's over, look back at who is looking at you: the camera.
- Never "comment" negatively, facially or verbally, on your performance.
- Leave happily.

CHAPTER 4

I asked him, "How do I get to where you are?" "Oh," he said, "that's impossible … but there are a million ways."

… Yale Whal, director, 1968

AGENTS, MONOLOGUES AND HEADSHOTS

First meetings with agents

Nothing ever goes as planned. Keeping that in mind:

In the waiting room, when they come to get me, this is the first glimpse they will get of me. It's an important moment. I always want to be doing something so that when they come to get me they interrupt my activity. I prefer to be standing, not sitting … looking at a painting, talking on the phone, reading a script, even pacing in the hall. To me, it's better not to be caught sitting small in a chair just staring waiting without activity. I think that makes me seem too needy. Timing this up can be problematic and sometimes means I have to do things over and over. Use your ingenuity. Make them come to you a little bit. Remember, you are at your most attractive when you are doing something.

> Note: What I wear to this meeting will be determined by what I was wearing when we met (if the meeting resulted from a social encounter) or my signature wardrobe which I used in my headshot. It will not be identical, but will strike the same note.

The overall impression I want to create (whether it's true or not) is that I'm professionally busy … that I've just come from a rehearsal or a meeting and right after I finish meeting with the agent I have some other obligation I must hurry to. For a meeting with an agent or a manager – as opposed to an audition, where you arrive as early as you need to – I like to arrive exactly on time or one or two minutes late. Never early. Never more than one or two minutes late. (Wait in the car if you have to.)

I try to make personal and specific contact with the receptionist (Twenty-Year Friend). This is a very important person. It's common for an agent, after a meeting with a potential client, to poll the receptionist: "What did *you* think of that person?" The receptionist will likely be busy when I first enter – they have their job to do – but there is always an opportunity, however small, to make some kind of contact. (Comment with humor on the reality of the moment. Share a thought about something that happened within the last ten minutes. Compare notes about life.) I don't flirt or hit on the person, I don't try to impress them. I just try to make true human contact.

> I had a student once, an admirably industrious young actress, who went in for a hard-won interview with an important agent she had heard great things about. Naturally, she was nervous about the meeting. When the actress arrived at the agency's impressive office, she was signed in by a receptionist behind the desk who kept intruding into her "focus" with small talk as she waited for the agent to come out. Not wanting to let anything distract her from her big moment, the actress was dismissive of the

receptionist's comments and gave them little attention. After a number of empty exchanges, the woman stood up abruptly and said, "Well, my dear, it was nice to meet you. Leave a picture and résumé and we'll give you a call." (Fat chance.) Turns out the "receptionist" was the agent! ... using the outer office for their meeting because of some mix-up in scheduling.

So, take a lesson. You never know.

We make people comfortable by making ourselves comfortable, by making ourselves at home. As the agent leads me to his/her office, I like to be already engaged in some communication ... Twenty-Year Friend, commenting with humor about myself or about what I'm just now observing or thinking in that moment. It's the only way I know of to be "true." I don't want to be led to an office in silence and have to break that silence after we're seated. Things seem to work out better if the conversation has already started.

I avoid "deep dish" chairs. They suck the energy right out of me. I become too passive. If that is all I'm offered, I will sit on the arm rest rather than sink back into its "black hole."

If I feel that "paralyzed" feeling as I am sitting, I'll change my sitting position, get up and walk around, even acknowledge with humor what I'm experiencing. Anything to get my body in the room.

Again, it doesn't matter what the agent and I talk about so long as I communicate my emotional relationship to whatever we're discussing through tone of voice and body language. (I do this best when I focus on a small detail that's of true and immediate interest to me within the context of the conversation.) My goal is to feel like I'm talking with my best friend or co-worker. I want to compare notes about life. I want to include within my focus the agent's life and experiences as well as my own ... just like with a good friend.

My sincerity, my work ethic, my background, my ambition, my credits, my professional acquaintances ... none of these are worthy subjects unto themselves. They will earn me no credit in the agent's eyes because all actors have these in spades. They're a dime a dozen. Ideally, when these categories come up (which they will) I find I imply more effectively a full complement of positive attributes by sharing and discussing one small detail. For example, I will convey *more* effectively that I am ambitious and sincere and industrious, and creative, and have a sense of humor, and am generally a nifty guy if I share honestly my experiences with, say, one speech of one character from one play than if I list *all* the plays or scenes I have ever done. The impression I make will be a function of my willingness to enjoy and share these details, rather than enumerating what's already on my résumé. The latter is always lifeless and without humanity. Another way of saying this is to focus on the essences that could *not* be conveyed about you in a written biography. Leave all that stuff for your résumé. And remember: Twenty-Year Friend!

Don't stay too long. Remember, you've got places to go and commitments to honor. Hang around too long, and you can talk yourself right out of it. If they introduce you to a colleague, it's a good sign. Most offices want to get a consensus that everyone likes you before they sign. But if they don't, don't worry about it. Rarely will they tell you there and then that they're interested.

AGENTS, YOU CAN'T LIVE WITH 'EM AND YOU CAN'T LIVE WITHOUT 'EM.

... Art Linson, producer

What is really happening is that you're interviewing the agent, not the other way around. If you guys like each other, everyone in that office will be working for *you*. You're just as much a key to the agent's overall success as the agent is to yours. If that agent likes you and sends you out and you score a good job, guess who starts losing sleep from then on worrying about keeping you as a client.

Your biggest enemy is the thought that you don't deserve an agent, that you would be lucky to get one, or that you're supposed to be something other than what you are. Every actor starts somewhere.

As long as you're in acting workshop studying hard, you have as much claim to prosper as anyone else. Trust yourself.

No agent holds the golden key and success doesn't drop into your lap like a winning lottery ticket. What you're looking for is a good "fit." The chances that you'll sign with the first agent you meet are remote. So try to relax and enjoy whatever happens. Finding an agent is a process, like looking for a house to buy … it's rarely the first one you look at. Yes, you'll naturally feel a sense of urgency about it. But the search most commonly unfolds as a series of steps, which in my life, anyway, no matter how earnestly I have pressed, has always been gradual and made perfect sense in retrospect. Remember to enjoy the ride. It will make you more attractive.

Monologues (for agents/managers/casting directors)

In all your on-camera professional career, it is likely that you will be asked to perform a monologue in only one particular circumstance: that is, as a newcomer, when an agent or a casting director takes an interest in you for whatever reason and he/she wants to determine whether you also are able to "act." Basically a monologue, in this circumstance, is an economical way for an agent or a casting director to evaluate your acting ability. Since it is likely that you will need a monologue at some juncture early in your career, it is a good idea to have one ready. You should also take the step to videotape your monologue as a possible adjunct to your "reel" or other internet applications (discussed in Chapter 16).

The following does *not* apply to stage auditions, rather to auditions that take place in an office, or on videotape, with the expressed intent to demonstrate to an agent or manager or some such person that you can act.

Here are my suggestions:

Make your choice contemporary. Ninety-nine percent of the parts you're likely to go out for in the early going will be of a contemporary nature. Even if you do a classic piece exquisitely, though it will be to your great credit, an agent will still want to see you do something contemporary, so that's probably a better place to start.

Trust yourself. Choose what's interesting or compelling or amusing to *you personally*. Do not be seduced by what you think will be impressive to them.

Don't confuse a monologue with a soliloquy. A monologue is not a stage manager talking to the audience, or a lawyer addressing a jury, or a character beseeching the heavens. A monologue involves one person talking to another person for a reason. The speaker is getting at something. He/she wants something from the other person, or wants the other person to understand something, etc.

Make it between one and two minutes long. Less than a minute and they will want to see more. More than two minutes, they will want it to be over.

A dramatic piece is good, but comedy is king (if you can actually make it funny). This is not to downgrade the merits of drama, but if you have two selections to pick from, both of equal merit, choose the comedic. We all love to find folks who can amuse us or make us laugh.

The piece should stand on its own. You owe no allegiance to the larger whole. In other words, don't feel you have to make certain choices based on what happened earlier or later in the piece the material comes from. Strive to make the piece work independently from the context of the source. You can edit it, you can omit sections, do whatever you want … they just want to see whether you can perform a given text in a compelling and believable way. In class, in some cases, I often urge students to identify, quite apart from the circumstances of the source, who it is they know personally that needs to know what they have to say using the text they have chosen.

Don't underestimate the importance of good writing, good material. It's to your advantage that the monologue be written in a way that is entertaining, fresh, compelling, funny, well crafted unto itself … quite apart from what your rendition will impart to it. The source can be anything: a play, a novel, a poem, a newspaper article, etc. Choose great material. But: Stay away from material that is well known or has already been performed brilliantly on stage or screen. For a number of reasons having nothing to do with your performance, you will likely suffer by comparison.

Writing your own monologue can be a very good move. But if you do, remember to respect both the writer and the actor in you. Be the writer, then respect the writer in you and become the actor, treating the material as if it were written by one of the greats. If, as the actor, you mix the two (because, after all, you are the writer, and it is your right to change it), the performance will get muddy. Be disciplined: Keep the two creative parts of you separate.

There is no need to identify the source of the piece unless they ask for it.

Deliver the monologue to camera. You have two choices: delivering the monologue to camera or to some imagined person in the room. I prefer the former. It is a stronger choice for whoever is watching later on the playback monitor. This takes some strategic planning. With very few exceptions (though I have heard of rare instances to the contrary) auditors want to *watch* you perform as opposed to being included in the action. As a general rule, making eye contact with the auditor during the scene confuses them … you will see it pass over their eyes: "Am I watching this scene or am I in it?!" If there's some question about this option, make your intentions known before you start. If they're putting it down on tape, I feel the stronger choice is to read to camera. Once in a while you may come across an auditor who will ask that you deliver your monologue to them. This is rare, but you should be prepared for it or have a well-founded alternative if you'd rather decline to do so.

One further note: You are going to be in an office performing for one person or maybe a small group of strangers who will be judging you. It is going to be strange. You will be nervous. Staging it might be weird. Think about this when you choose your monologue. It is a good strategy to match the theme and circumstances of the monologue to closely parallel the actual circumstances of your audition; i.e. what you are concerned with in your monologue has to do with being judged, or ugly, or misunderstood, or underestimated, or takes place in an office. This isn't essential, but it will help. If you are a novice, picking a monologue that requires an exotic or extreme setup or circumstance might mean asking too much of yourself.

Headshots

I witness many of my students getting quite nervous over this process, which is understandable since it is often an actor's first step into the business end of their aspirations. They want everything to be right. But there are few mistakes in life more easily correctible than your 8 × 10s. Of course you want it to go well, but if it doesn't, it is quite fixable. And, besides, the likelihood is great that you will be taking more 8 × 10s, for any number of reasons, within the next 18 months. So don't make the process too precious.

Let me make a few tangential points about headshots. This whole topic is actually not about acting at all … it's about marketing. In the largest view, trade and sales are what make the world go 'round, and marketing is the agency of this commerce. Being actors, many of us likely shrink from marketing ourselves. It makes us uncomfortable and feels pushy. (That's one of the reasons we seek agents or managers to do it for us.) But especially in the first few years of our careers, until we establish a relationship with a reliable and imaginative agent, we must understand that an important component of our activity will involve this aspect of self-promotion.

The key is persistence. I heard an applicable anecdote about sales that came out of the Harvard Business School. They did a study that observed that most corporate buyers did not make a purchase until after they had had at least five encounters with the sales representative. And, instructively, most sales representatives got discouraged and gave up after only two visits. Hummm.

Keep plugging. Go to seminars and seek out websites that address this issue. If something doesn't work, change it. YouTube, Facebook and whatever is next on the internet's horizon offer wide-open possibilities for innovative ways of making an impression on the powers that be.

Okay ... Headshots:

First off, and most importantly: We are looking for a shot of YOU. Not a corporate version of you. Not your mother's view of you. Not a formal, presentational version of you. YOU. Which to me means neither happy nor sad, nor situational, nor adorned of a "character's" nature ... but simply and directly the essence of you. Words fail, but I have no doubt that you will notice the quality I am talking about if you review headshots of other actors in casting books or online services.

We live in a digital world. Look to the casting services on the internet to identify for yourself the style of photograph you think competes best. To my mind, lately ("lately" because things change) it should be a color shot in close-up. These aesthetics are very subjective. Trust yourself. But definitely digital.

I prefer a photograph taken with a long lens (over 100 mm) so that the background, whatever it is, is well out of focus. I don't like to see vivid tree branches or brickwork or road signs over the shoulder of the subject ... these details compete with the actor's face for attention.

Once you pick a style you like – outdoors, natural lighting; indoors, artificial light; short lens, long lens – find several photographers whose style you like and go talk with them. When trying to decide what you are looking for, do not try to describe it … point to a photo in their "book" that captures what you want from them. This is the best way to communicate with any photographer about what you are getting at. If you don't find it in his/her "book," then that is not the photographer for you. Talking about it, trying to describe it, won't work.

You can expect to spend between $200 and $1000 for this shot. The price has nothing whatsoever to do with the success of the photograph (remember, you already like their style and quality). What *is* important … and what is very much worth paying extra money for … is the *simpatico* you feel with the photographer. If it comes down to you liking two equally, take the cheaper one. But if there is something about the manner or nature of the more expensive one, it is worth paying for.

Since we are looking for a picture of you, what we need to happen is you *feeling very comfortable in the presence of the photographer*, having an easy, natural conversation with him/her about anything and everything under the sun, while he/she takes your picture. A good photographer will be good at encouraging this to happen. You will not pose, or try to create a mood. (This is not modeling, which is the direct opposite of acting.) It is just you, totally comfortable, not making an effort at anything but merely responding to the conversation at hand just like with a good friend … while they snap your picture. It is their job to capture you, not yours. And they will, if you feel relaxed in their presence.

So if you feel any intimidation or strain or awkwardness, for whatever reason, when you interview the photographer – the smell, the location, the cigar, their nervous sense of humor, the cat … anything! – then they are not the photographer for you even though you like their craftsmanship.

Also ... there is nothing mystical about this. Be skeptical of photographers who delve in aromatherapy, or fifth-dimensional music, or hypnotism ... as if there is some psychological trick to all this. There isn't ... only to enjoy an engaging conversation with them while they photograph you.

"**It's all in the eyes**"

Of course your eyes will need to be vividly in focus. But what this phrase refers to is: you will ultimately be drawn to the photograph in which you are looking directly *out* from the picture, directly to the viewer. This quality will be "square one" in the criteria you will apply later to make your final selection. Again, refer to the headshots you deemed most effective in the casting collections. You will see they have this quality in common. Review "Looking back at who's looking at you" in Chapter 3.

To achieve this essential quality of looking "out" you must be looking directly and actively into the lens of the camera ... just as you do when you look into the eyes of somebody you are talking to ... rather than inward to your own thoughts. So don't drift off thinking about Tuscany or your grandmother's sugar cookies. Try to avoid the temptation to think about your face. This is not easy to do, especially under the somewhat exotic circumstances of a photo-shoot, where everything is so much about how you look. *Your task is to focus on having a true, natural, conversation with the photographer.* (This is why the *simpatico* issue is so important.) As you converse with the photographer, talk and respond, making contact with the lens of the camera, as if the lens were their eyes. Relax ... you do it every day!

Wardrobe

I suggest, unless you have a specific ambition for the photograph, three or four changes is enough. These changes should be selected, in concert with your photographer, a day or two before the shoot. Don't wait until the last minute to haul in your whole closet to decide, it draws too much energy away from the task at hand. Don't make selections you don't trust.

There are going to be a few shots other than the one you choose as your primary that show sides of yourself that might work well for specific parts. They are an effective way to suggest the range of your capacities on composites or websites, and are the principal reason for being photographed in more than one outfit.

Your *primary wardrobe choice* should be what I refer to as your "signature wardrobe." The others should be in contrast to or variations on that theme. Ask yourself, if you were going in to see an agent for the first time with no introduction, how would you want him/her to see you? What outfit represents most clearly and strongly your own personal style and at the same time suggests other possibilities if you were you dressed more upscale or more casually?

Don't choose some "cosmic" leather jacket or any other garment that is so distinct and of such a special quality that the photograph becomes about the clothes and not about you.

In all cases, make sure the garments you choose are "fresh." They don't have to be new, but I have seen many photographs sullied by garments that were threadbare or had seen too much laundering.

Don't be distracted by concerns about highlighting your "type" through wardrobe. There is no way you can escape your type no matter what you do or wear. Sure you have ideas, but the person who is least capable of determining your type … is you. It is an issue that will be determined by others as your career unfolds.

For women, if you have a good figure, at least one choice should include that fact without being overly suggestive.

Avoid jewelry that overwhelms the shot. Keep it simple. Remember, it's about your eyes.

The world is digital, and virtually all submissions by agents to casting directors are currently done via the internet. But you will still have use in the beginning of your career for hard copy 8 10s to persistently send out to agencies, and for postcards to advise possibly interested parties of an upcoming event you would like them to see you in.

I heard the great director Robert Altman once say that the way he edits his films is to show the rough cuts to friends and wherever he feels embarrassed he knows there is more work to be done. I take that as good advice: if you feel embarrassed as to the quality of your 8×10, or find yourself wanting to explain something when you show it to someone or send it out … time to get a new one.

Now let's begin to discuss an on-camera audition where there is an actual scene involved.

On-Camera
Audition Strategies

CHAPTER 5

I knew you were perfect for the part the moment you walked into the room

YOUR ON-CAMERA ENTRY

We've talked about factors to enhance your "general" on-camera interviews; now we're going to move on in the next chapters to the special considerations that come into play when you're auditioning on-camera for a specific role.

This chapter is about entering the audition room, which is a moment that is so important I am devoting an entire chapter to it.

The decision is made the instant they see you

This is huge. Huge! For all actors, but especially at the start of your career when you are an unknown entity, entering the casting director's office or the audition room – coming through the door, or when you first appear on the playback monitor – is by far and away the most important moment of your audition. You will hear it over and over throughout your career (I know I have):

I knew you were perfect for the part
the moment you walked into the room.

I remember reading an interview years ago of Peter Bogdanovitch, the director of the Academy Award-winning film *The Last Picture Show* (1971). He commented on this very phenomenon when referring to Jeff Bridges as the young actor walked in for his audition. In the article Mr Bogdanovitch said something like: "When he walked in I practically fell off my chair. He was perfect! I remember thinking to myself, 'God, please, I hope he can act.'"

In his long-standing book *Audition* (Bantam Books, page 230) Michael Shurtleff emphasizes the critical importance of an actor's entry when auditioning. He recounts the unforgettable impression Barbra Streisand made, a complete unknown at the time, as she walked on stage to audition for the Broadway production of *I Can Get It for You Wholesale*. She entered the bare stage to sing her song … in a raccoon coat, wearing mismatched shoes, chewing gum! She positioned herself on the lone stool in the middle of the stage and readied herself to begin: she sang two notes, paused and took the wad of gum out of her mouth and irreverently stuck it to the underside of the seat. Perfect! Then proceeded to sing her audition number.

For your on-camera auditions, because the decision-maker is going to be viewing your work on video playback with the fast-forward button in his or her hand, the following is particularly important. I have been in those tape-viewing sessions. Believe me when I tell you that many times the auditors don't even let you get to your slate before they send you off to the discard bin. You're out of it before they even see you "act the scene."

I illustrate the impact of the entry in the first meeting of my class. I like to wait until the classroom is full of students before I enter for the first time. Most of the students have never seen me before. They've heard stories perhaps but they don't know what to expect. Then I allude to this moment later in my introductory talk. I ask them to think back to when I first walked in, the impression I made on each of them the instant they saw me enter just by virtue of how I walked in, what I was doing, how I was dressed. I ask them to acknowledge that they each drew a specific conclusion about me, whether positive or negative. I either "looked the part" or I didn't.

You all know what I'm talking about. We experience this quite dramatically when, in life, we talk to a stranger on the phone, get a picture of them in our mind's eye, and then finally meet them in person. It can be a shock or a relief. In life we are all socialized to be tolerant and patient so we give a guy a break. But for the director of a film who also has a sense of what the character might look like in his mind's eye, this first impression, which he knows will register very emphatically with the audience, is critical.

I see it over and over: actors who enter the audition room and stand haplessly in front of the camera waiting for their audition to begin. When in fact the audition has *already* begun! It began outside before they came through the door. Next!

One of the telling clues as to what factors are paramount in winning a role is the fact that when you sit in the outer office waiting to be called in, all the other actors reading for your part will look pretty much like you. Very often they will have chosen to wear much the same as you in the way of wardrobe. The fact is you don't get the part because of what you look like: you may get the audition for that reason, but not the part.

Now, you cannot control what the director is imagining or how open he might be to new ideas, but there are definitely things you, the actor, can do to increase their chances. If you get the part it won't be luck. You will have intentionally done a whole sequence of things in your audition to win the role ... and the first thing will have been your entry.

In this chapter I'm going discuss "entering the audition room" in terms of five interdependent concepts that I have listed below. Keep in mind through this discussion, though, that as you actually enter for your audition all of these factors will be in play at the same time and will be happening simultaneously. (Just as in tennis: you keep your eye on the ball *and* move towards it *with* your weight forward *as* you draw your racket back all at the same time.) The problem is I have no choice but to discuss each component in a sequence of separate ideas. I will leave it to you to put them all together. Apart from actually performing your scene, the following factors are crucial to manifesting an effective on-camera audition entry.

The five concepts:

1. You are what you are doing
2. What creates "presence" on camera
3. The "entry verb"
4. "Character" is defined by what the individual *does*
5. Concentration

You are what you are doing

I like to start this discussion by asking my students: "In the broadest sense, when do people get crushes on you?" Think about it. Isn't it most often when you are so engrossed in doing something that you are unaware they are watching?

> *You are most interesting when you are*
> *totally involved in doing something.*

In your own life's experience, don't you find that it turns out you are most attractive or interesting to others when you're not trying to be attractive or interesting … but instead when your focus is elsewhere, when you are actually *doing something*? … mowing the lawn, giving a speech about something important to you, helping someone, actually reading. Whenever you sit on a bar stool caressing your deluxe coiffure trying to be fabulous, pretty generally no one ever comes knocking. Isn't that true? Isn't it?!?!

You are what you are doing. A physically grotesque person helping another person becomes a beautiful person. A gorgeous person stepping on another person's face becomes ugly. There's real knowledge in recognizing this is true. This goes all the way back to the Greeks.

> *TO BE IS TO DO.*
>
> ... Plato

Let's take this one baby step further. An anecdote I read some years ago illustrates what I mean by "doing something." Cybill Shepherd, the star of the hit 1980s TV series *Moonlighting*, was one of the biggest stars in the world when she was 18 or 20. She had been a model of international acclaim and then stared in the 1971 Oscar-winning film *The Last Picture Show*. She related in an interview how Orson Welles, the great film director, had asked her why, since she was such an international sensation, he never saw her on talk shows. She confided that it was because she didn't know how to "do" talk shows. He responded by saying that talk shows were easy. All she had to do was have a conversation with the host.

She didn't have to *be* witty or *be* beautiful, or *be* intelligent, or *be* entertaining. All she had to *do* was have a conversation with the host. This she could *do*. She focused on this and it immediately cleared up her whole problem.

So, the first concept is:

> *On-camera, strive to always be doing something as opposed to "being yourself."*

Because you are at your most attractive or most interesting when you are doing something, you need to be *doing* something as you come into the audition room.

We will discuss what that "doing" might be right after I make one other supporting observation.

What creates "presence" on camera

This is crucial: On camera, thinking is an action. The camera sees exactly what you are doing. No escape. If you're tying your shoe, that's what the camera sees. If you're *showing* us that you're tying your shoe that is again exactly what the camera sees: a person *showing us* that they're tying their shoe. If you're reading a newspaper but thinking about tying your shoe, the camera sees that you're thinking about something other than reading the newspaper. If you're thinking about the next line of dialogue, that is what the camera sees. If you're trying to look like you're thinking by thinking about how your face would look if you were really thinking … the camera sees that too. (I call that "Thinking about my face" and, incidentally, I personally don't do that in real life, think about my face, except in one circumstance … when I'm faking.)

On-camera presence is held by the actor with the most active thoughts. That's what generates presence: your mental focus on what the character is *doing*. In *Acting in Commercials* (page 35) Joan See combines Uta Hagan's well-known reflection, *to act is to do*, with her own succinct observations, leading us to the following synthesis:

> *To act is to do.*
> *To think is to do.*
> *To act is to think.*

Billy Bob Thornton was once asked what was the most difficult part he ever performed. He referred to a part that called for him to do nothing, mostly just be there and be still. He said what was so hard about it was that he had to have active thoughts all the time, which was difficult but essential, because the audience can tell when nothing is going on with a character.

Therefore, the second concept is:

> *Thinking is doing.*
> *This mental "doing" creates presence.*

Remember: *Do*, don't show. You want to have "presence" when you enter the audition room.

The "entry verb"

Now we are getting to "what to do." This is going to take a little time to explain, so stay with me. An equation is setting up here. 1) You're at your most attractive/interesting on-camera when you are doing something. 2) Thinking is doing. 3) Therefore always have a mental verb to enter with.

You always have to ask yourself when you prepare for a reading: "What am I going to be doing mentally as I enter the room? What problem am I going to be trying to solve? What is my mental attention going to be focused on?" That's why I call it the "**entry verb**." Never be without one. It will give you presence as you come through the door.

> **Important:** This is not an "improv." You're not showing in any way what you're doing. In fact you are essentially going to hide it. (You are going to "*tie* your shoe, not show us you are tying your shoe!") It doesn't involve talking, or exchanges with the casting people. It is something you're thinking about: an active mental task or problem to solve. The producers will not know what you're doing. They will simply see that "something is going on with you." That's what presence is. If they talk to you, you will take time out from your mental task to talk and respond to them. You will do so in whatever way is appropriate to the circumstance. But when the exchange is over, you go back to your mental objective … so that you are never on camera without your active mental task.

> Here is a life example to describe further the nature of what I am getting at: Imagine you're in a shopping mall and you have to make a phone call. Your cell is out of batteries so you're looking for a public phone. You happen to run into an old friend. You will take time out to greet and talk with your friend, cordially and fully, but

all the time in the back of your mind you will be thinking about having to make the call. Try as you might, the intention to find a phone and make the telephone call will affect the conversation. It will affect, however slightly, your behavior. If there is a lull in the conversation, you will possibly say, "Charlie, it is great to see you, but do you know where there's a phone? I have to make a call. Let me do that and then we'll have some coffee together." Mentally searching for the opportunity to make the phone call is, in this example, the "verb" I am talking about.

The third concept is:

> *Pick a mental objective that is doable but requires*
> *active mental attention to accomplish.*

And by this I do not mean counting backwards from 100 by sevens, or solving complicated long division problems. What do I mean? Read on …

"Character" is defined by what the individual does

Great novelists know this. It's what they mean when they say good writers "show" rather than "tell." In other words we learn who the character is by what we see him do. (And by the way, great writers do not trust adjectives. The power of good writing lies in the verbs the writer chooses.)

We are going to establish a working definition of "character" as: What the individual *does* in response to any given circumstance. As Shawn Nelson points out in his brilliant audiotape *The Impersonal Actor*, marital status, age, gender, limps, accents, past family trauma, poverty, hard luck stories, beauty, nationality, etc. … these are not character. These are the *circumstances* of the character. The character is what he *does*.

For example: as an individual walks down the street he is confronted by a mugger, the individual drops to his knees cringing, hides his eyes and holds out his wallet, begging the mugger to take it and be gone. That's one character. Same identical looking individual walks down the street, is confronted by a mugger, the individual hits the mugger with a right, slugs him in the balls, drops him with a knee to the chin, steps on his chest and goes whistling down the street leaving the mugger in a heap: same individual, totally different character. Again: same individual is confronted by the mugger, he makes a clever joke and the two go off and have a beer together ... see what I mean? The "character" is defined by what the individual does in a given situation.

Selecting what entry verb to use

To determine an effective entry verb, ask yourself what is the character doing just as the scene begins: Going to a party? Looking to get some rest? Trying to get some work done? Expecting to meet someone? What, and Where? Now, when I say "entry verb" I mean coming into the audition room with the mental intention of *doing what the character wants to do as the scene begins.*

The nature of the scene's opening situation will cue you as to what to enter with. Yes, something will happen as the scene unfolds that will cause a change (e.g. the character will be confronted by a mugger and react). That's how scenes go. But it is at the top of the scene, the beginning, where you look for an entry verb. (When you envisioned the character in the example with the mugger, what was he doing as he walked down the street? Shopping, going to meet a good friend, tired and going home? What did that mean he was thinking about, anticipating, or trying to solve? That's the entry verb!) You will come to realize that often when we audition for a scene on-camera we do not have the advantage of access to the whole script. All actors know that to do a scene well, you have to be aware of where the character has just been prior to the start of the scene; where he is coming from as the scene starts. This dovetails with establishing an entry verb.

Your entry verb is "your secret"

> *YOU ALWAYS HAVE TO WALK ON STAGE WITH A SECRET,*
> *SOMETHING THE AUDIENCE DOESN'T KNOW ABOUT ...*
> *IT MAGNIFIES YOU, MAKES YOU MORE INTERESTING ...*
>
> ... Emma Thompson, *LA Times*,
> Sunday, March 15, 1998, page 86

Trust Emma Thompson, for heavens' sake! What you are doing, your mental verb, is your secret, and you are not to tell it or to show it, only to *do* it. You will see, in the slightest but most vital way, it will affect how you behave in there.

The entry verb is not an adjective. It is not an attitude. It is an *action*.

For example, if the scene is about your character getting poisoned in the library, maybe a good choice (because it is your call) would be to enter the audition room mentally looking for the perfect place in the room to study. Or, if the scene were about you making an important phone call, enter the audition room looking for an opportunity to take time out to make the call. If the scene has you falling in love with someone you meet on a bus, then your entry verb might be looking for the best place in the room to sit down from your bus trip. (Don't sit down! Just covertly be looking for the best place.)

Consider the character's strategy. I used the word "strategy" earlier. Often the character has a strategy coming in the room. It is important, for instance, if the scene called for your character to confront the other character, or even to kill him with your bare hands, for you to consider what would be the most effective way for your character to enter, to make his point, or get close enough to wring his neck. It wouldn't include storming into the room, because that would telegraph your intentions to the other person and put them on the defensive. You would need to act more covertly to be effective. That's what Emma Thompson means by entering with a secret.

Important note: Make a socially positive or at least socially neutral choice for your entry verb. By this I mean, no matter how "bad" the character is, or how violent his intentions in the scene, do not make an anti-social entry. (Think about it: An ax murderer can be committing bloody mayhem in his room but in the midst of it all, if someone knocks on the door, he will suddenly become socially appropriate towards the intruder.) In my earnestness to do good work I made this mistake several times ... came thundering in looking to chew somebody's head off because I knew that was what the scene entailed. I acted abrasively toward anyone in my path all the way in from the parking lot ... until my agent called me and told me that everyone had concluded I was a total jerk. I complained to my agent: "I'm an actor! I'm doing a scene, for chrissake! Tell them not to take it personally!" But they *do* take it personally, they *will* take it personally. A negative (anti-social) entry choice will scare the auditors and/or put them off. The risk is they will take your demeanor personally and will consequently be distracted from seeing what it is you have to offer as the character. The truth is I was not only acting like a jerk, I was making ineffective clichéd choices for my entry; because in real life, if I acted that way, someone in my path would warn my adversary that I was on the march. They'd never let me in the door. The only effective way to get the upper hand would be to enter as harmlessly and as innocently as I possibly could. So be smart. Make the character cunning as to how he enters.

An example from one of my own auditions that worked great:

I was auditioning for the part of an incestuous child molester. It was for a Movie of the Week and the camera was rolling as I entered the audition room. My verb as I came in the room and chatted prior to doing the scene was to use a demeanor that would convince everyone in the room that I couldn't possibly be guilty of such a vile act. Worked like a charm. Colored everything I did.

So, the fourth concept is:

> *What you are doing mentally as you enter defines*
> *the character. It should be consonant with what the*
> *character is doing at the top of the scene.*
> *Keep it your secret.*

Let me say it again: What you enter with, what you are *doing* mentally as you enter and take time out from to talk with the folks in there … *is the character*. That's why the entry verb is so crucial. It's the first glimpse the casting people get of you; the defining moment. It's both a strategic and an aesthetic issue. When I help an actor prepare for an audition, we spend a good portion of time analyzing the content of the scene and our best estimate as to the overall nature of the story to determine what to "go in with," so as to make a strong initial impression that you are the character; you are "perfect" for the part.

Continue with this mental task all the way to and through the slate. You have no control over when they turn on the camera. (I have auditioned on occasion when the camera was running as I came in the room!) The first glimpse the viewers get of you as they watch your audition on the playback monitor is in essence your on-camera entry; again a defining moment.

Concentration

The fifth contributing factor for a good entry is concentration: your ability to involve yourself in what you are doing when you know that the camera is "watching." Acting teachers will often admonish you to "Concentrate!" What does that mean? (Have you ever been thinking so much about listening that you don't hear what is being said? Surely that can't be right.) What "concentration" means is to be involved in the circumstances of the scene or in the action you are doing so that you are no longer "watching yourself." This is why, because the camera is so perceptive, creating the circumstances, and posing them to yourself in terms of an action that you can actually do, is so important when acting for the camera. You have to know yourself. Remember, it is not an attitude, nor does it require an emotional disposition. It is a mental doing. You must choose an entry verb that is both suitable for the scene and compelling enough for you personally so that you can involve yourself with it even in the event that you feel "on stage."

> *NEVER LET THE PRODUCER SEE YOU OUT OF CHARACTER.*
>
> ... Peggy Feury

This is what the entry verb accomplishes. And don't forget, sometime during your entry you're going to take a moment and comment with humor on the reality of the moment.

There is an added benefit to a well-selected choice. As Stella Adler used to point out:

> *You get nervous (self-aware) when you*
> *don't have something to do.*

The entry verb not only gives you something to focus on doing as you enter and sets a "theme" for your portrayal of the character, but it also gives you something to turn to if any awkward pauses arise before the actual scene begins. It will help you take your attention off yourself and direct your energy to the task at hand. *It is not attitude, and it is not emotional.* In essence the scene starts with you out in the waiting room. The entry verb acts as a ramp up to whatever you intend to create, so you need only go from 45 mph to 60 mph rather than from 0 to 60 mph when at last you finally start the scene.

Therefore, the fifth concept is:

> *Select an entry verb that is not only appropriate for the*
> *scene, but that is also personally engaging enough for you*
> *to be able to concentrate on it even if you are nervous.*

In our initial classes I first put my students in certain on-camera situations to demonstrate how important body language and vocal tone are in communicating "who we are." This is what we discussed in the first chapter. I then follow up with the concept of working with a mental verb and how it can, among other things: create presence; overcome self-awareness; and dispel nerves.

Exercise: Working with "mental verbs"

To do this I have my students do one or two of the following on-camera exercises. I instruct them, as they sit down in front of the camera for the first time, to "just relax and be themselves." They cannot do it because no one in the world can do it … they start looking lost, or start to giggle, or become visibly self-aware. (If people could "just relax" there would be no such thing as stage fright. And paradoxically, "being" yourself, as Plato instructs us, is not something you can "do").

As a starting point, I then ask them to do one or two of the following – without gesture or in any way indicating what they are doing:

- Count backwards mentally from 100 to zero by sevens.
    This is a mental task they can get involved in. It can be done, but it takes concerted effort to do it.
- Sit quietly and listen to all the sounds they can hear, identifying the sound that is coming from furthest away.
- Telepathically – without talking – communicate to the camera the rules of baseball. (Don't gaze! Don't forget to blink!)
- Strive to make themselves at home.
- Imagine that they are, as they sit there, as "big as the room."
    Not physically, but rather that their energy, their chi, their aura, extends out from every side of them, top and bottom, to all the extremities of the room.

When students focus on these and other mental doings the transformation is often quite dramatic. Suddenly they fill the screen, they "belong" there, and we viewers are curious.

Note: The above choices are *demonstration* choices. It is *very unlikely* that they would pertain to a specific scene, but you might try them to see how all this works.

One further thought

You know how when you are acting well you have the distinct experience of being totally involved in the situation of the character. It includes knowing exactly why you are in the room. It is a great feeling, isn't it?

When an actor auditions well it is not only because they have the craft to pull off the audition scene, it is also because they have a conviction about the nature of the character and his situation in the first place ... they have a "connection" to the part, a "knowing." That knowing is evident as the actor enters. Believe me, casting people can "see it coming through the door." It is an unmistakable quality. And for the actor it can't help but include knowing "why the character is entering the room." The act of entering the audition room will be informed by what the character is trying to accomplish by being in the room in the first place. That's the "entry verb" I am talking about.

Summary

- The decision is made the instant they see you.
- You are at your most attractive/interesting when you are doing something. Focus on what you are doing rather than on "being yourself."
- On-camera presence is held by the actor with the most active thoughts. Therefore enter the room *doing* an active mental verb.
- Do not indicate in any way what it is you are doing, just do it.
- Select a mental activity that is consonant with what the character is doing at the top of the scene.

- Make a socially positive or neutral choice consonant with what the character is doing at the top of the scene.
- Do not confuse a verb with an attitude. Attitudes are defined by adjectives. Adjectives confine the character and they wear out fast. To be is to "do."
- As you enter and before you "settle," reflect with humor on the reality of the moment.

CHAPTER 6

Calm them by knowing what you want to do

HOW ON-CAMERA AUDITIONS GO

Let's get one thing straight right from the top: *an audition is a performance, a full out performance.* Your aim is either to get the job, or to make a strong impression.

The audition is not a suggestion, nor an approximation. They are looking for the actor who makes it work. It is your job to make it work right there in front of their very eyes. Your goal is to create a reality in the audition room on camera that supports the story being told.

In this chapter I will lay out sequentially what will happen in your auditions and make some recommendations as to how to deal with the various issues that will certainly arise. The chapters that follow will examine specific aspects of approaches to both strategy and preparation which, when marshaled together, will pave the way to inspired work.

The actual audition setup

When you walk into the audition room to read for a movie or television show, you are usually going to be walking into what is essentially someone's office … the casting director's or the producer's. The office will be large enough for you to do what you have come to do. Sometimes these office rooms are very spare and business-like, sometimes very plush. It won't be cramped or cluttered. On the other side of the room, opposite the door you enter will be a desk. Often the casting person will be sitting behind the desk facing you. Maybe there will be a window behind it; maybe a couch along one side of the room with a coffee table, perhaps some shelves along one of the walls. And there will be space for you to work in the center of the room, either standing or sitting on a chair that has been placed there for your use. There may be only one or two people in the room, sometimes more … the writers and the director could be watching from the couch. And, if they plan to videotape your audition, near the desk, aimed into the center of the room where you will be, will be a camera on a tripod. The person operating the camera will be standing behind it. (If it is different than this, you might find yourself commenting with humor on the difference.)

Even if the decision-makers are there in the room, the presence of the camera means that they're going to make their final decisions based on viewing the tape of your performance later. All of the on-camera issues are very much in play.

You are there to perform a scene, which usually means you are going to "read" with someone. They will play the other character. Sometimes they bring in a professional actor for this but usually it's one of the casting people who will fill in. The person who will read the other character will be standing or sitting to the side of the camera … or perhaps it will be the casting director sitting behind the desk. You will be the only one on camera, and you will no longer be talking directly to the camera, as you did for an on-camera interview, rather you will be acting as if the camera were not there.

When you audition on camera, the camera is shooting "the single"

To explain this further: when you watch movies or TV, you'll see that most scenes start out with a wide camera angle. This tells the audience where the action is taking place, and gives the audience a sense of the geometry of the action, who and where things are in relation to each other, so they can understand what's going on. (When the director chooses not to do this it's because he/she wants the audience to be disoriented or to wonder or be intrigued by what is unfolding.) Then conventionally – not always but usually – as the scene unfolds, the camera leaves the wide shot and moves in for emphasis. It isolates with closer shots what the director wants the audience to pay attention to. On the set, when you shoot the scene, you will perform it identically several times. At first it will include all of the players in the wide shot. Then they will move the camera in to isolate what they want to feature. (It's called "the single" or the "close-up" or the "two shot" … meaning only one or two of the actors are on camera.) The others will be playing the scene off-screen, actually standing next to the camera, depending on the geometry of the scene, and the actor who is on camera will be playing the scene to them in just the same way as in the wide shot. This, then, is the shot that's the audition scene. It's "*the single*."

Remember the frame-by-frame golf swing picture I alluded to in the preface? What follows is the general flow of how an audition goes. Its purpose is to guide you step by step through the details. But, as I said earlier, after you get the whole picture I must leave it to you to meld the steps together and "swing the club."

Read the chapter; study it; think about the ideas in it; but then let them go. Act the scene.

That having been said:

- You will enter with a verb.

- As you enter, you will "comment with humor on the reality of the moment."
- There may or may not be a brief chat.
- You will clear up any questions you have about the scene.
- You will identify with whom you are reading and make confirming eye contact with that person.
- You will confirm where in the script you will start and which character has the first line.
- They will have you "slate" (say your name to camera).
- Then you will "disappear" the camera and perform the scene as if it were just the two of you, you and the person playing the other character, in the room alone. Just like in the movies.

Make sense? Good. Now we've got work to do.

It is your audition. You belong there. Calm them by knowing what you want to do.

"They" might suggest other choices when you get in there, but go in with a definite plan about how you intend to use the room to perform the scene … e.g. sitting, standing, moving across the room, roaming, lying on the floor, leaning against the door, etc. Remember you are *collaborating* with them. An experienced actor comes in with specific ideas about what they want to do. It doesn't wear well to have you casting your eyes around the room trying to make up your mind as to whether you will sit "here or over there."

When I say plan, I do not mean a blueprint set in stone.

Also, don't ask permission. Simply inform them what you intend to do, if you expect to move about, so the camera person will be aware of what he needs to anticipate. In your rehearsals at home, visualize the likely physical realities of the audition space. Suffice it to say you will be in an office. There will be a door, a floor, a chair, perhaps a corner, perhaps a couch and coffee table. This is what you will have to work with. Usually there will be a chair in the middle of the room.

Its presence implies that you should sit. But that is up to you, the artist, as to whether or not to use it, and how you want to use it. Only experience will tell you what adjustments you might make. Come in with your own well-conceived preference as to how you are going to use the space but be prepared for possible alternatives. Usually you will be free to move about, or remain stationary, as you please. But I have heard of at least one casting director who absolutely insists that no matter what the content or action of the audition scene, she wants the actor sitting upright in a straight-back chair. So go figure.

Ask yourself: "What is it going to take to create a reality in there?" Remember, they are looking for the actor who makes the scene work. Moving within the "place" of the scene often is crucial. In the freedom and privacy of your rehearsal, once you have worked through the scene, explore what adjustments you would have to make if they required you to do it in an alternative way, i.e. sitting or standing in one spot.

One other note: To the uninitiated, the audition arrangement seems quite intimidating and constricting. I want to assure you that you may use the space within the office in whatever way you need to perform the scene as written. For example, if the scene calls for your character to die painfully of poisoning, then you may gag and quake as you crumple from your chair and writhe grotesquely across the floor until you succumb. If the scene calls for you to discover that your boyfriend is actually a vampire, feel free to back up to the corner of the room and shrink to a little ball as you scream in horror.

ON-CAMERA AUDITION STRATEGIES (STEP BY STEP)

Try to avoid going first

Sometimes it can't be helped – and you can indeed win the part going first – but try not to be first. Third or fourth is better. There are a lot of reasons for this but ask yourself, if you were judging a diving contest could you give the first person a "10"? Probably not. I have heard directors deny this but I know I am right ... and so does every other experienced actor in town. The main reason is, it often takes a while for the people in there to establish the best way to conduct an audition for a particular scene. The first couple of candidates are a little like guinea pigs. Things haven't taken a shape yet. Also, remember they are going to make their decision by watching the tape. It is going to take a while for everybody to settle down and concentrate in the viewing room. The first couple of candidates on the tape aren't going to get the viewers' full attention. So if you arrive at the appointed time and see on the sign-in sheet that you are first, take a walk down the hall, go primp a little in the rest room, try not to be the first one.

Do not come in the room until you know for certain that you have been called

Since your entry is the most important moment, you want to enter on your terms. Do not peek in to check whether you have been called, or to wonder why you haven't been called, or to make sure they haven't called you yet. If you do, you will blow your entry. If you are uncertain, don't worry, they will come and get you. They do not want you invading their space, or intruding on whatever they are doing in there, until they are ready for you. They will resent that intrusion. Entering before you have been called bungles the whole audition.

No need to shake hands

Ed Deckter, a prominent sit com director made this point at a symposium I attended years ago: Make your greetings kind of "Japanese style," a simple nod and acknowledgment with eye contact from across the room. They are seeing a lot of people. They don't want to shake a lot of clammy hands. They can't help but be distracted by the thought that they are bound to get sick.

Do not wear your technique on your sleeve

Do not make a big show out of "preparing" … going over into the corner and making a show of somberly gathering yourself. Nothing in the world is happening in that corner and you know it. If your entry verb is on target you should already be 75% there. Do not ask questions just to show off. Or say things that you think demonstrate a perceptive interpretation. Nobody cares how clever you are, they only want to see how you act the scene. Do only whatever it is you have to do in order to do what you have come to do. Stretch, move, acknowledge nerves but *never* "demonstrate" technique or process. Let your performance speak for you. It is the only thing that counts.

Read the chapter on "wardrobe"

This is an important component of a worthy audition.

You may ask questions, as long as they aren't dumb questions

The folks who are calling you in for the audition need and respect you, otherwise they wouldn't call you in.

Ninety-nine times out of a hundred, you and your acting coach (because every serious actor has a coach or someone of experience whose judgment they trust) will be able to formulate an approach to the scene you are going to read. But sometimes, when you are rehearsing a scene, there may be a question about the facts behind the circumstances of the scene, or the tone of the piece in general, which simply must be answered in order for you to make a specific choice.

You need to formulate this question in a simple sentence. No hand waving or hemming and hawing. And in your mind, you need to have already established that if the answer to your question is, for instance,

"A" you're going to do "C," if the answer is "B" you're going to do "D."

As I said, sometime after your greetings, someone will ask you if you have any questions.

You can ask this question in the audition room before you begin: "I am assuming thus and such is true. Am I on the right track?"

Or: As long as you don't make a pest of yourself, it is perfectly reasonable to call ahead to the casting office. Tell them who you are, what you're reading for and arrange for a good time to contact the casting director. When you talk to the casting director ask your question in a business-like way – meaning don't take a lot of time with self-indulgent small talk, apologies or explanations – just ask the question.

> However, be advised, if the question is self-evident or self-indulgent, or non-essential … you diminish their respect for you. They don't want to work with self-indulgent dummies.

> "Dumb questions" are questions whose answers make no difference in the acting choice you're making. Here's an example of a dumb question: "How long have they been friends?" It doesn't matter how long! If the answer were six months would it change the reading? They're friends! That's what matters! Ten years or ten weeks is not going to change what your character does.

Prepare them for whatever movements you are planning to do

As I said earlier: you calm them by knowing what you want to do.

You have to have a plan and have contingencies for last-minute changes (e.g. the director insists you do something else). You need to rehearse your plan and your contingencies, so you are ready for anything.

For example, your plan: I am going to start sitting, and then somewhere in here I am going to get up, walk over, and look out the window and from that point on I am not going to look at him until the last line.

Simpler is always better. Plan to do only what you *must* do to make the scene work. In the above example ask yourself if it would work just as well if you merely shifted in the chair and refused to look at him. Or if perhaps you only stood and turned away, without crossing to the window. See what I mean?

If you plan to move from your starting spot sometime in the scene, make sure you understand the frame of the shot: is it a medium shot (from the waist up)? A medium close-up (from the chest up)? A close-up (from the shoulders up)? What?

So there are no surprises about your movement, let the camera person know what you are planning to do so he can videotape you well. Do this before you slate, often in response to the "Do you have any questions?" exchange. "No, but I am going to move around a bit. I am going to start sitting, but then I'll be getting up and going over to the window."

If you know that you are being filmed in medium close-up or closer then you have to appreciate that if you move too quickly, the camera will not be able to follow. If you bolt from your chair, for instance, slow it down a little; "telegraph" the move just a little bit so the camera person can keep up.

They may put restrictions on this: "No, we want you sitting." In that case you adjust to your "plan B."

Paradox: You have to leave your "plan" outside the door

This next is important: You have to have a plan and you have to have contingencies … and paradoxically you have to leave your plan outside the door. What does this mean? It means all scenes have a physical component to them, meaning they happen in a real place, as the character is doing real things. When you rehearse at home, you will discover different possibilities for the scene when you experiment with different physical choices … e.g. if you play the scene walking around, or sitting in a chair, or getting dressed, or while taking a shower. Part of your rehearsal process should include experimenting this way. The different movements and actions will inform your readings, and inspire various choices and connections. You will arrive at one or two interpretations as your favorites … but you have to be ready and willing to drop it all in response to the reality you find in the audition room. The "choices" you developed in your rehearsals will be "in your body," even if you don't act on them in your audition. By making the scene work under a variety of different physical situations, you will be ready to create a reality in your audition, responding to whatever you spontaneously find in the audition room. *You have a plan, and yet you have no plan at all.* Does that make sense? It's like in athletics; you practice various moves over and over again. Then in the game they re-combine according to the instantaneous circumstance. That's the creativity of the moment. The impulses are not random … they take inspiration as variants of the options you have already explored during your rehearsals at home. In other words, in your rehearsals you are preparing for a variety of possibilities at any given juncture, and you therefore are prepared to respond creatively to whatever you, as the character, encounter at that moment in your audition when you are actually performing the scene.

There are basically three types of actor, whose approaches to acting correspond to the stages of each actor's own artistic development.

The first type filters the role through their memory of other performances they have seen, which they copy, imitating the selected effects in their own work. The second type explores the realities of the character's situation, drawing from their own unique imagination about the circumstances – which emerge in the security and privacy of their rehearsals at home – then resort, in the actual performance, to precisely imitating those rehearsed choices as the scene unfolds. In other words, they imitate the feelings and the line readings that emerged authentically in their rehearsals. The third type rehearses and rehearses, focusing on creating the circumstances of the character, and then when the curtain goes up, they embark on the scene, aware of the character's clear need to be there, and deal with the situation as if for the first time, responding in real time to whatever unfolds.

This is why interpreting the scene in terms of verbs as opposed to adjectives is the better approach. For example, the character chooses in the scene to: "try with all his might to get her to understand." That action is what defines the character … but within that action there are lots of creative options. How does he do that? The scene is going to "work" no matter which options he chooses, because the crux of the scene is that he gets her to understand. The actor has rehearsed a variety of options … then in the creative moment of performing the audition, some variation of one of them emerges as impulse.

So that's what I mean when I say: "You have to have a plan, and yet you have to leave your plan at the door."

Establish the size of the "camera frame" if need be

By this I mean: ask whoever is operating the camera "what's my frame?" Holding your hands out on either side of your head – he will tell you wider or narrower – will give you a sense of your range of motion within the frame. Most auditions are done in medium close-up, which implies that the edges of the frame are out about 18 inches on either side of your head.

Take a moment, if there is any question, to establish who you're going to read with, what scene is first, and who has the first line

If you get started wrong, because of some confusion about this, you will never recover. I have never landed a job when this happened. Making sure you both are on the same page and beginning at the same place is a good move.

Slate to camera "in character"

This goes back to the entry verb. Slate "through the verb." The temptation is to pop into mister or miss cutesy-pie. Rather, say your name to camera as you focus on your entry verb, i.e. what you came in with. Also, say your name as if to another human being. Remember you are actually saying your name to the person who is watching the monitor. This is something you might have to practice, making human contact with the camera.

As soon as the scene begins, you will make no eye contact with the camera, you will imagine it to disappear, and your intention will be focused solely on performing the scene, in the "place" (see Chapter 10) and circumstances as scripted, with whomever you are reading … just like in the movies.

Project your voice over the perceived distance

Actors trained for the stage, or who have been working recently on stage, sometimes have trouble making this adjustment. They have trained diligently to be able to project their voice expressively to the last row of the theater regardless of the circumstances of the scene.

Because there is a physical sensation associated with this practice – and a hard won practice it is – the actor integrates that sensation into his/her work. They grow to expect it to be there. The sensation of projecting becomes part of what it means to be acting. But acting for the camera often requires a much more intimate expression. That's one of the distinguishing features of the film medium. The audience is up close and personal.

> There is a famous story concerning the great film director George Cukor as he directed the sensational stage actor Jack Lemmon in the 1954 hit *It Should Happen to You*. It was Lemmon's first time on camera. Mr Cukor kept stopping the takes, exhorting him saying, "Less, Jack, less!" Finally the frustrated actor turned to the director and said, "My goodness, George, don't you want me to act at all?!" The director nodded with a big smile, saying, "*Now* you're getting the idea."

Remember, it's the distance perceived on the screen that is important, not the distance you actually are from the camera. So even though the camera may be many feet away, the shot may have you in close-up so that your voice need only be the volume that is required to travel 3 feet. It may sound like "stage heresy" but often in close-up, to mumble is the better choice. A medium shot (from the waist up) implies the listener is only between 5 and 8 feet away. A medium-long shot (from the knees up) implies 12 to 15 feet.

"Under" or "over" playing

> I have seen it many times: some actors have the misconception when they move from stage to screen that what is required for the camera is to "underplay" the part. This misunderstanding often leads to a muted performance, because the actor translates the meaning of the word "underplay" to be the equivalent of reducing the stakes or the emotional involvement in the circumstance. This is a misreading of what the camera requires. The involvement is the same, it is the *expression* of it that is

reduced. The character's issues are just as important, it's just that the *listener is closer*. If the tone of the project is for instance a broad comedy, watch accomplished screen actors: they definitely will not be "underplaying" it, even in a medium close-up. By the way, I suggest you ditch these two concepts of "under" or "over" playing altogether. They lead to bad acting on camera.

When you rehearse at home, and are speaking to an inanimate object as if it were a scene partner, or when you're practicing your monologues, put the object 3 feet away and see what it feels like to talk to it and no further. Same intensity, less projection. I have heard some acting coaches encourage their students when acting for the camera to be "lazier" with their voice, though this is an easy instruction to misunderstand, so too "to mumble." Remember, if I ask you to take an aspirin don't take the whole bottle. What I am getting at simply means release yourself from the sensation of over-projecting your voice.

Always audition with the script in your hand

Yes. An audition is a unique performance situation. You haven't had six weeks of rehearsal with the full cast as you do for a stage performance. Nor are there any re-takes when something goes wrong like on a movie set. You will be reading in a strange place with a non-actor-stranger, without benefit of a rehearsal. One take only. You will be nervous. If you get off track you will be glad you have the script at hand.

You do not have to memorize it. You do have to perform *it*

Let's be clear: you are not there to "*read*" the scene. You are there to *perform* it. There's a difference. We all can read. We don't need you to do it for us. On the other hand, you don't have to memorize it. You must be familiar enough with the action and the text so that you can perform it. Whatever that takes, and whatever that requires of you.

Every actor is afraid of forgetting his lines. It is literally the "actor's nightmare." But paradoxically you don't get the part because you say the lines right. I am not suggesting you can rewrite the script, but you need to know that a flub or two will not put you out of the running as long as you don't get flustered and "leave the scene." What wins the role is what you bring to the role, the interest you generate for the circumstance, the quality of your characterization, and the reality you create.

> *WHEN I HAVE TROUBLE MEMORIZING THE LINES*
> *IT IS USUALLY BECAUSE I DON'T KNOW WHAT*
> *MY CHARACTER IS DOING.*
>
> … James Caan

Be instructed by the above quote. If you think your job is about getting the lines right, and that's what you are focused on mentally, the camera will see exactly and only that: an actor trying to remember what he is supposed to say next. Your best choice is to focus on what the character wants, while using the script in your audition as a "prompt" when needed. Your rehearsal process should include referring to the text in this manner, especially if there are chunks you know will likely give you trouble.

Unexpected things will invariably happen in the audition, so even if you have it memorized cold, you should have the script in hand just in case.

An added bonus: There is an added psychological bonus that comes with performing with the script in hand. It implies that what you are doing is a "work in progress." It implies to the producers that your work will be even better when you are off book and on the set, even though that's not necessarily true. If you get the job by virtue of your audition, you will have performed well (or you wouldn't have gotten the part) and chances are that is as good as it is ever going to get. Be proud of that.

Props

Again, they're looking for the actor who makes it work. If you absolutely without question need to have a prop to make the scene work ... absolutely and essentially ... follow this guideline:

> *You may use whatever you carried with you on the street yesterday. Nothing more.* You may not come in with a lamp and a martini glass. You may not come in and rearrange the furniture. But you can use your wallet, or your cell phone, or a bottle of water, like that ... whatever you conventionally carry on your person ... but only if it is absolutely essential.

You want to come in the room with your script in your hand and little else. But if you had a purse or a satchel with you, you wouldn't leave it in the outer office ... you would bring it in with you and set it by the door. If it, or what is in it, can help to make the scene better, like a cell phone or a key ring, I say go ahead and include it as a prop in the scene.

Less is definitely more

There is a difference between using a prop because it makes you comfortable and using one because it is essential for the scene to work. Do not indulge yourself. The audition is not scene class or a stage play where you are working surrounded by a dressed set. My advice is to rehearse with whatever objects help you make the scene work, and then see how you can make it work by reducing or eliminating the props altogether.

Ask yourself what is essential to the sense of the scene.

For example: The script may describe your character as arguing with her sister about whether to see a certain guy. As the argument unfolds, the character is also trying to decide what to wear for her date with him. The script says her sister follows her around as she rummages frantically through her closet and dresser trying to pick a suitable outfit. But you, the actor, may chose to distill it down to wrestling with the decision as to "should I wear this scarf or not?", which you strategically chose to wear for the audition as part of your wardrobe.

Shrewd choices

Props bring life to a scene only when they present a true physical problem to be solved in real time by the character. Therefore, don't set things up or position anything too carefully ... make your character, for example, search for or untangle or arrange whatever prop he is dealing with for real. See "**What is the character literally physically doing at the beginning of the scene?**" (Chapter 13) for further discussion.

> To illustrate how solving a physical problem in real time affects a scene, Stella Adler used to have us cut out intricate paper dolls as we acted our scene. It had a profound effect on the results. It didn't take long for us to realize what a critical and strategic choice dealing with such a prop could be, and how effectively the right choice could enhance a scene.

> You must rehearse with the prop, but at the same time allow the prop to present little unsolved physical problems for the character during the actual performance. It will bring life to the scene. If it is all too practiced it will come across as staged. This is an art. Don't underestimate it.

If you are going to include a prop, use it!

One more observation about props. If you are going to include a prop, or a bit of "business" that involves a prop, *use it!* Don't just dispense with it within the first few lines of the scene. If you do that, why include it at all? A prop is essential to a scene only when you make it serve as a *metaphor for the character's situation*. In the above example of trying to decide about the scarf, the scarf has to serve as an embodiment of her values, or the impression she wants to make, or the indecision in her life, or the person she wants to get rid of, or the question of who she is or who she isn't, etc. Wearing it, discarding it, evaluating it, rearranging it, this way, that way, not at all! This action should be taking place throughout the scene as an expression of her situation and how she deals with her sister. If a prop doesn't have that kind of import, leave it out.

Further: Since a scene is an event, meaning something changes, the change can often be amplified by what happens to the prop ... she ditches it, or finally finds a satisfactory way to wear it, or gives up trying, or arranges it defiantly as a way of confronting her sister ... these choices say something! The choice should be emblematic of the event, the change in her, or what the audience discovers about her by watching the scene. Otherwise leave it out.

Again, less is more. Directors love to see this kind of inventiveness when it is artfully included. It signals a thinking actor who has ideas and knows how to convey them.

I have heard some casting directors say, "Oh, no. Never use props! Just sit in the chair and read from that position." I say they're wrong to be so rigid. No matter what they say, they're going to cast the person who makes it work. Sitting in the chair with no props? Fine, as long as you make the scene work. That's what is paramount. It is your audition. It's all you have. You are the artist. Trust yourself.

The script is most often your best prop

You will find that the script itself, which you will always have in hand, can serve very effectively for this purpose. It can be, for instance, a telescope, a hammer, a document, a photograph, a magazine, a hobby project, a sword, a club, a menu, a newspaper. It can be the money, or a note pad. It can be shredded in anger or thrown across the room. It can be an object of distraction or searched through to find something. Use your imagination.

*The **actual** object is usually not as important as the character's **involvement with** an object, any object.* The script as an object can serve this need to a tee. Use it to help you amplify the essence of the scene.

Speak through your involvement with the prop

If you are going to use a prop, or a bit of business, be involved with it. Since you are involved with it, speak through that involvement. That's what Stella was illustrating when she had us cutting out paper dolls.

I see it all the time in inexperienced actors: they stop doing what they are doing physically and talk; when they stop their talking, they resume their involvement in the business; then they stop with the business and they talk; then they do, then they stop, then they talk. Etc. This is no good.

If you are going to, for instance, tie your tie in the scene ... tie your tie! Keep doing it as you talk. Speak while you're doing it! Speak through the action! It will look like good acting.

A bit of business can help a line

Often we audition with little preparation time. There will be lines or exchanges that you simply, given the lack of time, aren't able to "solve." If you are at a loss ... have the character simply *do something* while you say the lines, a bit of business. Speak as you do the action. Gather your things, look for something in your purse, dial the phone, put on your sweater ... choose something that is consistent with the character's situation in the scene, but do that something as you speak. It will help a lot.

Avoid pantomime at all costs

Find another way. Enough said.

Positioning the script

Your rehearsals will reveal to you where you are having trouble with the text. Be smart. If you forecast that you might be likely to have trouble with a given speech, figure out a way to position the script strategically so that referring to it and looking to the other character requires little, if any, head movement. Be careful not to choose a position that is distracting or blocks the camera's view of you.

The scene is not over until they say it is over

Hang in there with whatever you have created until someone says "cut." You are not the one to say the scene is over. You stay with the action ... or the thought ... until *they* end it ... until you hear the words "cut" or they ask you to "post slate to camera," or until you hear them turn off the camera.

Exit frame if you can at all justify it

Without question, the best way to end an on-camera audition scene is, if it can be remotely justified, for the character to *exit frame*.

Once again: Before you begin the scene, tell them that's what you plan to do, otherwise the camera person may pan with you as you try to leave frame.

"Post slate"

Sometimes they don't ask for a "slate" (saying your name to camera) at the beginning of the audition. Sometimes they forget. Sometimes they want to set a different mood. In that case they will do what they call a "post slate."

If they ask for a "post slate," which means they want you to say your name on camera after the scene is over, say your name to camera *through the thoughts or concluding action of the character in the scene*. Do not leave the mood of the scene. Do not suddenly break from the mood, perk up and label the scene with your name. Rather, say your name as if you were still held by the resonance of whatever you created.

Leave happily

In fact, get out of there as quickly as you can, while *still being cordial*. Remember: never let them see you out of character. It is real easy to blow it after the scene is over. You're no longer in the mood of the character and you're no longer doing a verb. You will be all jazzed up having performed well, and you can chatty-chat-chat yourself right out of a job. Let your performance speak for you.

Summary

- Calm them by knowing exactly what you want to do.
- Try to avoid going first. Do not come in the room until you know for certain you have been called.
- If needed, prepare them for how you want to use the room, the general physical movements you intend.
- Establish the size of the "camera frame" if need be.
- Take a moment to establish with whom you're going to read and who has the first line.
- Slate to camera "in character" (through your entry verb).
- Limit your vocal projection to the perceived distance.
- Work with script in hand.

- Use only props that are absolutely essential; if you choose to use a prop, incorporate it thoroughly into the scene. Your script is your best prop.
- Exit frame to finish if at all possible.
- Leave the audition room happily.

AUDITIONING IN PAIRS

Enter in the relationship

Most projects, particularly television pilots, dramas and situation comedies (and certain commercials) involve two main characters. The producers are not going to make final casting decisions until they see the two characters together, to see how you look together, how you relate to one another, play off each other, and what, if any, your "chemistry" is like. Crucial:

> *When you audition as a twosome, you do not enter with a verb ... you enter and slate* in the relationship!

"We knew you two were right for the part the minute we saw you together." Here, especially, **Twenty-Year Friend** is huge. You and a stranger will be thrown together – as newlyweds, or old pals, or co-workers, or lovers, etc. – and with very little time to prepare you will be expected to enter as if you know each other intimately. You have got to get good at this. Upon entry:

- Do you talk to each other?
  or do you stand silently waiting?
- Do you stand close together?
  or do you stand a gulf apart?
- Do you enjoy one another?
  or are you stiff and mute?
- Do you look after one another?
  or are you isolated in your concern?
- Are you rooting for each other?
  or are you strangers unconnected?

- Do you touch each other?
  or keep your hands to yourself?
- Do you watch each other slate?
  or is it every man for himself?

A lesson about entering in the relationship

At the beginning of my working career I signed with a prominent commercial talent agency. They started sending me out like gangbusters, but I got nothing. Forty auditions went by without a bite. I thought they would drop me at any moment. One day they sent me in for a beer commercial that involved no speaking. The director was looking for three good friends, two girls and a guy who, in the commercial, would be scraping a boat in dry dock and enjoying a beer. As it happens I had a dog, Mr O'Neil, who just that week had been run over by a garbage truck. Mr O'Neil was my first dog ever, we had had some good adventures, and his death was harder on me than I ever expected. In the audition waiting room I began to tell the two actresses I was paired with about how much I missed my dog. In the middle of my story the casting director called us in. I was finishing my story as we entered and sort of huddled together on the mark. As I finished talking and before the director had a chance to even utter a word, we all three burst into tears. Just like really good friends. They hired us on the spot ... called our agents before we even left the room!

From that point on I learned to make a real and genuine connection to my audition partners: take a true interest in them; enjoy whatever is actually going on at the moment; share humor with them about the reality of the situation. I have real conversations with them; I have actually made dates standing on the mark; once I made arrangements to go bungee-jumping ... it's true!

The decision is made the instant they see you together. Therefore: Ask yourself, are the characters old friends or happy lovers? ... if so, you must enter *enjoying* each other ... they enter in mid-conversation, they joke with each other, one touches the other, they stand close together, they enjoy what each other says, they share glances, they look after each other. (Think Kurt Russell and Goldie Hawn standing on the podium at the Oscars.) Or perhaps the relationship is contentious, with each having a certain attitude towards one another? Other examples might be: one is innocent, the other is suspicious, or one is smug, the other is oblivious.

Identify the nature of their relationship. Use body language to express it as you walk in the room and take your place together on the mark.

One character might enter talking non-stop, while the other might have a non-verbal attitude about what is being said. One might stand slightly behind the other, glancing to the camera then to the unaware partner then back to camera, so as to convey a specific attitude ("He's my hero," or "Look what the cat dragged in"), or one might stand with arms folded, slightly turned away, while the other is very perky. One might follow the other like a little puppy. There are numerous variations. Don't over-exaggerate, be subtle, but be specific. Enter and slate in the relationship.

When you take your place on the mark, be aware that any space between the two of you (as little as four or six inches) shows up as a highly exaggerated spatial separation on the monitor. You want to control the impression this makes about the two of you. If your relationship is compatible, make sure you are standing close enough together so that you can feel the other's arm just barely brushing yours.

When slating to camera, be prepared for the following: As the two of you are standing next to each other settling onto the mark – communicating the nature of your relationship by how you are relating to one another – the camera person will be arranging the camera for the slate. He is likely to shoot the two of you in a medium-long two-shot and then zoom in to each of you individually. When he indicates which of you he is zooming in to first, the other should look at the person who is being slated, again with an attitude that conveys the relationship. This is off camera! … but after the actor who is being slated says their name to camera, the camera will pan to the other actor. This second actor should keep looking at their partner in character until they are sure the camera is on them (so the camera captures this look) *then* turn to camera and slate their name. Clear? This is a little touch that can have great effect. Share something visible to the camera during the slate.

This has to be *active*, active sharing, genuine enjoying or active discerning. You can't just aim your face at the other person … you must be making a genuine connection. Remember, the camera can see you thinking. It knows what's going on with you.

Now you see an added reason why **"Twenty-Year Friend"** is so important. You often are paired up with an utter stranger and must enter, four seconds later, as if you were old friends or newlyweds or siblings. You have to get good at this.

The scene itself

After the slate, the two of you will perform the scene. There will be one camera, and two of you. This means that the scene will be framed so that it contains both of you, in what is known as a medium to medium-long "two-shot." Standing or sitting, you will need to stay much closer together than feels comfortable or normal. "Two-shots" often require actors to stand so close together they are inside each other's focal distance. Get used to this. It is standard practice on camera. It looks perfectly normal on the monitor, but it makes you feel like you want to crane your neck to add some separation. (Bring plenty of breath mints.)

No matter how active the scene, the two of you will have to stay within an imaginary four-foot circle.

As you play the scene, the instinctive tendency will be to face one another in order to look each other in the eye. However, this locks you in profile. We won't see enough of your faces. What is preferred is for each of you to "open" 45 degrees to camera, and make eye contact in profile only when it is absolutely necessary. Take every opportunity to speak out toward the room, directing your responses not so much to the other character but rather "to the situation."

Playing a scene positioned so close to the other character can make an actor forget that the scene is happening in a given place, focusing only on the relationship. Make sure you include the place as a vital factor in the reality you are creating.

Inside the four-foot circle, pivoting away from the other character achieves the same impression on the monitor as walking away. Reaching out to turn the other character back toward you has the same effect as striding over and standing face to face.

You need to use your imagination in staging how to contain the physical requirements of the scene to remain inside the circle. For example, if a script calls for her to make a wild physical advance like chasing him around the office, she can accomplish the same effect by walking her fingers ever so slowly and seductively up his arm, or toying with a button on his shirt, or seductively taking off his tie. Such adjustments are commonly needed to accommodate the script to the physical restrictions of a producer's office.

CALLBACKS ON CAMERA

If you get called back, it means you did something right. Prepare to do it again … with one caveat. Let me explain.

They have seen your first audition on videotape. Something you did worked. But you can't be sure what it was. The powers that be want to see whether you can do whatever it was again, or whether you can make some adjustments that will improve the possibilities, or measure how you match up with other actors in the cast.

Definitely wear the same wardrobe as before. To the casting folks you are known as the "yellow sweater guy," or the blond with the "green belt." You want to maintain that identity.

Definitely work by creating the same "place" and acting on the same circumstances, relationships, and objectives.

But do *not* think "do it again" means *imitating identically* what you did or sounded like the first time. If you focus on behaving identically, which is very tempting, you will sacrifice the very things the camera requires: spontaneity and the flexibility to respond to the reality you find in the room. You will inhibit your ability to "play" and to make any requested adjustments.

The key to on-camera callbacks is to use your intuition and trust your impulses. Things will be different in that room. *You* will be different. Trust your preparation. It takes courage to leave all rigid plans outside the casting room door, but you must. You will enter with an objective in a situation … go in and get it. Focus on that. The choices you rehearsed will be there and they will emerge if they want to. Allow for them, but do not count on them or insist on them. If you do, you will give a mannered, lifeless reading.

> To illustrate: Let's say in the initial audition scene, reading for the bridesmaid, you chose, for instance: "having just found out that the groom is already married, to feign happiness as you get dressed, teasing your childhood friend, the bride, while looking for an opportunity to warn her." In the callback it does not matter what order you choose to put your clothes on or exactly when you check yourself in the mirror, or when exactly you give her a loving glance, or pause to assess how you will break the news to her. All of these things must happen in their own way, spontaneously, as the moments call for. However you end up doing these actions, the impression on the audience will be the same. The story will

still be told. Do the same things but do not hold yourself to doing them identically.

If you are paired up with a scene partner, rekindle Twenty-Year Friend and enter in the relationship, whatever form that takes. Look to re-create the circumstance you're in and your relationship to the other character. Re-identify your intentions and set out anew to do it in whatever way your intuition tells you, dealing with your scene partner. But do not require yourself to do things the way you did the first time. For example: if you choose to calm or reassure your "wife" in the scene. Yes, you will reassure her, but that does not mean you will focus on sounding the same or doing it in exactly the same way. Use your intuition. Allow for spontaneity.

When you are "called back," there will be decision-makers in the audition room. Remember: *you* are the one with the solution. You must still enter with your chosen intention, but make sure you do so warmly. Make the room yours, as if they are in *your* house. By this I mean treat them openly and generously as if they were your guests and they have come to you because they *need you* to solve their problem. Always remember that your primary function is to communicate your emotional relationships to whatever you are discussing. If the scene calls for an untoward intention, be very good at masking it until the scene begins.

Working with the director

One of the people in the room will be the director. Working with a director is an exercise in communication. More often than you might imagine, some directors are on shaky ground when it comes to working with actors. Many directors are secretly afraid of actors because they know nothing about what we do or about how to talk with us. (There are numerous books in circulation that aim to teach directors how to communicate with actors.) This fear can take strange forms and cause real problems. They have lots of fishy theories.

Don't let this distract you. Work with the director. Maintain a positive attitude. Show enthusiasm for the work. They need you as much as you need them. Acknowledge when you don't understand something. Support their efforts. Seek to help them communicate with you. The enemy is lack of clarity.

The best way to work successfully with a director is to be well prepared. This means that during your own rehearsals, you must try to anticipate possible alternatives the director might call for.

You will do well, during your rehearsals, to experiment with possible choices contrary to your own. Ask yourself, "What have I chosen for the character to be doing? What would happen to the scene if I did the opposite?" For example: if you choose to nurture, what would happen if you were to scold? Or if you were expressing concern, how would the scene go if you chose to be devil-may-care? Envisioning alternative choices is where a trusted acting coach or teacher can be of enormous help.

If, in your rehearsals, you have analyzed that the scene could go more than one way, let the director know what your assumptions are. But be careful not to talk too much. Let your acting speak for you.

The director will sometimes be looking for a certain result or effect. The best directors put their suggestions in the form of doable actions or intentions. But if the director requests a result, say for instance, for the character to be "nicer," your job is to transpose that result of being "nicer" into a doable form like: "take a greater interest in the well-being of the other." If the director wants you to "be sexy" you must find a way "to seduce," or "draw the other to you." If the director wants the character to "be jealous" you must find a way, possibly, to "steer the other to think only about you." If the director says he wants you to "be happy," you have to find a way to "enjoy yourself."

Note: A fundamental aspect of perusing the actor's craft is exploring and perfecting one's capacity to make these types of adjustment. It is one of the chief benefits of being in a scene study class, a necessity I keep harping on about. (You won't learn how to hit a curveball if you don't sharpen your skills in the batting cage.)

Directors sometimes give directions for no other reason than to see how you deal with them. Lighter/darker; faster/slower; louder/softer; bigger/smaller. If only as an exercise, part of your preparation should include adjustments that yield these ranges of result. This will help equip you to demonstrate your ability to take direction.

Always look for opportunities to inject humor into a scene. Notes of irony and/or self-deprecation make a character more intriguing.

In responding to a given direction: *Don't change: add!* Remember, when a director gives you a note, they just need to see the quality *somewhere* in the scene. Don't throw out everything you did in an effort to please. Add the referenced quality in a strategic place. The director's ideas can often be satisfied in a phrase or a look, rather than a complete reworking of the scene After all, you were doing something right or they would not have called you back. What is most likely needed is for one line or one small moment only to reflect or include the new interpretation.

An added note

Sometimes, in a callback, when you are auditioning in pairs, the director will seem to pay a lot of attention to the other actor and none at all to you. The tendency is to think, "What about me!? What am I, irrelevant?! How come they get all the attention? Aren't I worth any involvement?" If this happens, do not get distracted or defensive. When the director doesn't talk to you it means that what you are doing is *good*! Relax. Keep focused. Keep doing what you are doing. The director simply does not have time to fix what isn't broken, or to spend energy stroking your ego, commending you for competent work.

Never comment negatively on your performance.

Summary

Auditioning in pairs

- Enter "in the relationship." Use body language and conversation as you walk into the room and take your place together on the mark.
- Apply Twenty-Year Friend.
- Visibly enjoy each other – or visibly not – to the camera during the slate.
- Play within the imaginary four-foot circle. Close the gap.
- Avoid prolonged profiles. Open to camera at every opportunity.
- Refer to the "place" as a factor in the reality you are creating.

Callbacks

- Wear identical wardrobe.
- Trust your preparation and interpretation, then let it go.
- Be flexible. Use your instincts and intuition to adjust to the new conditions of the reading.
- Translate result-oriented directions to doable actions.
- In responding to a given direction, don't throw out everything you did in an effort to please. *Add* the referenced quality in a strategic place.

Now you have a general picture of how an audition unfolds and how you might deal with what you will encounter. Next we will focus on the actual performance of the scene … choices and techniques that will make it most effective.

CHAPTER 7

"I really really really want to get this part but I'm not sure how I should play it."

THE STRUCTURE OF DRAMA AND WHAT IT MEANS TO YOUR ACTING CHOICES

I am putting this chapter here, perhaps a little prematurely in the logical sequence of the topics, because I am afraid you will get bored with reading this book, put it down and never get the benefit of the perspectives this chapter contains. I don't know any other acting teacher who includes the following thoughts in their agenda. The ideas herein are crucial – how can I say this more emphatically? – to performing a winning audition. They have to do with substantiating a strategy for your acting choices.

The main point here is: Of course you will have to act well to get any part. But also, and very importantly: **Your choices will have to support the _story_**. If they don't, the producers will conclude you are a good actor but you're simply not right for the part.

When preparing for a role, an actor has two issues to solve: what to do and how to do it. "How to do it" has to do with the actor's craft, development of which is a life process and which I discuss in other chapters. This is the "What to do" portion, and deals with how having a sense of the basic structure of drama can help you make choices that support the story and therefore get you closer to being right for the part.

Read the following observation by Michael Douglas, from an interview on public television, "Inside the Actor's Studio," May 15, 2001; he discussed how working on the TV series *Streets of San Francisco* affected his approach to acting. There is considerable instruction in his conclusions.

> *UP UNTIL THAT TIME I APPROACHED ACTING AS BASICALLY*
> *A PROCESS OF REACTING. IN "STREETS," WE DID OVER*
> *100 EPISODES AND IT WAS THROUGH THIS PROCESS*
> *OF FOURTEEN-HOUR-DAYS-SIX-DAYS-A-WEEK-EPISODE-*
> *AFTER-EPISODE, THAT I BECAME AWARE OF WHAT I HAD*
> *TO DO TO MAKE THE STORY WORK AS A WHOLE. IT WAS*
> *A GREATER CONCERN THAN JUST MERELY REACTING.*
>
> … Michael Douglas

Again: your choices have to support the story. When a movie actor sits down with a television talk show host to promote his latest film, and is asked to tell the audience what the film is about, the actor can lay the story out very clearly. Believe me, he could tell it just as well before the filming began.

Here's a little secret: much of the effective (and consequently seemingly impressive) instruction your teachers impart to you in scene class is informed by their knowledge of the story the scene is from. They assign scenes from material they have read or seen in final form. They know what has to happen in the scene to make the story work and their instruction is enriched by that perspective.

When you audition, the writer will be in there watching you. Being the one who wrote the script, believe me, he has a very well-founded concept of how the story should unfold. In his mind, each scene is absolutely essential and is sequenced the way it is for very specific reasons. Each scene needs to be there, just where it is, to make the story work. He is counting on you, the actor, not only to bring the character to life, but also to do it in such a way that the story is clearly told. To him this means certain events have to happen and they have to happen in a certain order.

But you might say, "They never give me the whole script. I only get a scene or two when I read for the part." Yes, and that is why the subject of this chapter can be so helpful. You can't audition for a scene effectively if you don't have an orientation toward why the scene is there in the first place. You may be auditioning without knowing the story, but you should at least be contributing to *some* story, even if it is one you are venturing in your own mind. Being aware of the structure of drama will usually result in an estimate pretty close to the real thing, you'd be surprised. And how do you learn this?

I have many students who want and expect to become accomplished actors and yet they have no understanding of the form in which they are working. Drama has a shape. An actor needs to know it. Any actor of ambition should make it his goal to take at least one course in basic screenwriting sometime in the first five years of training. I personally recommend John Truby's screenwriting course. Look him up on the internet. It comes presented in a variety of formats. I strongly recommend Syd Field's book *Screenplay*, which is listed in the bibliography.

In his screenwriting classes, John Truby instructs:

> *Write about something that would change your life.*

An actor has to realize, that's what is happening to the main character(s): The protagonist is put in a circumstance that could change his life! Underline that. Your audition scene(s) therefore fit into a specific series of events that is going to change the protagonist's life. Think about it that way and you will make more dynamic choices, whether you are playing the lead and the change is happening to you, or whether you are playing a supporting role whose actions are in contrast to – or causing – the change.

Does the movie "work"?

Let me take just a moment to define what I mean by "works." When a producer test-screens a movie before its release he is trying to determine whether the movie "works." That is, does the audience come away with that "special feeling" we all are familiar with, or does it need more editing or alternate scenes in order for that to happen. Audiences pay a lot for that feeling. The laughing/crying masks that symbolize the theater pay tribute to what drama is meant to evoke. Some films won't work no matter what you do to them. They aren't plausible or don't make emotional sense or are too poorly crafted. Most films that do "work" rely on the dramatic structure that we are discussing here. But some, miracle of miracles, seem to break all the rules and still make emotional magic. It's unusual, but when that happens, the film gets an Academy Award for screenwriting. Because in that case all the screenwriters in Hollywood are looking up at the big silver saying, "Hey, how did he do that?!"

Now, back to the main issues.

Sometimes the scenes you are reading have been concocted specifically for the audition. But usually they will have been photocopied directly from the script itself. After you have auditioned professionally for a while, you will come to notice two things: first, you will come to see that if you are reading for the lead you will usually be reading three scenes; if for the villain, two scenes; if for a supporting character one or possibly two scenes. Secondly, that the Xeroxed scenes' page numbers (in the upper or lower right-hand corner) on the sides you are given are often pretty much the same depending on the nature of the role you are reading for. This is not a random coincidence. This is because the structure of drama, which is ancient, has a definite rhythm to it. In order for drama to have "dramatic" impact, certain categories of event have to happen at certain times and in a certain sequence. The audition scenes are chosen precisely because they are the ones that contain the events or revelations pivotal to the structure of how the story is being told.

Page numbers can tell the story

As I said, there will be many times when you will have only a few pages from the script you are to audition for. What I am suggesting is that *by virtue of the page numbers alone*, without benefit of reading the whole script, you can get a pretty good idea of what has to happen in the scene you are reading to make the story work. To do this you have to have a basic sense of how drama works, how the sequence of the basic action usually goes, how it's shaped.

That's what we are going to do now: take a look at the components of a screenplay, add that to the structure of drama in general, and see what that implies for the auditioning actor.

- The word "story" implies that something transpires, which means that the person the story is about – the protagonist – undergoes a *change* or causes a change to happen.
- A screenplay is a story told in a sequence of events.
- Each scene is an event. Define it as what the audience would identify as having taken place after it is over. (The word "event" implies a *change*, meaning something is different at the end of the scene from what it was at the beginning.)
- Most good screenplays are written in *three* acts and are about *one thing*, one major change.
- A good screenplay can usually be defined as being principally about *one person*, though sometimes it involves a group.
- Most good screenplays can be summarized in one or two well-composed sentences. For example:

    This is a comedy about a man – an out-of-work actor – who becomes a better man by becoming a woman.   *Tootsie*

This is a drama about a "bag man," lawyer, a "janitor," gifted at cleaning up the messy situations his firm's clients leave behind, who is forced, by the murder of his friend, to recognize the mess his own life has become, and uses the very talents he despises in himself to find redemption.   *Michael Clayton*

This is a comedy about a middle-aged writer, isolated by OCD and a crotchety cynicism, whose obsessive rituals entangle him in the lives of a single mom waitress, and a gay neighbor … whose unsettling world of emotional involvements leads him – against all odds – to seeking, accommodating, and accepting love.

As Good as It Gets

- One page of a screenplay represents one minute of screen time.
- Each act of a screenplay is roughly 30 to 40 minutes long, depending on the length and rhythm of the story.

General structure

> *RULES ARE MADE TO BE BROKEN, BUT WHEN*
> *YOU DO … PROCEED AT YOUR OWN RISK.*
>
> … Robert Blackmore, Colgate University

The structure of a screenplay is very powerful. Audiences often cannot tell the difference between good acting and the power inherent in any dramatic structure that works. In the context of a well-structured screenplay, very mediocre acting can look like dynamite. The converse is also true: if the script is no good, a brilliant actor will look inept. This is what Oscar nominees are referring to when they observe that it is the *role* that wins the big prize. They mean that the nature of the story and how dynamically it is told is a crucial factor in what makes for "good acting."

What follows is a description of what pretty much always happens. (For our purposes we will be talking about a 90- to 120-minute screenplay in three 30- to 40-minute acts. These numbers loosely expand or contract depending on the overall length of the script.) For your own edification, watch a DVD of a favorite movie and turn the "elapsed time" counter on. See if what I am about to tell you now isn't pretty generally true.

First act

The first (approximately) ten pages introduce the main characters and the "world" in which they live. On or about page 10, the equilibrium of this status quo is disrupted by some event.

From page 10 to approximately page 30 the protagonist attempts to deal with this disruption using every tool at their command. This is how we discover who this character is. We get a more complete picture of their nature, their skills, their resources, their relationships, and what others think of them.

On about page 28 to 30 another event occurs which is very much unexpected. This event is pivotal. It basically turns the protagonist's world upside down. This event, you could say, is what the story is about. It is this event that forces the protagonist to confront a circumstance, conflict or situation that is beyond their skill level or beyond their understanding of the way the world is. This event marks the end of the first act.

Second act

First half of the second act: The protagonist enters the second act shaken, isolated and alone. The protagonist scrambles for equilibrium. But s/he has been propelled into a situation, or "world," where none of his/her old ways pertain and none of his/her usual assessments can be trusted. This world can be an exotic, dangerous, faraway place. Or it can be a situation in the living room of the house they grew up in.

S/he would love to escape the situation – hide from it or run away – but there is some pressure, some value, which is easily understood by the audience (e.g. the need for revenge, justice, pride, safety, honor, money, freedom, love, etc.) that forces them to engage with this new, uncertain or dangerous condition. S/he is forced to establish some control over it.

S/he formulates and initiates a plan of action. *The plan never works*, because the plan is based on the capacities and values in force in the first act but which no longer apply to the "new condition" of the second act.

As the protagonist is driven forward, following their (unknown to them) futile plan, he/she encounters *new and unusual characters*. S/he encounters new perspectives. S/he comes away from each interlude, each scene, with bits of new information. S/he goes through a process of winnowing out new values, new truths, new skills, and realizations. S/he establishes new allies and forms new allegiances. It is a process full of trial and error.

Middle of the second act: In the middle of the second act (meaning on or about page 45 in a 90-page screenplay, or approximately page 60 in an 120-minute film) an event inspires a pivotal shift in the character's view of themselves, which results in either a crucial self-realization or the recognition of new or true love coming from an unexpected direction.

Second half of the second act: There is evidence of a change in the protagonist. The truth about themselves and the situation is starting to come into focus. Bits and pieces fall into place. S/he takes steps in the right direction. What they must do or come to terms with will dawn on them. The protagonist arrives at the end of the second act (on or about page 60 in a 90-minute screenplay, page 90 for 120-minute length) with a valid, but as yet untested assessment of the situation. S/he has solid evidence of what the true problem is and realizes what s/he must do.

Note: The length of the second act in relation to the length of the third varies depending on the rhythm of the story.

Third act

Fortified with the possibility of new love, or by the experiences they have had throughout the second act and what they have learned about themselves, the protagonist enters the third act ready to rectify the imbalance (injustice) that was imposed upon their world by the event at the end of the first act. This action, which often requires an act of destruction, is the subject of the third act.

Its successful completion results in the establishment of a new state of equilibrium. This equilibrium can be either higher or lower than the status quo that opened the story, depending on the theme of the story. The current tendency is for an "uplifting, happy" resolution, in which the evil forces are vanquished or eradicated; life is renewed; growth and perpetuity are confirmed; newfound love is fulfilled. Think *Rocky I*. But sometimes, though not currently the fashion, the protagonist arrives at a lower equilibrium. Think *Godfather II* or *Cool Hand Luke* or *Bonnie and Clyde*, in which the protagonist pays a price for choices that leave him dead or emotionally wounded.

Example: Rain Man

Let's take a look at the general shape of this example and see how it conforms to what I have outlined above.

This 1988 comedy-drama was directed by Barry Levinson, with Dustin Hoffman, Tom Cruise, Valeria Golino, Gerald R. Molen; written by Barry Morrow and Ronald Bass. It won Academy Awards for best picture, director, screenplay, and actor, Dustin Hoffman.

> **Act one:** *The first 10 pages introduce the main characters and the "world" in which they live. On or about page 10, the status quo is disrupted by some event.*

>> **During the first ten minutes:** We meet Charlie Babbitt, his business partner, and his girlfriend. Charlie is a materialistic hotshot business guy. It's all about the fancy cars, the import

deal that is going sour, the money pressure he is under, the slick talk and the wheeling and dealing.

He and his girlfriend intend to drive to Palm Springs, all during which she complains how emotionally closed off he is, that he never shares what he is thinking …

At page 10, the 10-minute mark: he gets a phone call … his father's died. No reaction, very matter-of-fact. With the news, he swerves his car back in the opposite direction.

From page 10 to page 30, the protagonist attempts to deal with this disruption, using every tool at their command. This is how we discover who this character is. We get a more complete picture of their nature, their skills, their resources, their relationships, and what others think of them.

During the remainder of the first act we will come to find out a great deal about Charlie Babbitt, his nature, and his relationships. We see him in Cincinnati, aloof and distant, at his father's funeral. With his girlfriend in tow, we see the house he grew up in, hear stories about his past, including the Fireball Eight convertible that was so symbolic of his troubled relationship with his father. And also, we hear him refer to the "Rain Man," an imaginary friend that gave him comfort as a child.

At the reading of his father's will, we see his resentment when he finds that he is left only the car and the roses … but that the entire estate, three million dollars, is to go into trust to an unidentified party.

Charlie Babbitt does what he does best. At the hall of records, he slickly wheels and deals his way to getting the trust information, including the whereabouts of the mysterious stranger.

He drives the Fireball Eight to the designated address ... which turns out to be a sanitarium populated by a weird assemblage. In conversations with the director, he finds out he has a brother, an autistic savant whom no one ever told him about.

Throughout the scenes in the remaining part of the first act, we see that Tom Cruise's Charlie Babbitt is cold, unfeeling, and without any common sympathy for his older brother, Dustin Hoffman's Raymond. His attitude towards Raymond is almost mocking. Charlie's girlfriend is unsettled by his lack of feeling. But Charlie's sole focus is on the injustice of his father's will, and the money he has been cheated out of.

At about the 30-minute mark, he devises a plan: Against every warning, Charlie kidnaps Raymond in order to get his half of the inheritance. To all but Charlie – with Raymond's special needs – this is clearly a bad idea. This event marks the end of the first act.

First half of the second act: *The protagonist enters the second act shaken, isolated and alone. S/he has been propelled into a situation where none of his/her old ways pertain and none of his/her usual assessments can be trusted. S/he would love to escape the situation, but some value forces him/her to engage this new condition and establish some control over it.*

Here we see what Charlie has gotten himself into. Charlie is entirely unable to cope. Raymond's routines are demanding to the extreme and without compromise. Special diet, special bedtime arrangements, special TV programs; Charlie explodes with frustration and unsympathetic contempt for his brother ... so much so that his girlfriend, disgusted with his behavior, leaves him.

In this section of the story, because of Raymond's demanding needs, Charlie, now alone to care for Raymond, is forced to alter his plans: he must drive all the way to Los Angeles. Three days in a car with weird Raymond. It is during this cross-country journey, through a series of small-town situations and encounters, that we see Charlie's exasperation continue to grow. His business situation in LA deteriorates ... while Raymond's special gifts go unnoticed as frustrating annoyances.

Middle of the second act: *In the middle of the second act (meaning on or about page 45 in a 90-page screenplay, or approximately page 60 in an 120-minute film) an event inspires a pivotal shift in the character's view of themselves, which results in either a crucial self-realization or the recognition of new or true love coming from an unexpected direction.*

Charlie is marooned by rain in a motel room. Everything is falling apart for Charlie when, at the 68th minute – pretty much dead center of the screenplay – Charlie makes a stunning discovery: that Raymond is, in fact, the Rain Man, his beloved childhood protector.

Second half of the second act: *There is evidence of a change in the protagonist. Bits and pieces begin to fall into place. What they must do or come to terms with begins to dawn on them. They take steps in the right direction. They gain solid evidence as to what the true problem is and realize what they must do to put things right.*

At the beginning of this section, Charlie is at the end of his rope. His business is bankrupt and every material thing he cared about is lost. But his realization about Raymond has changed him. He takes steps to reconcile with his girlfriend, and has a new, caring attitude toward Raymond.

Which leads Charlie to bond with Raymond – "make a connection" – as they unite in a card counting scheme in Las Vegas. Through this section of the story the two grow closer, they become brothers with a special bond. Charlie treats his bother with respect and caring, and in so doing discovers himself.

By the end of the second act, Charlie arrives in Los Angeles reunited with his girlfriend, has somewhat restored his bank account, and has made a commitment to his relationship with Raymond.

The third act: *Its successful completion results in the establishment of a new state of equilibrium.*

Charlie has expansive plans to devote himself to taking care of Raymond, set up an apartment, and have Raymond live with him. In his meeting with the sanitarium director he declares that he no longer wants the ransom money, he has learned that what he truly wants is "connection" ... he has tempered his resentment towards his father, and now wants custody of Raymond. But realities are stubborn things. As the third act unfolds it becomes clear that his plans would not be best for his brother. He must sacrifice his own desires for his brother's wellbeing. In the final scene, as Raymond embarks to return by train back to Cincinnati, it is clear that their bond has opened Charlie's heart, and the connection he has made with his brother will be for life.

End

Further observations

A well-written screenplay is a very tight form. Nothing is wasted. Nothing is incidental. *Every* scene and *every* character (even the doorman) makes a vital contribution to the story. Each is important ... indispensable even. Strive to make this true of your own work in every scene.

It is always better to be "mediocre" in a hit than "fabulous" in a dud. Therefore, always strive to make performance choices that will make the *project* successful, rather than being distracted by concerns over making yourself look good.

The audience will accept anything they see in the opening scene of a film. It is the "setting" of the story and the baseline of the story's reality. For example, if people are levitating in the opening scene, the audience will accept that the story takes place in a world where people levitate.

The same can be said of a character's initial appearance. The initial impression the character makes will be emblematic of the entire role. Especially at this moment, when the audience first sees you, make a bold choice as to what you are engaged in and your attitude towards it.

> Directors use this device all the time, especially if they are concerned that the audience might not "buy" the actor in the part. In any case, it is an effective way to impress the viewer with the character's essential quality. First photograph the character from behind, or with their face obscured, doing an emblematic action impressively, show how other characters react to their action, *then* come around with the camera to reveal who it is. For example, take a look at the opening to *Raiders of the Lost Ark*. Indiana Jones does several cool things … we see his boots trekking through the dense jungle; we see the determined figure he cuts as he leads his porters up the trail; we see his hand examine then dismiss a blow-dart stuck in a tree; we see that his porters are afraid to enter the zone they are invading; we see the back of his head as he surveys the jungle landscape, then hearing the click of a revolver, suddenly whirls and uses his nifty bullwhip to deftly disarm the threat, crack! … *then* he turns around and it is revealed to be Harrison Ford doing all this brave stuff.

Be aware of the potential of this option for your auditions as well. Let us see you *do* something characteristic, *then* initiate the dialogue.

The passage of a character from one state of being to another is called the "arc" of the character. With the best writers, every character in the screenplay goes through an arc to some greater or lesser degree. For a supporting character to go through such an arc he must appear in at least two scenes.

When you have at least two scenes in your supporting role, always look to create a contrast, or arc, between the character as we perceive him initially and the one we witness evolving or emerging later. This change in our initial perception of the character is usually most perceptible in the character's last scene. This change will often not be written in. *It is the actor who creates it. In the audition!*

How page numbers can inform your choices

> *GOOD ARTISTS POSITION THEMSELVES WELL*
> *BEFORE THEY LEAP.*
>
> … Charles Arnoldi, artist

Warning: The following is *not* a fool-proof formula for success. It represents suggestions, *by virtue of dramatic structure*, as to what you might explore in order to "make it work." But beware, nothing in art is *always* true.

You are the artist. We in the audience love it when you surprise us. But in order to surprise us you have to establish a certain expectation. That is what conventions and stereotypes do. (The sweet little librarian turns out to be the assassin!) Robert Blackmore's admonition on page 119 implies that if you are going to break rules and stray from convention, you ought to at least know what you are straying from.

Okay, so let's take this general dramatic shape we discussed above and see what it implies for our acting choices.

If the scene you are reading is in the first act

(Pages 1 through 28/30)

These scenes depict values and/or conflicts within the status quo, the initial equilibrium.

For the protagonist:

This is where the protagonist must come from to get to where he has to go.

Things only exist insofar as they are in contrast to other things. e.g. we have no way of depicting honesty if we have no deceit. We have no courage if we have no fear.

The protagonist is about to embark on a "journey," which can be physical or psychological or both. Make sure, by what you choose your character to be guided by in the first act, that a clear contrast will exist between that and the end point. e.g. a downtrodden person is going to get rich; an isolated person is going to find community; a fierce warrior will soften; the confident will be humbled, etc.

For all supporting characters introduced in the first act:

These characters are tied to the initial status quo. The nature of these characters throughout the first act allows us to estimate the nature of the protagonist by how they treat him, think of him, or are in contrast with him. Even though this situation will be shattered, create it as vital and true. The more fully these initial scenes are actualized, the greater the eventual impact of the story.

For the antagonist:

In these scenes the antagonist is strong, benevolent, expansive, and confidently in control.

Day players:

If this is the character's *only* scene, play the stereotype. The audience has to know right away who and what you are.

Any seemingly innocuous character introduced in the first act and *with one later scene* will often prove to be an important story element … e.g. a fearful witness, or a character who somehow provides a missing piece of the puzzle. This is often a memorable part in the eyes of the audience because the character plays a crucial role in unfolding or resolving the story.

If your character is introduced in the first act and dies by the end of the second act:

This character is a valued part of the protagonist's life. He represents the painful cost for the protagonist … the thing we value greatly which must be lost or exchanged for something we value even more. *This is a very sympathetic role.* The audience will love you. They will think you are a great actor! If you are reading for a character who is introduced in the first act, who is an ally of the protagonist, and who dies at the end of the second act: take the part big time. Don't quibble about money. Make any sacrifice to get the part. It will lead to better things.

If your character dies in the first act:

It is the death that is important … the role calls for a stereotype.

Play "good guy" or "bad guy".

If the scene you are reading is in the first half of the second act

(Pages 30 through approximately 45 or 60)

For the protagonist:

Here the protagonist has been thrown into a world or situation s/he doesn't understand. These scenes are about misconceptions, misinformation, deceptions, manipulation, half-truths. Old habits, shortcomings, foibles, ineptitudes rule.

S/he initiates a plan (which is not going to work). S/he starts to realize they are up against something unexpected or beyond their control. They must learn to observe and to listen.

Supporting characters:

In this section all supporting characters *put pressure on the protagonist*. In a dramaturgical sense, that's what supporting characters do. Their actions or nature push the protagonist to deal with a difficult situation ... to fold up tent or to press on ... initiating a journey or pursuit.

If the supporting character was introduced in Act 1:

The character is tied to the initial status quo. Therefore, in the second act, they likely serve, by contrast to the protagonist, to show how far the protagonist is straying from his initial (first act) self. Often in the second act these characters are urging the protagonist to "Come back, you're headed for trouble."

If the character is *introduced* in the first half of the second act:

These characters function to expose the protagonist to a new world or new viewpoints. These characters are eccentric, even bizarre in their values or lifestyles.

The audience sees the story through the eyes of the protagonist. If the "situation and its people" are intended to be strange to the protagonist, they need to be strange to the viewer as well. Do your research. Make a bold choice. Look to create a clear contrast between your character's values and those values established by the characters in the first act.

Because of their distinctive natures, these are memorable characters. They are a gold-mine of opportunity for an actor. Here is where many film-acting careers are born.

If it is the supporting character's *only* scene:

Again, look to play unconventional values with conviction. The character often plays a "role," or has "an attitude." Attitude can be an effective choice, but be careful: an attitude becomes static – too rigid to carry for more than about half a page. If the scene is longer, look to the character's eccentric actions or values to guide your choices.

If the character has *one or more later* scenes: All of the above is true, plus: a good story will not return to a character simply for more factual information. The new information must be accompanied by a perceivable (if slight) change (an arc) in the supporting character the second time we see him.

As I mentioned earlier, often it is *the actor, not the writer*, who will supply this change. The audition allows you to demonstrate to the director, by virtue of your performance choices, what you see to be the nature of this change.

Note: If you cannot create a change … any slight change at all … a change of heart, a change of outlook … defeat or collapse is a change, coming to terms with it is even more of a change … then the writing and your character likely serve to be but a foil for the aggrandizement of the hero. Okay, but it does not offer as powerful a possibility as a character that manifests a change.

For the antagonist:

The antagonist and his cronies are in full command. Here we often see how the antagonist's power has been corrupted.

If the scene is pretty much dead center in the screenplay

For the protagonist:

This is the scene where the protagonist comes face-to-face with an elemental truth about himself. It is often a *love scene*, often "the kiss." It may read like a simple conversation, but don't be fooled. In this scene, the protagonist discovers something pivotal in his own nature or discovers love coming from an unexpected direction. It may be subtle, it may be filial, but it is definitely a fulcrum point in the telling of the story.

Sometimes the protagonist activates it, sometimes they resist it, sometimes they are oblivious to it – the variations are numerous – but it *is* a "love" scene where the protagonist, in spite of themselves, comes face-to-face with something crucial about themselves through this encounter.

In this scene, the **supporting character** provides the counterpart to this exchange. Allow them to embody more "knowing" than the protagonist.

If the scene you are reading is in the second half of the second act

For the protagonist:

We see evidence of a change in the protagonist. The truth is starting to congeal. What he must do or come to terms with will dawn on him. Towards the end of the second act he will correctly identify the true enemy and initiate a plan of action.

For a supporting character:

If it is a supporting role, in this section of the story the character will often confront or present the protagonist with what he doesn't yet realize he needs to face or know.

For the antagonist:

Often, toward the end of the second act the protagonist (or his trusted ally) will face or confront the antagonist. Either here or in the third act the antagonist will state his case. The antagonist's equilibrium is disturbed. The antagonist will miscalculate, make a wrong move.

The third act

Except when reading for the villain, I have never been asked to audition for a scene taking place in the third act. A writer/producer friend of mine, James Lee, explained: "Acting-wise, if it isn't happening by then, it isn't gonna happen." For the dramatist, the final scenes are the most important part of the story. They determine what the audience leaves the theater with. (Would we pay so much attention to "Oedipus Rex" if he didn't claw his own eyes out at the end?) But for the actors, the last act will not unfold with dramatic impact if the earlier acts are not well crafted, well cast, and well acted. If the earlier scenes are played effectively, the actors' scenes in the third act will fall into place very naturally.

For the protagonist:

The character takes action: which leads either to victory, resolution, self-realization, love, a new a new and higher equilibrium … or, depending on the theme of the story, downward to a darker or more ambivalent state of being.

For the antagonist:

If not at the end of the second act, here the antagonist states his case. For the villain and his cronies these scenes involve exposure, miscalculation, desperation, ruin, confession, banishment, death.

Summary

This chapter is about how understanding the structure of drama can be a guide towards informed acting choices, choices that not only are compelling but also contribute to telling the story. As suggested earlier, rules are made to be broken; however, you would do well to consider the following:

If you are reading for the lead, it is common to be asked to read three scenes.

- The first will often be toward the beginning of the screenplay where we identify the status quo and the initial nature of the protagonist.

- The second is often around the end of the first act to dramatize what challenges the protagonist must confront in the story.
- The third audition scene is often dead center in the screenplay where the protagonist realizes something fundamental to what he must discover in order to solve the challenge he is confronted with. This scene often involves new-found love.

If you are reading for the villain, it is common to be asked to read two scenes.

- The first will usually be in the first act to demonstrate the control the character has on the status quo.
- The second will often be at the end of the second or third act, depending on how the story is being told, to dramatize how the villain's plan has been shaken and/or what motivations were behind his schemes in the first place.

If you are reading for a main supporting character, you will often be asked to read two scenes.

- The first will be where your character is first introduced as an ally whose relationship to the protagonist is emblematic of the values at sway in the initial status quo.
- The second will be a scene, usually toward the end of the second act, in which you cause the protagonist – by confronting your pal or by symbolizing a contrast to him – to identify the fundamental issue facing the protagonist.

If you are reading for a supporting character introduced in the second act.

- With *one scene* only, you represent the strange world the protagonist has been thrown into. Your choices need to personify the nature of the unfamiliar world confronting the protagonist.
- *If your character also has a later scene*, strive to create a contrast between the two scenes you appear in. This is a golden opportunity. It is where film careers get made. Think of this change as representing a story unto itself.

If the role involves a romantic theme:

- You will definitely be asked to read the scene where you two first meet, which often brings into focus the circumstances that keep you two apart.
- You will also read the "love scene" in the middle of the screenplay, where newly recognized love turns the direction of the story.

All **minor supporting characters** contribute to highlighting the nature of the protagonist or what he is dealing with.

So now you know.

CHAPTER 8

He buys his ties in the city

WARDROBE STRATEGIES FOR ON-CAMERA AUDITIONS

Just as performing a play is not a social visit with the audience, an audition is not a social visit with the auditors. It is work. Your work. And it is best understood as being a full-out performance. Every single little detail of it.

In the theater the "dress rehearsal" is traditionally one of the last steps in the preparation process. Stella Adler used to talk about how her weeks of theater rehearsals would culminate in the final days before opening night with putting on the character's wardrobe, finally dressing the part. She said, "You rehearse and rehearse and rehearse and then at the very end you put on the costume and you become the character." This traditional sequence tends to delay the effect of wardrobe to the end of our preparation process.

Our initial training as actors, which correctly emphasizes our internal emotional state and our openness to the situation and circumstances of the character, also de-emphasizes the importance of wardrobe. I actually used to think when I started studying acting that wardrobe was unimportant in my process. It was exterior and therefore not the "essence of the issue" for the actor. It didn't matter what I wore so long as I was experiencing and feeling what the character felt and experienced. Wardrobe was extra. Window dressing. A bonus. I have come to learn I was way off on that one. In fact the opposite is true.

When we were children playing the princess or the king, we played dress-up. It affected us in our fantasies, made them more vivid to us. To be the tiger, make the face of the tiger.

> *I USUALLY START PRETTY WELL OUTSIDE. I'LL*
> *START THINKING ABOUT THE CLOTHING AND*
> *THINGS LIKE THAT, AND THEN MOVEMENT. BIT*
> *BY BIT THE OTHER THINGS KIND OF FOLLOW.*
>
> ... Sean Penn,
> *LA Times*, Calendar, Jan 6, 2002, p. 88

Try this: *Make your commitment to what you will wear early in your process of preparing for your audition.* It will definitely contribute to making you read more effectively.

But be mindful of my semantics. **By wardrobe, I do *not* mean costume.** To clarify the difference: out on the street, to a passer-by, "wardrobe" goes totally unnoticed. "Costume" sticks out like a sore thumb. It is an issue of subtle suggestion. *Never audition in costume.* Never show up as a cowboy with chaps and a hat and a rope. Never show up in the full regalia of a naval lieutenant, or in a nurse's outfit complete with little white hat and blood pressure monitor. If you do you will not get the part. For a million reasons such an approach just doesn't work.

What we're talking about is a strategy with regard to grooming and clothing that, while looking "normal" on the street, in the context of the audition will enhance both your commitment to your performance and the effect of your performance and will *suggest* to the auditors the instant they see you that if you were in costume, you would be perfect. It all has to look totally natural, yet nothing be left to chance. This concerns your overall look, of course, but also might include touches in the details such as slightly mismatched socks, the literal or metaphorical graphics of your shirt design, a ball-pen stain on your breast pocket, an ever so slight hair adjustment, a missing button. Even the unseen counts ... your undergarments, for instance ... pampering and luxurious? or threadbare? Unlaundered even. It all counts. It will affect you, however subtly ... in ways that you should calculate. Believe me, they will see the effect. The slightest detail. It will register.

To further clarify: If you are a student and the character you are reading for is a student, it is not enough to "dress like I normally dress." I am urging you to commit to very conscious choices. Wardrobe is a very creative component in the actor's art. It is a category for the Academy Awards, remember, and should be pro-actively included in your audition strategy. Your choices will affect your performance in the same way that feeling fat or lean affects your behavior and disposition in everyday life. Significantly. (Sometimes the disquieting effect of your character's poor taste or of being overweight is exactly right for the character's situation.)

Usually you don't have to go out and buy anything. Use creatively what's in your closet, it's most often the best source for wardrobe. Yes, I have on a few occasions gone to a fancy department store, bought a fabulous overcoat or sweater, tucked the tags out of view, auditioned, and then returned the item. But in my case this has always backfired. When I have done that I have always gotten comments like, "Great reading" (which means I'm not getting the part) "But what a great coat! Where did you get that coat!?" So, you're on your own here.

Wardrobe choices are one of your strongest tools for playing with or against "*type*" in your auditions. The word "stereotype" is derived from a nineteenth-century French printing process that allowed an image to be replicated over and over again. A *cliché* was the small metal gizmo that held the stereotype in place. Work for or against the stereotype. But avoid the clichés. Don't be original, be specific.

In commercials, auditioning in type is absolutely essential. We need to know exactly what you are the instant we see you. In feature films, the opposite is often true ... it depends on the part.

Often the script or sides will include a wardrobe description. Do not feel you must follow these instructions precisely. Take the *sense* of what the description implies as your lead rather than an exact rendering of it, and apply it to the character's circumstances.

For example: I was auditioning for a character once who was described as being very wealthy and powerful. In the story he wanted to divorce his wife but avoid paying a lot of alimony. The scene involved a conversation between my character and his newly retained lawyer. "Wealthy and powerful" ... I came dressed to the nines ... $2000 suit, cufflinks, pinky ring, silk shirt, money clip, perfect hair, the works. I looked fabulous. The job had come down to being between me and another actor. I was sitting in the waiting room looking very wealthy and very powerful, when my competition walked in. What a jolt! It was genius. He came wearing a tattered pair of Bermudas, old sneakers with no socks, a faded knit shirt and a ball cap. He looked like a poor schlubb about to do his yard work ... exactly what a man *would* wear if he wanted to get out of paying heavy money. I went home empty-handed that day ... "wealthy and powerful" ... and a little wiser.

Along these lines also, there is a famous anecdote about Chekhov scowling after reviewing a dress rehearsal of one of his plays. The crestfallen director asked the playwright what was upsetting him and he said, "It's preposterous! Why is that character, a simple woodsman, dressed like such a dandy?" "But sir," said the director, "you've written right here in the text ... 'He buys his ties in the city.'" "Yes, that's exactly what I wrote," answered the playwright. "He buys his *ties* in the city." (Meaning *only* his ties.)

Again, don't be original, be specific

A word about looking good: Movie stars look great up there on the big silver. So I think, "If I'm going to be a star I've got to look great too." Not necessarily. To "meet," yes. To audition, it depends on the part.

One of my first parts in television was that of a patrolman on the hit series *Beretta*. I was inexperienced and very nervous to do well. I had one line like "stick 'em up" but they had called me in and gotten me into wardrobe and makeup what turned out to be 10 hours before I was actually needed. All that time while I was waiting to work I was worried about the creases in my uniform, worrying about looking crisp and groomed. It was torture. We were on location: a muddy junk yard with grime on every surface. I didn't lie down, I didn't sit down, I didn't want to rumple myself for my big performance. After about nine hours of this I saw Robert Blake, an Academy Award nominee, who was playing the title role of the show, arrive on location and go into his trailer to get ready for his scenes. He emerged a few minutes later in wardrobe, paused for a moment and looked down disapprovingly at himself. I watched dropped-jawed as suddenly he threw himself to the ground and slithered around in the muddy gravel on his stomach and back, then got up thoroughly soiled, dusted himself off, and said, "There, now I'm ready to work." Boy, was I confused.

> *JOE, WHEN ARE YOU GOING TO REALIZE THAT*
> *ACTING IS NOT SOMETHING YOU COMB YOUR*
> *HAIR AND WASH YOUR FACE TO DO?*
>
> … Peggy Feury

Along these same lines, at about the same time years ago I was in the "looking good" frame of mind and I was preparing to do a scene in workshop. I was wearing this ultra luxurious drop-dead cable knit sweater. Peggy saw me on the stairs going up to rehearsal and said, "Too bad about that sweater." Meaning I looked fabulous. I thought, "Wow, I look great, my sweater's great, my hair's great, I'm going to look great for the scene therefore I will be great in the scene." (That's the point, after all, isn't it ... looking great?) After the scene was over, I sat down for notes and was thoroughly flummoxed when she said: "Joe, why the hell are you wearing that sweater!? And what's with the perfect hair?!"

The point is that wardrobe and grooming – or the lack of it – have to fit the circumstances of the character. And that *is* what it's all about, after all ... the character. It is not about me, Joe. It is about me, the character. That's who the audience sees. That's who the story is about: the *character*. Duh ... Many of you already know this, but I'm embarrassed to admit this is something that took me a long time to learn. I couldn't stand not to look good on my own terms. (None of my characters were ever as cool as I was.) And it took everything I had to resist the thought that the character's appearance was a reflection on me personally.

FOR THE ACTOR, VANITY IS THE ENEMY.

... Robert De Niro

I see it all the time. Young actors who want to make a special effort to do well in a scene equate that effort with spiffed-up clothes and a faultless hairdo. They come in, just like I used to, looking like they're presenting themselves for a job at some fancy law firm, all shiny and clean and put together. It can be spooky. And it's all totally wrong. Again: wardrobe and grooming have to fit the circumstances of the character and the nature of the scene. It's not about you. It's about the character.

Sometimes in the early going of your career, neither your agent nor the casting directors will have a clear idea of what you're right for. If I am reading for a part where I feel strongly that that is true ... (I will never get cast as a Hell's Angel, for instance) ... I will dress so that as I enter, the casting director will see me as what I *am* right for, and then as I settle I will add or subtract a garment appropriate for the part I am reading for. In other words, I will take off a sport coat to audition for a lumberjack (which part I will never get because of my physical appearance) or put on a scarf or take off sunglasses or strip down to a tank top, or whatever, so that they get at least a glimpse of me both ways … The part I am reading for and the part I should be reading for.

Further notes

Wardrobe and soap operas: For a soap opera audition, no matter what the part, no matter what the circumstance, think sexy. Careful: this word means different things to different people. By "sexy" I do not mean underwear. I mean dress in whatever way you would dress if under the circumstances of the scene, you were also trying to make this appeal to the other person; that being sexually attractive was a component of what you were trying to effect. Add this element as a consideration in your wardrobe choice.

For an interview from your 8 × 10: When you go in for an interview that was initiated by someone having seen your picture, wear the same tone or style of clothes. Do not wear the identical outfit. That would be weird. But keep in mind they liked something about you in the picture. What you wore had something to do with that, your casualness or your formality. Pick clothes that strike the same note.

For a callback: When you audition for a role, if you are in contention they will call you back in to read a second time. You did something right. Who knows what? Dress identically.

Wardrobe and commercials: It's important to keep in mind that commercials are driven by demographics and rely on instantly identifiable stereotypes. Especially if you're going to audition for commercials, both men and women, you're going to need a high-quality business suit, and at least one hip "upscale, casual" outfit along with your everyday wardrobe. It's the business. You'll need it if you want to work just as surely as you need an 8 10. Along with these, you'll need to identify for yourself what I call "your signature wardrobe" which is the versatile outfit that is "You." It is the wardrobe that compliments your type and makes you feel confident just to wear it … one that "can go both to Paris or the beach." I describe it to my students as what you might wear for a blind date with a special person. It defines your nature simply by wearing it. (And by this I do *not* mean your jogging sweats or your favorite serape.) It is versatile in that with slight adjustments it can be made to fit a wide variety of situations. You will use this outfit when you don't know what "they" are looking for.

One other thing: Pay attention to what I call my "25%" rule. For commercial auditions only, dress *up* by a factor of about 25% above what you think is realistic for the situation. In commercials (unless it is a character which the audience is supposed to find ridiculous, for instance if the foolish character doesn't use the product or works ineptly for the competition) women wear nice clothes to do housework. Men mow the lawn in spanking clean trousers. If you have two contrasting auditions in one day and circumstances are such that you can't change or adjust what you're wearing, wear the better clothes to both rather than the other way around. You're more likely to get a callback for a mechanic when wearing a business suit, than you are to get a callback for a businessman dressed as a mechanic.

In closing: Years ago I ran into a director, Melvin Solkoski, with whom I had worked numerous times. We were chatting and he mentioned in the course of our conversation that he had seen me on a certain show. It was an episode of *Charlie's Angels*, a trifle that was on the top of the charts for a few seasons in the 1970s. I hadn't been real pleased with what I had done with the part. I had "phoned it in," as they say. And, as a way to disown it, I said, "Oh, come on, Melvin, that doesn't count." His answer to me was: "Joe, everything counts." I have come to realize that it is absolutely true … everything counts. Ultimately, that's what our careers amount to: an accumulation of everything we have done … every scene, every audition, every show. Stella used to exhort us to grasp that "We actors don't own anything

We don't own the script, or the set, or the cameras, or the clothes on our back. All we own is our performance." I see it time and time again. The good actors always seem to be good. I have come to realize that this is not so much because they are inherently good – they have talent, of course – but, then, so do you. It is, rather, because they have a work ethic. They work hard to be good. They strive in every scene in every line to do their best and to accomplish something specific. Taking the step to commit to specific wardrobe choices is part of your work. Take the step. Do it early in your process. You will reap benefits.

A last note: I just this moment got a call from a student who was very excited about an audition she had just finished. I had coached her for the reading. We had spent a good deal of time considering what she should wear for the audition. She was playing a young teacher who was also connected to a religious order in Hawaii. We settled on a white dress shirt buttoned to the neck, a blue blazer, and khaki or dark matching skirt; sensible dark leather shoes. She told me that she felt a little uncertain about her choice while sitting in the outside office because all the other young actresses who were reading for the part were dressed in cutoffs and tank tops. (Hawaii, after all.) Upon entering the room she reported that a producer literally exclaimed: "Finally! An actor who has some regard for wardrobe!"

I don't know if she got the part. Too early to tell. But I do know that they will for evermore hold her in high regard. You'd be surprised how long people hold on to first impressions.

Further update: She thought she read well; she did not get the part. But two weeks later she was called in to read for a feature film based solely on the impression she made … as an actor who has made a serious commitment to her craft and pays attention to detail.

CHAPTER 9

Your eyes/your thoughts

THE IMPORTANCE OF WHERE YOUR CHARACTER LOOKS

Tom Cruise said in a televised James Lipton interview ("Inside the Actors Studio") that the job of the film actor is to create subtext. I suggest what he meant by this was – once again – that the essence of most movie scenes lies in what the characters are thinking or experiencing, not what they are saying. Stories are about change. On the stage the changes are registered by what a character says. On screen, they are registered by the character's *reaction* to what is said. I have heard this same idea put another way: the essence of acting on stage is found in the lines; the essence of acting on film is found in the spaces *between* the lines.

To be effective on stage, an actor must learn to contain and communicate their reactions through their voice. This can take years. In consummate stage acting the voice does not render a reaction, it *is* a reaction. Film acting requires something different. The actor reacts in mind and body, then speaks.

> **Film acting note #1:** Watch a film closely and you will see that before an actor stops talking, the editor will often have cut to the other character so that the audience can see how the second character reacts to what is being said. That is why, when you prepare your scenes for an actual production, it is vital that you recognize what word or phrase in your counterpart's speech grabs

your attention and causes you to begin to react or visibly formulate an opinion. Observe yourself in life. As a listener, your reaction starts before the speaker finishes. It is the same way with film acting. As a speaker, the intent of your speech lingers on after your lines are delivered.

Film acting note #2: I noted this in Chapter 6, but it bears repeating. Some instructors put heavy emphasis on the idea that screen acting is "smaller" in size than stage acting; that it requires "less" because the screen is so big or so close. I think this is misleading. It suggests that a scene should be "underplayed." But "underplaying" is no more valid than "overplaying." The result is that actors often dampen their intensity; they mute their reactions to a point where nothing vital is actually going on. My advice is to maintain intensity, but bring the listener closer. Part of your preparation should be to rehearse your scenes with all conditions equal, but put the listener less than three feet away.

Film acting note #3: It has been well observed that with regard to close-up reaction shots, the actor enjoys a vast privacy. In other words, when isolated in a close-up, whatever registers as a reaction on the face of the character is strictly between the character and the audience. It is as if no one else in the scene can see it. For your close-up reaction shots it is important that you react visibly, however subtly, though facial gestures, slight movements, or expressions.

For an actor, the most important part of a film scene lies in the thoughts aroused in the character as he tries to deal with the situation, the place, and the dynamics of the relationships rather than in the literal content of the spoken text.

In film, the actor needs to be able to convey that his character is reacting to what is being said, or what he is observing in his counterpart, or is having thoughts aroused by his physical surroundings. Accomplished film actors give their characters active minds. Their characters are always evaluating, reacting, considering, strategizing, etc. Obviously much of a character's thought process is revealed through the subtle changes of expression on the character's face; but not so obvious is how much is revealed in the character's eyes: *what* he looks at and *when*. These choices have a substantial impact on the viewer.

The test is in the other person

Many young actors tend to think, because of the emphasis put on it in our early training, that our most fundamental function is to react emotionally, using the text – to "respond from our center" (as many acting teachers put it.) Make no mistake, this is an essential starting point in our training. It is a skill that must be mastered. For some it can take years. But in life we don't go around talking without thinking. We don't go around seeking the emotional truth about ourselves in every exchange. We gauge, amend, and edit what we say. Let your characters do this too. In life we say things for effect; we "manipulate" those around us by our tone of voice and choice of words in order to control how others perceive us. Let your characters do the same. The *Practical Handbook for the Actor* (Vintage, 1986) suggests, "The test lies in the other person." In other words, when we talk we are trying to achieve a purpose by talking – talking is an action – and we must often look (but not always) to check whether or how the other person is reacting to what we say so that we can communicate effectively. In life, how the other person reacts often determines what we say next. Let your character devote energy to this process as well. It invariably involves a mental calculation, a thought process, an evaluation, which is an activity the camera likes.

Most importantly: this thought process is made apparent to the viewer by where the character is looking, and when he does it. On stage, a character's thought process is revealed by how he says his next line. On camera, the character's thought process is revealed in his eyes often before he speaks.

Looking at your script

When you are auditioning on camera, if you have your eyes continually downcast to the script you are depriving the viewer of being able to observe the most revealing component of your exchanges. Therefore if you, the actor, have to look down after every sentence to check for your next line, the viewer loses the ability to see your character's thought process. We are not able to see you observe the effect your words are having on the other character. And we are not able to observe your reactions to what is being said. Especially at crucial moments, we need to see your character's eyes.

This does not mean that you, the actor, have to be completely "off book" to audition well (and even if you were, you would still work with the script in hand). But on camera you need to have reasonably large chunks of the text known to you, so that you don't constantly have to look down at your script. Use your script to *cue* yourself, rather than read directly from it.

> **Important note:** When you do look down to check a line – and you will – don't "leave the scene" to do it. Don't subtract yourself from the situation. Glancing down should be integrated to the situation, as if the pause is part of the character's thought process. In life we sometimes stutter, we stall, we have unexpected thoughts, we search for what we want to say … so do your characters on occasion.

Motion and change

This next point is easy to illustrate on the screen, but hard to explain in words, so stick with me.

At what and when? Next time you watch TV, observe what it is that grabs your attention as a viewer. You will see that your attention is captured by raw *movement* itself on the screen; the fact of it. It's drawn to what is *changing visually*. (We humans are in effect like frogs that leap to eat a bug only when they see the insect move. Remember the dinosaurs in Stephen Spielberg's *Jurassic Park*? It was an important plot point that the monsters couldn't see the humans if the humans remained motionless.) This physiological phenomenon is why chase scenes, for instance, are so purely cinematic. There is lots of movement and visual change. It is also why stage directors will insist you be physically still while the other character is talking, otherwise your movement will draw attention away from the speaker and "upstage" them. Simple dialogue scenes can be much enhanced – made more visual – by editing or camera movement. Our current wave of young film directors sometimes takes this to the extreme dizzying us with their excessive quick cutting.

In conjunction with this, a major aspect of the film editor's art is to calculate when to cut and what image to switch to in order to highlight what the viewer pays attention to … it is a vital factor in good cinematic story telling. You will also notice that when the editor cuts from actor "a" to actor "b," it will be just a fraction of a second before actor "b" moves or shifts or glances or twitches. The movement however slight, is what we are drawn to.

When you're auditioning, you'll be playing the scene with another person. But unlike in a finished film where the editing will switch back and forth between the two of you – which in effect creates movement – in the audition it will be only you on camera for the entire take. There will be no editor to pick and choose what or when movement should be created or highlighted. But movement will happen – for example when you enter, when you sit down, when you yawn, blink, smile, sniffle, shift your weight, whenever you move in any way – our eyes will be drawn to it. The viewer will also be drawn by the movement of your eyes: *when and where and what you look at.*

An actor needs to be aware that his character is somewhere trying to accomplish something important and that *what he's looking at and* **when** *he does this* is an important – you could even say strategic – acting choice. It enhances what the viewer interprets the character to be thinking: whether, for example, it's into the eyes of the other person, or instead at some other aspect of the person (e.g. their hair or body or their garment), or at some aspect of the place (e.g. the height of the building or the footprints in the snow).

Where the character is looking has meaning. When he looks at something, the viewer gives it "weight" … it implies a thought. When you work in film, typically you may hear a director say something like: "Darling, when you say that line, don't look at him, look down at your glass of wine." The director knows this will imply a thought. (This is, by the way, why smoking cigarettes on film works so well … the pause to take a drag and the manner in which the character does it imply that thinking is going on.)

When you look at what you look at is also important. The *movement* of your eyes … the *movement* to the next place of interest, impacts the viewer. (Along the same lines, if the camera were positioned behind you and we could only see the back of your head, if you were to turn your head, our interest would be drawn to what we project you to be looking at. The editor would cut to see what you were looking at immediately. The audience's curiosity would require it.)

"Looking" has the most meaning when the viewer sees you do it.

Particularly in an audition for a love scene, for example, the natural choice is for the two lovers to gaze deeply into each other's eyes. This is a very tempting choice for the actor because it feels so "connected." And it is! *But because there is no editing back and forth in the on-camera audition, after a time this gaze loses its impact.* I call it "The Tunnel." It feels great – very connected – for the *actor*, but for the viewer it soon becomes a lifeless stare. So in this example, I urge my actors to "look to the room": find the promise of love, for instance, in the fine bones of her hand, or in the sparkle of the glassware behind the bar. That way when you *do* move your eyes to look into hers, the viewer will see it vividly. Be aware that in all instances if you look at something for too long, if your looking turns into a gaze, its power is lost, it goes stale. How long is too long? Just as in real life, "too long" is when it stops being "real looking," when you no longer are seeing – and in seeing, having real thoughts – but merely have your eyes pointed at something. (I know you know what I mean.) And, of course, at the same time, eyes that flit around without actually seeing anything at all isn't the goal either.

I find many beginning actors who have trained only on the stage tend to enter frame, immediately park themselves somewhere and from that moment on, to the exclusion of everything else, look only at the script or the person they're talking to. They lose all sense of where the scene is taking place or what they or the other person is doing physically, or what's going on around them. They drop it like it doesn't exist. It's as if they are frozen in place and the only thing that matters is their voice and the words they speak. On camera, in a medium close-up this definitely does not work.

Again: you have to *look* at what's around you, *see* what's around you, *have thoughts* about what's around you.

In your rehearsals you have to calculate the character's strategy as to when it is most important to look at the other person … and when not to. (By the way, "not to" can include looking down at your script … if your script is an object of your thoughts, rather than the next line.) If for instance you are playing a corrupt congressman, sitting on a yacht angling for a bribe from a lobbyist, of course you will glance at him casually as you talk, but don't fix on him exclusively. Have thoughts as you look out at the water (thinking: "A rising tide raises all boats, even my own."). Relish the lap of luxury in the teakwood deck chairs ("So *this* is how it's going to be for me."). Listen to the flags flapping in the wind as you talk ("The winds of fortune are blowing my way.") Feel the warmth of the sun ("Ah, money, what a comfort.") Look at him occasionally as you talk, of course … But wait to *nail him* with a penetrating look at the perfect moment.

Let me give another example. Let's say the scene calls for the character to tell her lover that she's leaving him. She's getting dressed as she does this. The character can either sit upright and motionless on the edge of the bed and deliver all of her lines to him ... her whole speech directly to him without ever breaking eye contact ... or she can say many of the things she has to say while dealing with gathering her things (so she can start a new life), putting on her shoes (the ones she's going to walk away in) and only look directly into his eyes at crucial moments. I am telling you this latter type of approach has a more dynamic effect in an on-camera audition where there is no editor cutting away from you.

See what I'm getting at? But let's be clear ... there's nothing exotic about this! This is actually what we do in real life. Our minds are active and our eyes move naturally from thought to thought. We look directly at someone to make a point only under specific circumstances, and even then if we hang on too long we become self-conscious about it, don't we? In life, even within our most heartfelt appeals, not all sentences carry the same weight. When you make and hold eye contact, it makes a special statement. Let the same be true of your characters in on-camera auditions as well.

For a terrific example of this type of on-camera work, watch Glenn Close in *Fatal Attraction* (1987). She is a consummate master at gauging eye contact. Your on-camera auditions will have greater impact if, as you rehearse, you keep these ideas in mind and incorporate them into your audition.

The "middle distance"

There is one more important note about registering a thought or realization with our eyes. It is called "looking to the middle distance." Shawn Nelson, in his collection of very illuminating audiotapes, "The Impersonal Actor," instructs that this term refers to the act of looking with our mind's eye, when faced with a realization, to the immediate past or the immediate future. It is a gesture that connotes seeking the deeper implications of a situation. It equates to being vulnerable to a meaning beyond what is being said. We are all familiar with this common human phenomenon. This spot – this "middle distance" – is located about three feet in front of us, slightly down and slightly off to one side. Look for it. To the camera, the impression is that we're not focused on some object in the room, or on the other person, but rather on what we're seeing in our thoughts; a deeper meaning; a memory or an idea. We humans do this all the time when we're concerned about the outcome of an upcoming event; or are referring to something important that happened in our past. When the character recognizes what is there in his thoughts in the middle distance, he is referencing a consequence or vision of major significance to him. This can be a very powerful on-camera tool – your eyes/your thoughts – signifying a realization or an unshakeable personal truth that can not be argued with.

> **For example:** Imagine saying: "I don't know" directly into the eyes of another person. Compare this to saying "I don't know" to the middle distance as to a thought in your head. The impact of the utterance is entirely different.

Speaking to middle distance is another example of where a character might be looking other than directly into the eyes of his counterpart. It can come into play particularly during those exchanges where the character is accounting for his behavior, stating why he is doing (or did) something. It's especially useful, if strategically applied, for the one line in the scene that seems just too naked to utter directly. Caution: Use the middle distance with integrity and discretion. If your overdo it, it loses its power.

CHAPTER 10

The place/your thoughts

THE PLACE *IS* THE CIRCUMSTANCE

This chapter deals with the problem of converting the audition space – the typical environment of the producer's office – into the "place" as written in the script. All well-performed audition scenes include this component, i.e. we viewers can tell by the character's behavior where the scene is happening.

In the preceding chapter we discussed how, in an un-edited medium close-up of an on-camera audition, an unbroken gaze into the eyes of one's scene partner is an ineffective choice. But when the actor is not making eye contact, where is he looking? And what meaning do the objects of his attention lend to the scene? The objects must be a source of genuine thought, so that the actor, as the character, will actually have real thoughts in real time as he is playing the scene in a producer's office. I call this source "The Metaphor of the Place."

Let me circle in on this.

A film actor cannot get away with pretending that he is thinking or feeling. Such affectation might work for a character in some situational comedies, but in a dramatic role this "pretending" is what the camera emphatically interprets as bad acting. We want to avoid this at all costs.

Dustin Hoffman sums up the actor's conundrum:

> *I MIGHT LOOK DIFFERENT, I MIGHT MOVE DIFFERENTLY,*
> *I MIGHT EVEN APPEAR TO BEHAVE DIFFERENTLY ...*
> *BUT I THINK AND FEEL JUST THE SAME AS MYSELF.*
> *THIS I CANNOT CHANGE.*
>
> ... Dustin Hoffman

As Hoffman points out in the above quote, an actor cannot choose to have given thoughts or emotions. He can only have those which he actually has. The actor's process, then, however he does it, is basically to put himself in the character's situation so that he can respond to it authentically. Invariably this involves a process of interpreting the scripted circumstances in such a way as to highlight or encourage specific emotional points of view.

Next step: Look to the place.

> *THE TRUTH LIES IN THE PLACE.*
>
> ... Stanislavski

The truth lies in the place. The truth lies in the place. Why do they keep saying that!?

I cannot over-emphasize the following: In film media particularly, if you only play the scene according to what you detect from the dialogue, the scene will play flat. Of course, every line of dialogue is crucial to understanding the nature of the character, but I implore you to look to the circumstances and the implications of the place to find the reality of the scene.

> *THE PLACE IS THE CIRCUMSTANCE!*
>
> ... Stella used to holler at us

I remember when I first learned the impact of "looking to the place." I was working on scenes from Horton Foote's teleplay *Old Man*. I remember it as if it were yesterday. The title refers to the Mississippi River and involves an escaped convict who comes upon a whole variety of eccentric characters (and a beautiful girl for whom he eventually sacrifices his own freedom) as he tries to escape down the river. We were doing the play on a bare stage, which meant there was no real raft, no real river. (The situation was much like what you will encounter when auditioning for many of your film roles in a producer's office.) To make the physical circumstances real for myself I had to focus my imagination on the river: the banks of it, the color of it, the flow of it, the expanse of it, the challenge of it. The more I invested in "creating the river" the more "the river" gave back to me … eventually becoming the whole of life's mysterious paradoxes and all that implies. I involved myself in the river and the thoughts it inspired. All my dialogue, the exchanges I had with the other characters, came through those thoughts and emotions. I didn't care what the audience thought. I cared only to say what the river was telling me. You could say the river gave me truth.

Trust this. Try it.

When I coach an actor, I always start by having them read the scene out loud to me. Invariably they start by plunging into the dialogue. I have to stop them and ask them to read the scene heading very slowly. Every single word. For instance: "INTERIOR. HOSPITAL. WAITING ROOM. NIGHT" and we spend time talking about that. Why is the character there? Why at night? How late at night? How did the character get there? How long has he been there? Who else is there? What are his relationships to them? What was he doing before he came there? Is this an emergency or something routine for him? Why is the place empty or populated? What's strange about the place? What's unexpected? What's the temperature, the lighting, the furniture? Is it quiet, or is there a hubbub? What does it smell like in there? What does that smell mean? … sanitary or polluted … and so on: identifying and exploring all of the physical elements – *and what they imply* – that would indeed be present in reality.

We are looking to develop connections between those aspects of the character's circumstances that are reflected in "the place" and those that will arouse authentic thoughts and dispositions in the actor himself. Establishing this connection is a practice well known to disciplined actors; and when you are filming "on location" it won't present much of a problem. The reality of "the place" will be all around you. The question is, since "the place" is so important in creating a reality for your on-camera auditions, how can we tap into it authentically when we are auditioning in the sterile environment of a producer's office? Put another way: how can I find the Mississippi River, for example, in the producer's bookshelf or out of his office window? The next step, which I call establishing the **Metaphor of the Place**, will enrich your on-camera audition performances.

This approach was inspired by a single sentence that Thomas Harris wrote in his novel *The Red Dragon* (1986). In this story Harris astutely observes that we humans get ideas from what we see in front of us. I am applying this well-observed human phenomenon and using it to make us better on-camera actors. It works.

> *Metaphor:*
>
> *noun:* a figure of speech containing an implied comparison, in which a word or phrase ordinarily and primarily used of one thing is applied to another (Examples: the curtain of night; "all the world's a stage")
>
> *noun:* a figure of speech in which an expression is used to refer to something that it does not literally denote in order to suggest a similarity.
>
> (http://dictionary.reference.com)

Metaphor of the place

A stormy night suggests that something ominous is approaching. A scene that takes place in the rain signals that events of dire consequence are unfolding. Sunshine and flowers promote a happy ending. Canyons or tunnels suggest there is only one way out. Jagged rocks and tremors portend danger. Gleaming high-rise office spires speak of unshakable power. Clutter can mean chaos or unimaginable creativity.

Ask yourself what does "the place" represent to you personally, the actor, in relation to the story? In the example of the hospital waiting room: is this hospital setting a metaphor for lost causes, or redemption? Or is this where miracles are supposed to occur, or the crossroads of fate? Or is this place like a tool or a workbench in which you ply your craft? I encourage the actor to look at the situation of the character and then be aware that there exists a metaphorical connection between the actor himself as he auditions in the office and the place where the events of the scene unfold.

Picture it: the producer's office will have at minimum a floor, a door, a window, a chair, a corner, a desk, a phone. There will be other objects as well. So, what is it about the space – the actual physical reality of the producer's office and its contents – that will be equivalent to or in contrast with the physical circumstances as written in the script?

See, the question is what are you actually going to *do* in your on-camera audition? ... and don't tell me, "Say the lines right." That won't be enough. Or that you're going to "feel" a certain way about the events. Planning how you'll feel will only result in a phony affectation. We're looking for you to have an active mind and authentic emotions. I'm telling you that you'll find a source for these thoughts, real thoughts, "in the place." If you invest in developing an awareness of the metaphorical or symbolic connection between the place as scripted and what it means to you personally ... you will find the metaphorical equivalent of the scripted place on camera in the producer's office!

To illustrate what I mean using the "hospital" example, as you act the scene in the producer's office and you look around "the hospital room" you will find connections between the "hospital" and the objects in the producer's audition room. The office itself and its contents will be, then, a metaphor for lost causes, or redemption, or where miracles are supposed to occur, or a workbench on which you ply your craft! See what I mean?

WHERE *YOU ARE IS* WHO *YOU ARE.*

… Stella Adler

Years ago I read an article about Kevin Costner which included an anecdote about his successful audition for the lead in the1988 film *Bull Durham*, a film about a minor league baseball player. He insisted that the producer's audition take place in the batting cage of a local baseball field. Very few of us are in a position to make such a request, but clearly Mr Costner understood the importance the place plays in how a scene unfolds.

Many of the missteps I made in past auditions were because I failed to identify a meaningful connection between my character's circumstance as written in the script and my own situation as an actor auditioning for a producer in his office. I failed to see for example that such an office can represent "a place of opportunity"; or it can represent "at long last a promise fulfilled"; or it can be metaphorically "too shabby a place in which to save the world"; or "an ironically strange place to find a lover." See what I mean? There will be a connection either in the similarity or ironic oppositeness between what you find in the "office" and the physical setting of the scene as written. Include these thoughts, speak through them as well as to the other character in the scene.

What do I mean by "speak through them?" In class recently we were working on a scene in which a character in a holding cell was being interrogated by his lawyer about a crime he didn't commit. For the first go around the actor delivered his lines to the lawyer, responding only to what the lawyer said, looking at the lawyer only, while defending himself as best he could. Then we included an added dimension. We let him move around in the audition space. We considered the walls – "the place" – of the audition space and how they represented the walls of his character's imprisonment – how intractable they were, how unjustly they held him. But not only that; how those walls metaphorically limited him the actor as well; how they represented all the obstacles that limited him in his abilities and kept him from his dreams; how unjust it was and how frustrating; and how he could never seem to get outside the boundaries they set for him. Real thoughts! ... about things he, the actor, really cared about. The scene was much enriched by including these metaphorical connections along with those implied by the bare facts of the scene's text. All the frustration came through as he responded not only to the lawyer but to the realities presented by the metaphor of the walls, speaking through the thoughts and emotions they aroused in him, as opposed to those limited by his mere reactions to the accusations of the lawyer.

If the scene, to take another example, takes place between you and another character in a car as you drive in the middle of the night down a dark Texas highway ... what does that darkness represent? What future lies beyond the illumination of your headlights? What lies in the past out the rear view mirror? What are you escaping? What are you seeking? Why is it always dark when you most need it to be light? Can you see the connection between these questions and the physical audition itself?

As with my own experience in Horton Foote's *Old Man* in my earlier example of the river and how it spoke to me, speak through the thoughts you invest in the place. The world outside the office window turns out to be in fact the infinite possibilities and ironies of life. The bookshelf actually is like the river, a symbol of all we wish we could know and be. The audition itself is indeed the obstacle that stands between us and the freedom we desire.

A word of caution: I hear acting teachers urge their students to "Listen!" I have come to the conclusion that's not what the teacher actually means. I know for myself that the harder I try to listen the less I hear. I focus so hard on the *act* of listening I don't hear a thing. I know you know what I mean. What we really are wanting, when we talk about listening, is for the actor to have and respond to actual thoughts, actual opinions, about what is being said to them. And it's the same way with seeing. It's not so much an issue of *looking* at some object we have "created in our imagination." Because I know if I look too hard it is never there! I start behaving *as if* I see it, which doesn't work at all. In that case what I typically wind up doing is demonstrating that I am "looking." No good. Rather, the aim is to consider whatever is in front of you, as Thomas Harris instructs, and allow for how it – whatever it is – connects metaphorically to the circumstances implied by the place as written in the scene.

Let's refer to the above "hospital" example one last time. First of all, if the scripted scene has your character sitting, then play the audition sitting. If standing, then don't sit down. If the scripted scene has you moving about, then move about it in your audition. As you sit or stand, what are you doing ... Waiting? Searching? Fulfilling a routine job requirement? What? Now, for example, what about the chair in the producer's office? Is there a chair in the "hospital" scene as written? And if there is, how does the audition chair compare to it? Strangely, or just what you would expect? Is it an adequate agent of support, or not? And where are the nurses and why is everything so quiet? That camera is looking awfully technical, is that a new medical gadget? Is the character in a situation beyond his control? And might that not be true as well for you, the actor, as you audition?

Concluding thought

Investing in the "metaphor of the place" not only encourages your having real thoughts on camera. It also encourages a more organic involvement with your surroundings as you look at or touch things, and in so doing include them as reflections on the character's circumstances. One of the most glaring shortcomings of novice actors is their failure to "use the place" in their on-camera auditions, to move freely within the place, and to react viscerally to the physical reality of the character's circumstance. The novice often feels boxed in by the presence of the camera and tends to focus their attention solely on the other character. Developing the metaphor of the place tends to loosen this up. Work with this. It will enrich your performances.

Summary

- Look to the circumstances and the implications of the place to find the reality of the scene.
- Investigate the connection between the character's circumstances as reflected in "the place" and those that arouse authentic thoughts and dispositions in you, the actor.
- Develop an awareness of the metaphorical connection between "the place" as scripted, what "the place" means to you personally, and the metaphorical equivalent in the typical producer's office.
- Include the reality of the place as a vital component of your audition.

Scene Preparation for On-Camera Auditions

CHAPTER 11

How to paint a nose

BASIC PHILOSOPHY

– 1 –

Accomplished acting is the primary issue in any audition. All of the considerations addressed in this book are meant to support your capacity to perform the part. Since this book lays out the sequence of what must unfold to manifest a worthy on-camera audition, it would be incomplete without addressing the craft itself.

Let's start by saying everyone wants to be special and have things come easy. But there are laws in the universe and woe to anyone who thinks they can short-change the universe. The "secret" for success? Ask any successful artist and they will answer: First comes work, then comes luck, then comes talent. Success can't possibly happen if you don't show up well prepared.

The single most important contributor to being well prepared is consistent participation in an acting workshop or local theater where you can pursue and express your craft. Actors are like athletes: they must work out every day. They don't sit idle all week and expect to win the tournament that weekend. If you are an actor you have to be *acting*. You cannot sit around and wait. If you do, you will not be ready when an opportunity comes. And believe me, they come and go in a flash.

Former students often call me for my advice or coaching for a part they suddenly have an opportunity to audition for, and if in the course of our session they acknowledge to me that they have not been in workshop, I inwardly know they are probably not going to get the part. Like it or lump it, that's the way it is.

That said, in this chapter I am going to attempt "a raid on the inarticulate" as T.S. Eliot so perfectly put it. I am going to outline what I have learned about the acting process itself and also give a summary of what clues an actor might pursue to bring his work to life. You are the artist. I venture this as a starting point that might be helpful to you in cobbling a process for yourself. The following is an assemblage of thoughts, anecdotes and approaches that might help if you need it. I know I did.

> **Note:** I have had the blessing of studying with some truly great teachers: principally Stella Adler and Peggy Feury, but also Sean Nelson, Peter Flood, Jeff Cory, to name a few. I confess I am humbled when I venture to address the subject, eclectic as it is, which has been so brilliantly espoused by these gifted mentors. For an excellent and thorough exploration of the acting process I vigorously recommend the following:
>
> > The Intent to Live, Larry Moss, Bantam, 2005.
> > Directing Actors, Judith Weston, M. Wiese Productions, 1996
> > Stella Adler, The Art of Acting, H. Kissel, Applause Books, 2000
> > The Impersonal Actor (Audiotapes), Shawn Nelson, 1994
> > Acting in Commercials, Joan See, Backstage, 1993

Andrew Wyeth, the great American artist, was once asked if he ever took art classes. "No," he said, "I was afraid someone would teach me how to paint a nose." He didn't want to know "how." Indeed he wanted to discover "how" anew with each and every nose. And that is the way it should be for your acting; and it most certainly will be. There isn't a "way." No one can teach you how to act. You will have to teach yourself. But … in the beginning, most of us do not have a clue as to what we are doing and crave some guideposts to get us off in the right direction. Or we are aware that there are holes in our preparation for our on-camera auditions but don't know where to look to fill them.

I want to start this discussion by relating an event that happened to me years ago. It may seem oblique to the subject but it actually cuts right to the heart of the matter.

Jennifer Part was a casting director working out of Screen Gems who was very supportive of my work, meaning she called me in to read for anything I was remotely right for. She was clearly in my corner as evidenced by the number of times I auditioned for projects she was casting. But I wasn't landing any parts. One day, with the sides in my hands, as I was going in to read yet again for another project, she stopped me on the stairs that led up to the producers' offices. After cordial greetings she said: "Joe, I have been thinking about you. I've been wanting to tell you something." "What, Jennifer?" I asked with mild curiosity. She looked at me with warm eyes and said, "Joe, I have never seen you give a bad audition." "Why, thank you, Jennifer," I said. And then she shook me to my bones when she said with a genuinely kind tone as she patted me on my wrist: "Unfortunately, darling, that's not a compliment." Then she went toodling on down the stairs … "Bye!" … leaving me standing there in a state of stunned bewilderment. What in the world did she mean by that? "I have never seen you give a bad audition and that is not a compliment." I was like you. I ached with ambition. I was studying like crazy, working on scene study every night, going to acting exercise class twice weekly. I was in great shape. I was moderate in my excesses. I was very talented at looking great and sounding natural. (That was my idea of acting at the time, I am embarrassed to say.) I was cool, very cool, too cool for TV, as they say. Never made a fool of myself. Always cool, always looking good. (I hope you hear a note of self-derision.) Producers were calling me in all the time. I was very active professionally. What in the world did Jennifer Part mean?!

Looking great and acting natural, yes. That's what I was doing. Back then I knew *how* to do everything but I didn't know *what* to do. See, I thought my job in an audition was to show them I could do whatever it was "they" wanted me to do. If you think about it, what that meant was I basically had to come from the neutral center. I had no point of view. It took me a long time to understand what Jennifer was getting at. I remember a note that Peggy gave me in class once. She said when great actors are bad, they are very bad. What she meant was, and this is the whole point, our characters are meant to be *real people*, actual people, caught in the circumstances of the story … and those circumstances are not "everyday" circumstances. They are *special*, *unusual* circumstances; because otherwise we don't have a story. The choices that an actor makes have to live up to the unusualness of the character's situation. The characters are pushed out "on the edge" as it were … not in the center, which is where I was playing it (in my effort to be natural). When a great actor – who is great partially because he knows this – goofs, it is because he is out on the edge, but it is the "wrong" edge, and that's why it looks so bad. That's the risk an actor takes. But being out there is also where courage and greatness lies. *This* I was not doing.

I was not doing it because I had not yet devoted a portion of my preparation to identifying why I, Joe, personally (and with some passion) wanted to do the scene. I wasn't investing myself personally in the work. I had a passion for being professional and accomplished in my craft. But I didn't, in the beginning, have a *passion for the character and the situation he was in*. I spent not one calorie of energy establishing for myself what it was about the character and his situation that I personally wanted to express. I just wanted to be good.

I know for your auditions you are going to be all wrapped up getting the lines right and sounding the way you want to sound … but I urge you to focus with all your muscles on what it is about the situation and the nature of the character that you personally want to express and therefore bring to life.

I can tell you that when you audition well, one of the main reasons will be because you have an insight or an enthusiasm for some aspect of the scene: the predicament or tactics of the character, or the theme of the story. This can be as simple as: "I would love to play a part in a scary movie. I'll make it just like my nightmares." Or "There is so much needless violence in the world. Why do we treat each other this way?" Or "I was at a wedding once, my sister's ... it was hilarious! A total catastrophe!" Or "God, it would be awful to be in that situation, and I know why." You need a connection to the scene/screenplay that excites and interests and challenges you such that you look forward to the audition as an opportunity of expression rather than a booby trap.

Larry Moss addresses this issue with an anecdote in his book *Intent to Live*. He describes how as a young acting student he felt completely insecure, confused and doomed to humiliation as he tried to prepare a Chekhov scene for class the next morning. Then it struck him to his bones that the catastrophe he was forecasting for himself was exactly parallel to the social situation of the character in the scene. Once he embraced that point of view, the entire scene along with every impulse fell into place for him.

Stella Adler used to say that an actor's talent does not lie in mastering the actor's craft; rather it manifests itself in the actor's choices.

And where do we find these choices? There is only one guide to lead you: yourself. Look to what you, the artist, through your own life experience and imagination, find compelling, funny or interesting in the scene. Believe in it. It is, after all, the key to what you have to offer as an artist. It is all you have, actually. Try not to be distracted by what you think "They" want; rather look inward, to yourself, as if you yourself were the producer of the project driven by a passion for its theme, and you the actor were perfect for the part. Show them exactly how the part should be played.

– 2 –

A really precise definition of the word "talent" eludes me. I made the glib comment the other day that talent is: "You do it, I like it." In the same conversation a teaching colleague, Lora Zane, offered a more instructive definition: that talent was the ability of the actor to be in the character's situation; to be the doctor attending a patient, the student falling in love, the outcast seeking revenge … to be whatever the screenplay required. This dovetails with Sandy Meisner's definition of acting: living truthfully under imaginary circumstances.

Every once in a while I have a student who doesn't know the first thing about acting who comes in and knocks my socks off. As an "actor" he doesn't know what he is doing … but he knows exactly what the character is doing! In other words he throws himself completely into the situation and makes believe! He doesn't seem to have trouble memorizing his lines, because he instinctively connects them to what the character is doing, what the actual human dynamic of the circumstance is. He loses all self-consciousness, because he is absorbed completely in the reality he has created. He is not wondering if what he is doing is any good or not, or what the audience is thinking of him as he does it. Just like when we were kids. He's thoroughly engrossed in making believe.

That is the goal … to put yourself in the situation the script calls for and live inside of it … just like you did when you were a child making believe. When we were kids we would build a fort and ready ourselves for the bad guys, or we would paint our faces, fashion a tomahawk and live in a teepee, or present ourselves to the Queen of England to receive the honors of a Knight of the Realm. And while we were doing this never once did we break the spell of what we had created or doubt for an instant that we were anything but what we were pretending to be. This is acting at its best. This is the goal. All the rest is subordinate to this … whatever it takes.

I read a *Playboy* interview with Dustin Hoffman in which he said (what's with the *always* Dustin Hoffman!?) in association with his work on the film *Lenny* that the work for an actor gets harder, not easier, because the actor becomes more and more demanding that his work include this total involvement. It is both elusive and essential. He was alluding to the fact that an actor becomes increasingly self-critical – he knows when he is faking – as he seeks an authentic involvement in the character's situation. This is what critics are referring to when they castigate an actor, usually a star, who simply "phoned in" his performance. They mean by this criticism, and it is a very harsh one, that the actor clearly was not involved in his work but chose instead to rely on his well-worn reserve of acting tricks to manner the performance, rather than devoting himself to the requirements of the part. Peggy once related in class that Marlon Brando during his run of *A Streetcar Named Desire* had to arrive at the theater earlier and earlier to ready himself for the role of Stanley. His life was changing with his exploding fame, and to get back to what the role required took more and more time.

Whatever it takes. There is a famous exchange between (again) Dustin Hoffman and this time the legendary Laurence Olivier that occurred during the filming of *Marathon Man*. As the story goes, the scene they were shooting involved the dramatic confrontation between Hoffman, the victimized protagonist, and Olivier the evil Nazi war criminal. The screenplay had Hoffman's character on the run and going without sleep for three days, thus the title. As the actors assembled to rehearse the scene, Olivier looked at Hoffman and said, "You look terrible, what's the matter?" Hoffman told him he hadn't let himself sleep for three days so he could shoot the scene. Olivier commented, "My goodness, why don't you try acting?" It wasn't a put-down. It was comment on how differently actors approach their challenges. Some work from the outside in, as Sean Penn suggested in the quote in the section on wardrobe, others work from the inside out. Most, of course, do a combination of both.

A further example of this dynamic involves a soliloquy I saw Olivier perform on the early-50s television variety show *The Ed Sullivan Show*. I was no more than nine years old. I watched Olivier walk out on the bare television stage, unadorned, and deliver the final soliloquy of Oedipus the King as he recognizes the agonizing truth: that, as the fates had foretold, he had indeed murdered his father and slept with his mother and thus was the one to bring disaster to Athens. I remember in chilling detail how his tongue stretched out as he screamed, like the woman in Picasso's apocalyptic painting *Guernica*. I have never forgotten that moment. I remember at the time instinctively knowing that I was witnessing something a great deal more profound than *Steamboat Willy*. It gives me goosebumps even now. Curiously, perhaps 20 years later, as an acting student, I read an interview of the renowned actor. Like so many such interviews, he was asked about his process. In the course of his answer he alluded to the time many years before when he played Oedipus. And with an appealing self-deprecation he recalled how he, as an actor, was totally at a loss as to how he was going to let out a scream that would authentically express the degree of agony embodied in the character's wretched defilement. Olivier, of course, had never slept with his mother, nor killed his father … and yet he had to bring himself to scream as if for the sake of all humankind. Olivier related with some amusement how he ducked the moment all through rehearsals. He would abandon the scene and walk off the rehearsal stage just at the crucial moment, hiding under the cloak of being a "big star." But he admitted he hadn't the slightest idea of how he was going to solve his problem … until quite by chance he read a magazine article about how the farmers in Siberia at the time would trap ermine. The pure white pelts of this mink-like creature were considered the most luxurious of all furs. According to the article, the farmers would put out salt licks in the dead of winter when the animals' coats were at their thickest. The little creatures would be drawn by their need for the salt, lick the block, and would be stuck to the frozen salt by their tongues. (Believe it or not, a rabbit can scream louder than a human being!) This was the image Olivier brought to the character's moment, a humble creature trapped in its horrifying fate by its own tongue.

Some actors find their way into make-believe through a change or sensation in their bodies – a limp or an accent or a physical sensation – the change allows them to believe their creation. For some it is their rhythm of speech, or a thought or a memory from a similar situation in their own lives; for some it lies in the wardrobe, for some it's a musical theme; or it might be a connection between themselves and the moral issue or dilemma that the character faces. Some focus on the physical nature of the situation, the cold or the drunkenness. For some it is an "as if," meaning this situation is "as if" some equivalent event from their own familiar life was unfolding. For some, like Olivier in the above example, an image puts them in touch, or a photograph; for some it's focusing on an action or an intention, or on solving a physical problem that lies within the scene for the character. Or, as is many times the case, it is the effect of a combination of several of these influences.

– 3 –

Given that the purpose of acting is to tell a story, what an actor needs to create in any given scene is involvement in some aspect of the character's situation that so engrosses him that he loses self-awareness. This focus on something other than the "self" is often referred to as "concentration." And the actor's dealing with this aspect of the situation is what acting teachers call "being in the moment."

The following list can be helpful in unlocking the essence of a scene for an actor. You can find such lists in a million acting books.

- What do you think this scene is about?
- What is the event of this scene? What happens in the scene?
- How does this event contribute to the overall story?
- Where is the scene taking place? What is the physical nature of the place?

- Why is the character there? Where was he just prior?
- What aspect of the character's background comes into play in th
  scene?
- What is his relationship to the other characters?
- What is at issue for the character?
- What is the character literally doing when the scene starts?
- What is the character seeking or wants to have happen?
- What is he doing to get it?
- Why is it important?
- What is standing in his way?
- Why doesn't the character just walk out?

It is fruitless to arrive at factually and intellectually correct answers t
each of the questions if they are "dry" answers. "Dry" will not serv
you. We are looking for something that lights you up, somethin
"juicy," an angle, an answer which, by virtue of some person
enthusiasm, point of view, or experience, connects you, the actor, t
what is going on for the character in the scene. One answer to ar
one of the above questions will work if it is meaningful enough. An
one can unlock the answer to the crucial question: "What is th
scene about for you?"

CHAPTER 12

What needs to happen

ANALYZING THE STORY/THE SCENE

Given the basics we have just discussed, where do we begin preparing for an on-camera audition? Remember, we are looking for a personal connection to the material that lights us up. As I said before, it is this specific personal energy that is at the core of what we have to offer the project. Without it we have little to bring to the story as a performing artist. Without it our work, our audition, will fall flat. Or at best we will come in second to the actor who has it.

Look to the circumstances

I will repeat it numerous times: in a screenplay (as opposed to a stage play) you will rarely find the key to effective choices though interpretation of the dialogue. Look to the *situation*, the *circumstances* of the character, to inspire your choices. For your on-camera work, look to create the reality of the circumstances.

Start by telling the story ...

Out loud to another person, or to the bedpost if no one is around – in such a way that it is interesting to the listener (or you). In as great a detail as possible, from what the script or the "sides" give you, try to create the quality of: "Yeah? ... and then what happens!?" To do this you will have to use words and images that are dramatic and engaging. These word choices will influence and set the tone for what you will seek to play. They will imply what is compelling or dynamic or funny about the action. They will also starkly show you where the "holes" are in your own understanding of the story and what makes it worth telling. When you only have the scenes unaccompanied by a complete script – called the "sides" – this can be sketchy, but you still have to make choices based on your instinctive guess as to what the plot probably is and how the scene you are reading is indispensable to telling the story. If you only have sides, then pay attention to the chapter on structure as a guide to formulate this speculation, remembering that a good screenplay is a sequence of scenes each of which is crucial to the story.

Explore your sense of the "world" in which the story takes place, your character's relationship to it and to the people who inhabit it

To get an idea of what I am talking about, take a look at promotional blurbs on the back of DVDs or VCR tapes at the video rental store. There will be an enticing summary of the film in question, a paragraph or two that describes the movie in such a way that will make you want to watch it. It will indicate the **Genre** (comedy, drama, thriller, suspense, adventure, etc.) and will involve the **Setting**, the **Era** and the **Professional Milieu** the story depicts. These will imply what socio-economic values are in play. This is different from the plot, which is the sequence of how the story unfolds.

For example:

> In this shocking tragedy, Oedipus Rex, the esteemed king of ancient Athens, seeks to know the cause of a dark emergency, why his beloved city is beset by cruel pestilence. Sending his

minions throughout the realm uncovers mysterious clues to the source of the evil, whose secret ultimately lies in the cryptic prediction of a long-forgotten oracle … and to the very foot of the throne itself.

Another example, in this case *The Devil Wears Prada*:

This is a comedy about a young woman, high achiever Andy Sachs, who lands a job "a million girls would die for" … assistant to the demanding editor of a glitzy New York fashion magazine. Against her better nature, she lets herself be seduced by the challenges of this fast and glamorous world, leaving everyone to doubt whether she will be able to find her way back to herself and the journalism work she is truly proud of.

By doing this you will often identify what the protagonist wants or values in the broadest sense. Acting teachers identify this as the character's **super objective**; the driving force, a seeking, that is threaded throughout the tale. If you are reading for a supporting character or the antagonist, this summary will give you an idea as to how your character either promotes or inhibits the "journey" of the protagonist.

The scene itself … why this one?

Think: *Why did "they" choose this particular scene for your audition*? Part of the answer might be because of practical concerns … that it lends itself physically to being performed in an office. But there will be other more critical reasons as well: the nature of the character; a sequence that demonstrates a change in the protagonist; the nature of their relationships; the unfolding of a pivotal plot point. No matter what your role, the scene you audition for is chosen because it highlights a crucial aspect of the character or a pivotal event in the story. You need to have a feel for what that is and how the audition scene (or sequence of scenes) contributes to telling the overall story.

Pay attention to the logic of dramatic structure as discussed in Chapter 7.

Every scene or sequence of scenes you audition for will start with the protagonist in a given situation or frame of mind and something will happen to change that situation and propel – or nudge – the character in a new direction. Count on it.

You will be reading for either the protagonist or a supporting role. If you are reading for a supporting role, your character will put a kind of pressure on the protagonist, or complicate his situation. That's what supporting characters do. For example: the pressure of forcing him out of his preconceptions, the pressure of calling him back out of danger; the pressure in giving him new information; the pressure to conform; the pressure to take action; or the complication of his liking you or being sympathetic to you or finding you repulsive. If you are reading for a supporting character, ask yourself: What is my reality? What do I want? What's at stake for me? Or what is the jeopardy in the situation? What problem does the circumstance cause me to solve, or give me an opportunity to do? And how might my choices about these issues highlight or enhance the theme of the story from the central character's point of view? In other words, what pressure does my behavior put on the protagonist so that as a "supporting" character, I actually do *support* the story?

> **Note:** Some stories are about a group where each character has equal weight in the story. In this case, the challenge is for each character to participate in the overall objective of the group, but to exhibit qualities and concerns that are distinct from the others. Think *Steel Magnolias*, *City Slickers*, *The Big Chill*.

Ask yourself: What happens in the scene? Where does it take place? What is the situation? What results from the scene, what does it lead to? If I am the protagonist, what changes? If I am a supporting character, what change or complication do I, however incrementally, contribute to?

Summary

Breaking down a scene/terms

In schematic form, this is how a scene often unfolds:

- The character is in a specific **Place**, in a specific **Situation or Circumstance**.
- He wants something that is his **Objective**.
- How he plans to go about getting his objective is his **Intention**.
- The subsets of his intention are the **Tools** he uses.
- The importance of getting what he wants is called the **Stakes** … the bad thing that will result if he doesn't get it.
- Something is in his way: the **Obstacle**, which is either an outside force or person, or a value within himself.
- Then some element in the situation will change, and that change will advance the story.

For example:

The situation is: Your character has a chance for a date with the woman of his dreams, but he has to babysit his little sister. He is at a restaurant where he arranged to have lunch with his older brother. The woman, his "date," is due to show up any minute.

His objective is to get his brother to take care of the little girl for him.

The obstacle is his brother has had a fight with the little girl and refuses.

The stakes are he's desperate, she is a knockout. He's in love!

He intends to do whatever is necessary to get his brother to comply.

He tries all sorts of *tools*: begging, cajoling, humoring, lying … but nothing works. Finally he bribes his brother with every last cent he has.

The change is his brother relents, says okay and takes all his money.

His date arrives. She is a knockout. She is expecting a very extravagant evening. Now our hero is broke and needs to borrow a couple of bucks.

CHAPTER 13

Acting is doing. Meaningful acting is doing in an emotional context

CREATING THE CHARACTER: ACTIONS AND CIRCUMSTANCES

– 1 –

Of all the terms that are used in acting classes, the question of what is meant by the word "character" is to me the most vexing to define; that is, to define it in a way that informs an approach to our work. Definitely one size does not fit all. And definitely "character" is a composite of numerous dynamics and influences.

I have played many roles. Often I worked hard but struggled awkwardly to find a connection to the character and make whatever I was doing believable to myself; sometimes I knew the character inside and out and knew exactly what "he would do"; but only on two occasions in 35 years – and then only for a very fleeting length of time – did I truly have the experience of feeling that I actually *was* the character. Actually somebody else. It was an experience of unique quality, and so rare to me that I wonder if it is reasonable to evaluat my efforts against that criterion.

I have heard it put this way: that your character is a "version of you. "The character" is very much you, and at the same time is not you You are the source of the character, and yet the character stand apart. Jack Nicholson quotes his teacher Jeff Cory as saying that th character is "85% completely identical to you." Peggy Feury onc observed that the really good film actors understand that th difference between themselves and the character is very smal Recall what Dustin Hoffman said: No matter how he moves an behaves, "he thinks and feels just as himself, this he cannot change Safe to say there are many seemingly paradoxical concepts floatin around. All we can say for sure is that the source for creating "th character" definitely changes from part to part.

Acting is an eclectic process. Look for whatever works. Kee reviewing the circumstances and the theme of the story. Let th character come to you. Elements will assert themselves, e.g. wha she looks like; her background and class; how she moves; her basi concerns; her connections to your own past experiences; perhap she's like a person you know … the list is unending. This proces never unfolds in a straight line. My beloved teacher, Peggy Feur related once in class how her actor friend, the great Collee Dewhurst, once secreted herself away in a cabin vowing not t emerge until she "found the character," then finally telephoned Pegg saying ecstatically, "I found her! She's in her hands!" Dustin Hoffma said once: he knows the character when he gets how he walk When Anthony Hopkins says he reads a script never less than 30 times, this is what he is doing: searching, and imagining, and allowin I guess you could say how an actor approaches creating a charact is tantamount to defining him as an artist.

Actions

For a starting point I am defining "character" as being: **What the individual does and how he does it in response to a given circumstance.**

In life, how do we measure a person's character? It is by what they *do*, isn't it? Certainly their appearance and their ambitions, their background, their capacities, their relationships and how they feel about it all are contributing factors to understanding a person, but in the end it is what they *do* that determines their character. John Wooden, the great UCLA basketball coach, used to say that sports did not build character, they revealed character. His observation reinforces the focus on what an individual does in any give circumstance as the determining factor in estimating character.

> *ACTING IS DOING. MEANINGFUL ACTING IS*
> *DOING IN AN EMOTIONAL CONTEXT.*
>
> … Sandy Meisner

So I am going to start our discussion on creating a character by discussing actions. I will follow with identifying many of the factors that contribute to the circumstances.

In any given scene, an actor's focus has to be on something a person can actually do … an action described as a verb, rather than on a quality of being, which is an adjective. We are called the "actors" because we do the *action*. We are not called the "pretenders," or the "behaviorists" or the "emoters."

An action can be physical or mental. To seduce, charm, shake, tease, mock, confront, insult, suggest, inform, encourage, hint, etc. are examples of actions. On-camera thinking is an action. For instance, to: strategize, appraise, discern, see the irony, scheme, regret, evaluate, plot, mislead, conclude, seek, yearn, etc. These are all actions. Experienced actors know the thesaurus can be a helpful source for identifying verbs whose synonyms have special meaning for you. Acting teachers advise to look for verbs that energize you verbs that fuel your imagination and your choices.

Look for **proactive,** *as opposed to* **reactive** *choices for the character*

This means your reaction to another character is not solely a function of raw emotional reflexes, but rather is combined with – given the circumstances – what your character wants to do or have happen.

Let me explain: In our early acting training, the object of our efforts most often is focused on encouraging ourselves, in the midst of a lot of nervousness and self-consciousness, to be emotionally open and expressive; to do this "in public" as it were. For many this takes a lot of work and it is an extremely important component of our training. But this leads many actors to believe that acting is really a function of reacting reflexively to the other character, i.e. to be "connected" to and expressive of however we feel. We conclude, since that is the aim of many early acting exercises – and we get a lot of praise for doing it – that we are doing our job if we are "in touch with" what we are feeling and express it. But this is not what we do in real life, nor is it what our characters are most often doing. Or ever do! … except for perhaps once or twice in the story at a pivotal moment.

The protagonist never finds the truth where he thinks he will find it. He never discovers it to be what he thought it would be.

Here's what I mean by "reacting proactively with purpose:" This is what actually just happened right now as I write this. My wife just walked in. I love her dearly and she is a very special person to me. But I am in the middle of something important in my work, I am really focused and I don't want to be disturbed. It upsets me that she has interrupted my work. I think: "Doesn't she have any respect for what I am doing?!" She "just wants to talk." Typical! If I indulge what I am *really* feeling and allow myself to get upset with her, it will only serve to cause a quarrel and if that happens it will take me even longer to settle down and get back to where I was in my work. So I contain myself, I stay calm and talk for a few minutes. I treat her lovingly (not because I love her at the moment but because I want her to go!). I indulge the chat; but all the while my real purpose is to get her to leave without much disruption so I can get back to what I really want to do. This never leaves my mind. It colors my every reaction to whatever she says or does. This is what I mean by "*reacting proactively, with purpose, rather than just reactively*." How I get her to leave says a lot about me as a person. (And by the way, it worked pretty well. I was spectacular. She left happily. Now I can get back to what I really wanted all the while.)

Explore what the character wants, why she wants it, and what she does to get it

Try to make your character proactive rather than passive to the circumstances. So ask yourself: "What is she doing, what does she want and how does she go about trying to get it?"

Add to this: As you identify what your character wants or what she is "getting at," give her every ability, every cleverness, using what the writer gives you as the circumstance, to get it. If you focus on this you will often arrive at much more interesting choices than what comes from relying on a purely emotional or reflexive reaction.

Underestimating the character: big mistake

Here is a corollary to the above approach: We know that drama is about human frailty. We know this because when we sit in the audience and look up onto the screen we witness the frailties operating. So we think we are on the right track to imbue our characters with frailties. Once we identify them, as actors, we feel compelled to demonstrate them for the audience … since we are the ones who know what the story is about. Big mistake.

This is falling into the trap that dogged me for years: thinking that as an actor, part of my task was to show the audience what was *wrong* with the character. This is actually a form of contempt for the character. Try this instead: *within the character's circumstances as defined by the writer*, give your character the tools and capabilities they need to get what they want. Make your characters as cunning, perceptive, and capable as the circumstances allow. Ask yourself: "If they behaved this way, would they get what they want?"

Shawn Nelson admonishes us to make our characters smarter and more perceptive than ourselves. Do not hobble the character with shortcomings, or points of view you yourself have no conviction towards, in order to accommodate what you, the actor, know to be the outcome of the story. *The writer will take care of that*. If my wife, in the above example, had suspected that I was insincere or manipulating her, the whole morning would have blown up in a quarrel. My day's work would have been lost. I had to be very good at getting her to leave. If the character comes up short, make it be because of the plot the writer constructs rather than because of the choices you as the actor burden the character with. To take my "wife" example one step further: if the morning *does* blow up with a quarrel, it should not be because I am transparently insincere; it needs to be because even though I was "spectacular," she saw through it! That's what I mean by letting the writer do it. This approach makes for much more creative choices, you will see.

If the character is a coward, don't worry, he will run away no matter how cleverly he pretends to be brave. The writer will make him do that. You don't have to act "afraid," because the character will be seeing the danger no matter how you play him. If he is a rat, he will betray his friends no matter how loyally he treats them. If he is a klutz and you allow him to be graceful, he will spill his drink anyway. You will see, this approach often leads to much more interesting choices than deciding what is wrong with the character, defining him by the corresponding adjective, and then setting out to demonstrate it for the audience.

Especially on camera, because the camera sees all, it doesn't make for good work to "show" us what is "wrong" or "what you know" or "intellectually understand" about the character. Remember: the story isn't about you, it is about the character.

One of the great things about acting is that your characters teach you things about being a human being. Put yourself in the character's circumstances and work from there. Choose for the character to be at their most able, caught in the circumstances, doing the best they can with what the writer gives them. Identify the character's intention and then ask yourself: how must they behave in order to be totally successful at accomplishing their goal? So that they would *actually* succeed? Then stick to it through thick and thin until the script derails you.

Example: From an article entitled: "Character Building, TV-Style," *LA Sunday Times* Calendar Section, Sunday, March 2, 1997, p. 7. Michael Richards talks about his character, Kramer, in the hit show *Seinfeld:*

"The real key came about eight or nine shows in. I had been playing Kramer as if he were slow-witted – always one step behind what everyone else was saying. Then I learned to play Kramer as if he were blocks ahead of what everyone's saying, and I had him."

Example: Paraphrased from story in *LA Times*, September 24, 1996:

"A man committed suicide at a gun range yesterday. Because of the new gun law that requires a waiting period at the time of purchase, proprietors at target range rental facilities have had to be on alert when renting pistols to new customers. When asked about the suicide, the owner of the gun range said: 'I had never seen him before, so I looked him up and down pretty good. I looked for the smallest sign of anything fishy about the guy … but I didn't spot a thing. Not a twitch. Never in a million years did I suspect he was going in there to blow his brains out.'"

(Now, there was a man who wanted to succeed.)

Example: Paraphrased from a TV interview of an actress who was very proud of herself and excited that the following worked so well

> The actress had to do a striptease. She said, "I definitely did not go out there with the goal to turn the guys on. I could never have done that. My mother would kill me. What I chose as my goal was ... through an ancient and timeless ritual ... long ago choreographed in every detail ... my goal was to hypnotize every man in the audience. To put every man into a trance. To cast a spell over each and every one of them."

Identify "the problem"

Especially in an audition, it is not enough to go in planning to merely react to the other character in the scene. In an audition you will most often be reading with a casting assistant of mediocre abilities. Plus, your off-screen partner will be distracted by wanting to watch *your* performance. Their full focus will not be on playing the scene.

An auditioning actor must be prepared to go in and react with a clear goal. No wishy-washy "let's wing it and see how it goes." This approach depends too much on the playing abilities of the scene partner. The results will be predictable. The scene won't go anywhere. And neither will you ... until you learn to read with a clear, easily explained purpose to drive the scene.

Many actors pace the floor, repeating their lines over and over in an effort to sound "natural." This is a waste of precious time. "Natural" but devoid of a driving purpose is totally blah. And besides, focusing on sounding "natural" leaves you completely dependent on flow and rhythm, lost without the words. The whole house of cards is too easily disrupted under the unrehearsed circumstances of an audition. Use your rehearsal time to focus on identifying what the character actively wants, using the text to get it.

When analyzing a scene, ask yourself why the character is there, or why he doesn't simply leave. The answer to this question will often indicate an obstacle or problem (sometimes physical, sometimes mental, which the character must solve in real time, i.e. actively, as the actual audition scene unfolds). Examples might be: the character has to finish getting dressed … he can't leave the room naked!; or the character has to put his best foot forward no matter what; or the character wants to leave his lover but in so doing he wants her still to love him; or he has to find out "who did it" without tipping his hand by being confrontational. Such problems exist in real time, so that no matter what the actor encounters from the auditor he is reading against, the character must think about how to deal with it and how next to proceed. The camera loves an active mind. If you can interpret a scene as a problem to solve in real time it will bring compelling "life" to your reading.

What is the character literally physically doing at the beginning of the scene?

To carry our discussion concerning actions further:

Your audition scene will always have your character in a place doing something. Sounds simple enough. In a screenplay no character is "just" doing anything. When I ask an actor what the character is doing and if he answers, for instance: "He's just sitting there," right away we have a problem with scene interpretation. What the character is doing and what he does or says in response to a given situation, and how the character behaves in the situation defines "the character." This is "who he is." Remember how Tom Hanks sat down to wait for his son after delivering him to the school bus in the closing scene of the 1994 film *Forrest Gump*? He definitely was not "just sitting."

In the scene, the character will have an intention to do something (which goes back to our "entry verb") and then something will change that. In your audition scene, identify what the character is literally physically doing or wanting to do as the scene begins. Let them continue to pursue this, even though something will change, diverting their attention to something else, or at least making it difficult for them to continue what they are doing. This interruption (or change) is most often caused by some action of the other character. But you, the actor, will enhance the illusion of the reality of the scene if you keep doing the literal physical action until the circumstances of the scene or the action of the other character(s) makes it impossible or too difficult for you to continue. Don't give it up easily. If the character, for instance, is reading a newspaper, don't throw down the paper the instant the other character comes in and starts to talk. Let your character split his attention between trying to finish his article and what the other person is saying. Of course you will talk to the other character, but allow yourself to be distracted in your responses by your reading. *Let your character speak through the physical action for as long as it lasts, or until it is interrupted by something more important.*

To illustrate: If at the beginning of the scene your character is getting dressed for a wedding and a bomb goes off in the next room, try to finish fastening your cufflinks or slip on your shoes as you race out! Or take one last look in the mirror! These touches give the illusion of reality. Another example: notice that if, in real life, you are walking down the street late for an appointment and have a dizzy spell, the spell has to get pretty bad before you actually let yourself stop and take a moment. Or, if you are preparing a special dinner and something interrupts your work, you keep focused on completing the preparation until the interruption simply must be attended to.

Remember the scene in *The Godfather I* when Marlon Brando, now an old man and retired from being the Mafia don, was playing in the tomato garden with his grandson? He was teasing the boy and was chasing after him in amongst the rows of tomato plants when he was struck by a heart attack. Watch him. He keeps chasing after the boy until the heart attack stops him, but he doesn't stop right away. There is a moment when he doesn't accept what is happening and keeps chasing after the boy even though he can feel his heart giving out.

We all want to finish what we start. So do your characters. This is a very human detail. Including it will help your auditions.

Attitude

Attitude is a powerful communicator. It can be very effective in anchoring the first impression of the character. (Masha in Chekhov's *The Seagull* comes to mind. She enters her first scene saying, "I'm in mourning for my life.") But attitude will only work well for about half a page … then it will go thin. All attitudes are invariably defined by adjectives, and adjectives contain no movement or active thought. An attitude can feel like a good choice – and it can be – but it must soon turn into an action. Use it as a springboard to an action. For example if you, the actor, envision the character as being "filled with self-loathing," for instance … then let the character see everything and everyone around him as being "in the belly of the beast" and identify mentally what needs to be acted upon or changed to correct the status quo.

Look to what the character wants and what he needs to do to get it. Look for what the adjectives say about the *movement* in the character, *what change or action or intention* the adjectives imply are happening in the character as the story unfolds, or the barrier to movement the character might present. It is the change or action, what the character discovers or what the character does or causes, that should be the focus of your interest. It is these actions that define the character.

Circumstances

So now, having addressed strategies with regard to the character's actions, let's look at the other side of the equation, namely the character's circumstances.

Research

Find out what you need to know in order to make specific doable choices. The goal is not to be original; it is, rather, to be specific. An actor can't imagine they are dying of cancer, for instance, but they can imagine that their chemotherapy has made them so weak and nauseous they have to fight to keep from vomiting. Research can help you determine what dynamic exists within an exotic situation which you can focus on to make it "real" for yourself and true to the circumstances.

> **Note:** Remember, the *art* of acting lies in the choices. Your research should lead you not only to a doable and specific truth, but also to one that is compelling (theatrical) to you personally.

The character's relationships

Within the boundaries of what the script gives you, what is the nature of the relationships between the characters in the scene you are auditioning? Not all people treat their sisters the same.

Within the range of a story, relationships evolve, they change. These changes are a principal component in any well-told story. Indeed, in many cases – in "love stories" or "buddy movies" for instance – these changes are pretty much what the stories are about. The audience can only identify the impact and themes of these changes by the evident contrasts between the characters themselves and how these contrasts change as the story unfolds. When you are auditioning without benefit of having read the entire script, look to the principles of structure in Chapter 7 to guide you as to what aspects of the relationship are featured in the audition scene. Do not trust adjectives, they tempt an actor to "play" them. Be guided by the other categories of consideration discussed in this chapter when thinking about the "relationships." Work to identify specifically, by virtue of the relationship, the contrasts between what the situation looks like from your character's point of view and that of your playing partner(s). And: look to define how the nature of the relationship shapes your character's knowledge and expectations of the other.

Social standing, *occupation*, *background* are dynamics that contribute vividly to the audience's perception of a character. They are most clearly evidenced in the nature of the character's relationships and how those relationships conform to or violate stereotypical expectations. Explore these dynamics as circumstances rather than as innate aspects of the character himself.

Note: Trust what the *other* characters say about you as a guide to your character's nature. Do not trust what characters say about themselves.

The character's physical circumstances

Physical circumstances of the character such as inebriation, temperature, time of day, private or public situation, etc. need to be included as part of the circumstances of the scene. How the character behaves in relation to the physical circumstances says a great deal about his nature.

Inebriation often allows a character to express themselves in ways they ordinarily would not by virtue of the relationship or the setting.

Where the scene takes place: As we discussed in Chapter 10, converting the space of the audition room into the "place" as written in the script requires the actor to be aware of how the physical surroundings of the scene as indicated in the script are affecting him. In well-performed auditions this component of the reality of the situation is always clearly conveyed.

A scene taking place in a public venue such as a crowded restaurant often restricts the degree of expressiveness a character might allow themselves in their exchanges with the other.

A scene that takes place in an office just as the work day has begun is distinctly different in tone from one that takes place late at night after everyone has gone home.

A scene that takes place on a snowy street corner will not play the same as would the identical dialogue in a sweltering train station.

Distinct physical characteristics such as a regional accent or an unusual physical attribute will affect the character's behavior; certainly his mannerisms. Many actors find their characters centered in a specific physical expression in their body ... posture, hand gesture, etc. This is definitely true for acting on stage.

The character's issue

A screenplay (or scene) will be about something important ... certainly important to the characters. When you formulate what the story is about, as exemplified in the blurb for *The Devil Wears Prada*, you will see there is an issue that the story demands that the protagonist deal with. In this case it is: which professional direction should this young woman go to satisfy her ambition to excel, and at what personal cost? Call this the "Issue." Once you identify it you will find that each scene and each character frames the issue or a facet of it in some new light or permutation. Each character has an issue. Whether it is a comedy or drama, each is struggling with some aspect of their own nature. The issue, and how the character is positioned relative to it, can tell you a lot about a character. It establishes your character's personal point of view, and thus is germane to creating a character.

Dramatic writers sometimes identify this aspect of the character as the character's "ghost," a theme of unfinished business that "haunts" the character, which they carry from their past and has yet to be resolved.

When I visit the class of my esteemed colleague, Mary Joan Negro, I hear her continually admonishing her students as they rehearse a play: "Tell the story! Make sure you're telling the story!" … which means the actor's choices have to be oriented around bringing the issue at hand into focus.

The task of the actor is to identify or establish a personal connection to the character's issue. (We always get back to this "personal" thing.) It seems to me the principal benefit of writing a "back story," as many instructors suggest, is that it encourages the recognition of a value or dynamic which the actor genuinely has in common with the character. Without this connection it is hard to imagine that an actor could make a vivid contribution to the story or would understand what part of themselves needs to be unveiled and expressed.

Identifying the strong personal connection that exists between the actor and the character – *vis à vis* the issue they have in common – puts the actor on track to establishing a vivid point of view.

Ask yourself what issue the scene allows you to address. All characters in all scenes can be interpreted to be dealing with an issue. Such as: Why don't other people like me? Or: Am I really destined to be a coward? Or: All human beings deserve respect. Or: Don't judge me by my looks. Or: Good friends are loyal. Or: I can't forgive the unforgivable. Or: A person is asking for trouble when they stick their neck out. If you can find an issue in the character that you yourself strongly identify with, emotion will never be hard to come by.

Note: Look to Chapter 15, which discusses auditioning for the villain, to examine the notion of the issue further.

Note: The most compelling emotion on camera is shame. Its expression implies that the character has come to recognize he has allowed his actions to assume a dimension out of proportion to his issue. It is a precursor to redemption, something we all long for.

Wardrobe

Read Chapter 8 on wardrobe. Determine what specific wardrobe choices affect the behavior and disposition of the character or the way we the audience perceive them.

Rehearse in wardrobe. It will help you get in touch with the character's circumstances.

– 2 –

DEALING WITH PRECONCEPTIONS

Your agent will call you, or you will get a fax or email that contains the sides or the script for an audition. Get as much information as you can. Often this doesn't amount to much. Of course you will read every word of the sides you are given, but also pay attention to those which are crossed out, the fragments of scenes which you are not reading for but which might happen to be intermixed with yours on the sides. There are often tidbits in there; glimpses of other characters, other important circumstances, hints as to the tone of the piece, the milieu it deals with, the class of people.

There will be adjectives. *Discard them.* It takes self-discipline not to be seduced by them.

Script breakdowns commonly describe characters in terms of adjectives: as being, for instance, some version of "bad" or "lovable" or "kind." But you can't "be" bad, you can only "do" bad. Sometimes you are going to have a reflexive impression – a stereotype, if you will – of what the character must be like. Sometimes this impression is exactly the juice you are looking for to create the character. Great, go for it. But other times the impression, the picture in your imagination, says to you that you are not right for the part. You basically instinctively "type yourself out" of the project.

It is easy for us actors to react to these descriptions very prejudicially. Either we conclude instantly, based on the description alone, that we are totally wrong for the part. Or, more commonly, we will make a judgment, however subtle, about how the character must be played based on our preconceptions about the describing words: about how our "powerful" or "evil" or "alluringly handsome" or "intelligent" or "slim and beautiful" character must behave in order to live up to the description. *Trying to fit yourself to the character description does not work.* Doing so inevitably results in superficial, phony choices.

The adjectives are there for the reader – for the banker, or the agency, or the investor, or the line producer – not for the actor nor for the director. They are there to set a tone, they are *not* instructions. They are meant to give whoever is *reading* the script a sense of how it *might* all go. *They are not meant as a blueprint for the actor.* Adjectives limit the resourcefulness of your character; they tend to restrict your choices to the boundaries implied by the definition of the describing words. Rather, when thinking about the character, focus on what the character wants, how he goes about getting it, and what is getting in his way.

If you find yourself reflexively thinking you are not right for the part, acknowledge it to yourself and ask yourself why. Answer with cold objectivity. Consult your acting coach, talk to a friend. You have got to challenge your own preconceptions and find a way to make your "shortcomings" interesting alternatives.

Assume you are physically perfect for the part

If they ask you how old you are, the only answer is: "The same age as the character."

Start with the premise that the screenplay *insists* that you are *physically perfect for the part*. Take the step to make it work on your terms, with you as the character. Your character is capable of all things ... all treachery, all insight, all love, all evil, all charm, all accomplishments. Don't be distracted by adjectives you deem essential for the character that you think you don't have. If the character is, for instance, a thug gang leader and you are a 90-pound weakling, make the character overcompensate, or make him very smart and perceptive, or give him his leadership through special skills. I ask you, does Bill Gates look like the richest man in the world? Is Barbra Streisand actually beautiful? Can't a lumberjack be a dandy? Can't a dandy be a lumberjack?

Be guided by the situation the character is in and his ambitions. Go about it *your* way. Identify the issues at stake. Find an aspect of the character that lights you up, and then calculate how you yourself would proactively and effectively go about getting what the character wants, guided by values that you yourself respect. Guided by your personal enthusiasms, you must bring what you and only you can bring to the part. Your perspective. This is your fundamental contribution to the project.

Be honest with yourself

Especially, acknowledge any elements in the character, or his situation, that you simply cannot believe could be true or that don't make sense to you. Identify your reasons for these judgments. State them clearly. Confront them. An actor's reflex is often to proceed through the scene as if these sticking points were not there. We go ahead and just do what the script says, despite our secret misgivings. But ducking these contradictions or inconsistencies leads to "stock" choices and phony performances. State your preconceptions clearly. Dealing with them is the bedrock of an actor's job. Solving them will often prove to be the source for your most specific and inspired choices. Adjusting preconceptions to make these inconsistencies work honestly will be the basis for all your best performances.

If you follow this advice, you will audition intelligently and with originality and honesty. Even if "they" don't think you are right for the part and don't cast you, they will remember you. You will have displayed your true capacities, and they will have a much better estimate of what you would be right for in their next project.

Exercise: Create a character portfolio

Here's what you need to do. This will pay big dividends. All substantial libraries have extensive collections of photography deemed to be fine art. Collections of the great photographers: Julia Margaret Cameron, Alfred Stieglitz, Paul Strand, Weston, Adams, Lartigue, Cartier-Bresson … the list is long and glorious and extends right up to last month. Here's the assignment: look through these volumes. Spend some time. Put together a photocopied portfolio of about 20 to 25 photographs. What you are looking for are photographs of *people you know you could play **at this time** even though nobody else might realize it.* It's just you and the person in the picture: a particular soldier in a foxhole, a woman kissing her lover in a Paris bistro, a nurse in a Civil War hospital, a member of the 1932 Polish national women's volleyball team, the governor of a distant state, a peasant waiting in a food line … a wrangler, a debutante, a prostitute, a cab driver, the young man in the second row, third from the right of the graduating class of 1947, a housewife hanging out the laundry … and on and on. Some will look like you, some won't. But each will be one that resonates specifically in their own private way with you. Look for the truth. There will be heroes and scoundrels; rich and poor; local and worldly; powerful and humble. It's personal and private. You will never have to defend or explain your choices. Focus not on people you wish you could play, but folks who you privately know you could play with conviction, no matter what anybody else might expect by looking at you or knowing you. Some will be your type, some will not. Avoid famous personalities, actors, sports heroes. They don't work. We are looking for real people, not those contaminated by a public persona. Photography was invented in the 1850s. The collection should cut across history, social strata, cultures, and continents. Or maybe it won't.

And from now on, whenever you read a magazine or a newspaper, be on the lookout for additions to your collection. As time goes by, new characters will filter in and others will fade away for you.

Now, once you have this collection, here is how you will use it. When you first read a scene or a monologue and feel only a vague (or no) authentic connection to the character speaking … look the character up in your book and see if they are there. If they are – some will be, some won't – a triangulation will set up. The photograph is the character, you have a special relationship to the photograph … allow your resonance with the photograph to connect you to the character in the scene. Read the material into the eyes of the character in the photograph. Do this repeatedly … seeking, allowing, opening to it. Your connection to the photograph will begin to emerge in yourself. It will suggest background details, enthusiasm, attitudes, and perspectives. The person in the photograph will guide you to places your own imagination or personal experiences were blind to.

Keep the image fixed in your mind as you begin to put the scene on its feet. Move around the room as you study your lines. Let the image have its way. Add wardrobe touches that enhance the connection between you and the character in the photograph.

Experiment with this. If it happens that when you read a character breakdown and you immediately conclude there is no way in the world you are what they are looking for … open your book of characters. You will see, the door of possibilities might be open wider than you think.

Note: There will likely be a photograph in your collection of an individual who is isolated, disenfranchised, ugly, angry, pathetic, alone. (Your mother would be aghast to imagine that you are drawn to playing this person!) Pay particular attention to this compelling character. Include this character in your process. Derived from an insight by Dr. Phil Stutz, this character is a depiction of what can be identified as your "Shadow Self." All humans have one; and we all keep a tight lid on it because we instinctively think it makes us too vulnerable to ridicule. The shadow self, in an effort to remain hidden, informs all the other selves in us how to behave so as to conceal its very existence. Therefore you could say it is calling the shots for all the other characters in your book. Read your scene into the eyes of your shadow self to discover what in your character's nature emerges that needs to be concealed.

Summary

Preparation for dramatic roles:

- Assume you are physically perfect for the part.
- The character is defined by what the individual does in response to a given circumstance.
- Explore what the character wants and what he does to get it.
- Identify what is at stake and what will happen if the character doesn't get it.
- Within what the writer provides, do not underestimate the character's capacities.
- Look for *proactive*, as opposed to *reactive* choices.
- See whether you can identify a problem that the character can be trying to solve in real time.

- Explore the implications of:
  - the nature of character's relationships and whether they are changing
  - the character's physical circumstances, e.g. physical infirmities; inebriation; environment; etc.
  - what the character is literally physically doing at the beginning of the scene
  - the character's issue.
- Create a character portfolio. Rehearse into the eyes of the photograph.

– 3 –

LOVE SCENES AND FURTHER NOTES

THERE ARE TWO THINGS YOU CAN'T ACT:
YOU CAN'T ACT YOUNG, AND YOU CAN'T ACT SEXY.

... Stella Adler

When it is clear by reading the sides that "these two are going to get together," we actors instinctively feel we have to make the character attractive to the other. Even worse, if you're like me, you are actually thinking you have to make your character attractive to the *audience* (even worse, to the producers!) so that everyone involved will understand why the other character is attracted to you. We feel a certain pressure to do this, don't we?

Pay attention to Stella's quoted admonition above. Trying to be attractive rarely yields attractive results. Rather, it usually leads to all sorts of goofy self-conscious posturing, thinking about your face, and manifesting behavior that has nothing whatsoever to do with what people actually find attractive in you.

Remember:

The *script* says he or she likes you. No matter what you do, the two of you are going to get together. You do have to want something, but you don't have to earn it. It is going to happen no matter what you do. The script says so.

An important observation about the meeting of lovers

Question: When is a love story over? The answer is: when they get together. That's when they live happily ever after and we see them riding off into the sunset. The engaging aspect of the story is how they overcome some crucial barrier that keeps them apart. Now, nothing is always true, but when these two first meet, look to see what will keep them apart. Sometimes this barrier can appear to be insurmountable. One character or the other, or both, will be very much aware of it. It will be something like another relationship, fear of commitment, divergent social status, professional obligations, cultural differences, pre-conceptions, reputation, divergent ambitions ... something. This is an important aspect of each of the characters' circumstances with regard to the other. Do not lose sight of it. During their initial exchange, this factor will intrude. Sometimes this factor will predominate, and will eclipse their attraction for the other. If that's the case, somewhere in the scene we will need to see a glimmer of the attraction. On the other hand, if it is the attraction that predominates, we need to see, in a sentence or a look, an awareness of what keeps them apart.

In either case:

Speak through what is in front of you:

- The situation: In the scene where we see you together for the first time, what are you physically doing in the scene just before you meet? Try to create a contrast between your disposition in this activity and how you are then affected by the presence of the other character. Negative to positive is a more apparent change (and easier to manifest) than neutral to positive. In other words, your positive reaction to the other character will be easier for the audience to perceive if you are preoccupied or distracted, or frustrated for some reason right before the other person comes into your life.

- What is attractive about the other person? Their fragrance, a physical detail, a certain intelligence, their humor. This is personal and specific, and might be quite different from what the script implies. Allow yourself to focus on this alluring alternative to your current situation.
- The facts are not important. Speak through the quality that attracts you to the other person. For example, think "My god, your hair is beautiful" as you say, "Let me help you."

Exercise: Speak Through What Attracts You

Do the following out loud now: without pre-formulating a solution in your head, use the words "Let me help you" to express "My god, your hair is beautiful." You will see what I mean by "speaking through what attracts you." Focus on the other's hair and its beauty and express *that*, rather than on how the words "Let me help you" would sound logically.

"Enjoy the dance," meaning this interlude has played itself out a thousand times. Just as when you, in your own life, meet a person you hit it off with … you can't make a mistake. Even if you are initially at odds with one another, the union is going to happen. Watch with bemusement how intractably it unfolds.

- Refer to yourself with self-deprecating humor.
- Allow yourself to be nervous if you are. After all, a person like this doesn't come along every day. You don't have to be cool. Just don't underestimate your character. Try to put your best foot forward. The other character is going to like you no matter what. And men: it is not attractive to women to be *overly* confident. This disposition implies a narcissism that will only be effective as an *antagonist* rather than protagonist.

Further notes for scene preparation

Do something in real life as the character. Often, in the beginning of our careers, we are given little time to prepare. At best we have but overnight. But if there is time, try the following: shop for groceries, for example, or ask directions of a stranger, as the character.

Rehearse "in the place." If the scene takes place in a coffee shop, go rehearse in a coffee shop; or in the car, or out on the street corner, if that's what the scene calls for. Get a feel for how the physical circumstances influence the scene. It will also give you a chance to contemplate the "metaphor of the place." Pay attention to how the place influences your choices with regard to your posture, your vocal projection, your sense of privacy or lack of it, etc.

Rehearse with a live human being, at least once, preferably more. I cannot over-emphasize the importance of this. *This is essential.* Even if it is the 11-year-old neighbor, do this. (I never want to. It makes me feel stupid and naked. But I have to. It challenges my power of concentration and shows me where the holes are. If I don't, I will not get the job.) It is a huge mistake to go into an audition without having experienced what shape the scene takes when you are reading with an actual (and therefore unpredictable) live human being. No matter how well you know the scene, you will be scrambling mentally the first few times you do this. You've got to get this stage of preparation out of the way before you actually audition. Sooner or later, you must ... simply must ... read with another human being.

One clear choice: You can't put the whole character in one scene. The performance will get muddy. Rather, each scene reveals an *aspect* of the character by how he deals with the circumstances in that particular scene. If you are asked to audition more than one scene, that will be your chance to express the other evolving facets of the character, as well as (possibly) evidence of change.

CHAPTER 14

Somewhere, someone thinks it's funny

COMEDY: SOME GUIDELINES

In this chapter I am going to take a little detour and explore the topic of auditioning for a comedy from a wider perspective; meaning the following holds for both live and on-camera comedy auditions.

Comedy is king. It's unlikely, unless you become a huge dramatic star early in your career, that you will be able to sustain a living wage as an actor over an extended career without being able to do comedy. If things go for you as they did for me, substantially more than half of your auditions will be for comedy. The following pages focus on situation comedies – after all, most scripted comedies are situational – but these guidelines will undoubtedly be helpful when you explore any comedic genre.

> *DRAMA IS A LOT OF FUN TO DO. BUT COMEDY? ...*
> *NO, COMEDY IS VERY SERIOUS BUSINESS.*
> ... Milton Berle, TV's "Mister Saturday Night

What Milton Berle, the premier television comedian of the 1950s, is referring to is the precision required in comedy. In my experience, it is possible – actually desired – to get swept away while acting a drama. But in comedy this rarely happened for me; there is too much to think about in terms of the mechanics of the scene, what must happen, exactly when, and to what degree, to make the comedy work. It seems to me to be as much a science as an art. My credits include about a dozen comedic roles. I'm able to do well if the script is well written. When it is, I focus on vividly creating the circumstances and the stakes and it will play out. But I have never had the talent to make a poor script funny: as they say, "to make chicken salad out of chicken poop." I am no Bill Murray. I don't have that kind of talent.

Some people are just plain funny. They do something and it's funny. I remember reading in *Truffaut on Hitchcock* (1962) how the great director, commenting on the importance of casting, complained that Robert Cummings, an actor with this inherent comedic lilt, ruined the seriousness of one of the director's early suspense melodramas just by virtue of the impression he made on the audience. Hitchcock complained that the actor could aim a revolver at you and you would swear it was made of licorice … you simply could not take his character seriously. In the same vein, I once saw Judge Reinhold, of *Fast Times at Ridgemont High* and *Beverly Hills Cop* fame, working out at the gym I frequented. He was on the stationary bike, unaware that anyone was watching … he was funny. Then I watched him go over and do some sit-ups … it was funny. I don't know why.

A lot of us, most definitely myself included, are not "funny." But hard work at comedy will pay dividends. My advice is to get into a comedy workshop and stay there until you have a firm grasp of an approach that works for you. It's hard work and can be very frustrating, humiliating even, when it doesn't go well. But remember, almost all material, even the darkest drama, can be enhanced by including humor. So the guidelines I offer in this chapter are worth investigating.

But before we begin that discussion, I want to make a few general observations about the audition process as they apply to comedies. Many years ago I went to a seminar conducted by Ed Deckter, a prominent comedy writer and director, just to check whether what I was telling my students about the audition process had been observed by other professionals. Turned out Mr Deckter and concurred on about 98 percent of the central issues. Here are some of the highlights of what he said. They reinforce thoughts expressed in other sections of this book; and refresh our contextual view of the audition situation.

- Auditioning well and getting a part is *not luck.* There are definite things you can do to increase your success ratio. You can complain about the process all you want, how thoughtless and unfair it is, but the process is the process, it's not going to change. You have to focus on how you can prosper within the constraints of the way it goes.
- If you don't learn how to cope and audition well, you simply won't work.
- Actors have no control over what Mr Deckter called the "typecasting" problem. He observed that 95 percent of the time the actor is going to be the wrong type and will lose as they come in the door. They will be "typed out," as he put it. So an actor must score on the other 5 percent of the opportunities.

    My note: I think the "type" issue can be helped a lot by choosing the right entry verb … a concept Mr Deckter is totally unaware of.

  Mr Deckter put a lot of emphasis on something I also emphasize; whether or not an actor gets the job can depend on the impression of competence and professionalism the actor exhibits.
- Some parts demand a specific type, others don't. Especially in the early going, or when the actor is not "right" for the part, their job is not so much to get the part as to establish that they are a good actor who knows what they're doing so they will get called in for other material.
- Do not chat. Let the reading speak for you.
- Enter as the character only if you have got it totally nailed.

    My note: I have asked many casting directors their opinion concerning entering in character and I never get the same answer. It is a judgment call. Mr Deckter defines "character" in terms of physical manifestations (limps, gum chewing, accents). My advice is to enter with the energy of the intention consonant with the character at the top of the scene. Then let the physical manifestations of the character emerge as the reading gets under way.

- Don't frighten people. If you're going to read an angry scene or play the role of a heavy, do not enter the audition with a negative or overly aggressive verb.

- Don't rearrange the furniture. Don't take possession of props in the room. Don't sit at the desk, or use their stuff.

    *My note: I think you can if you ask permission, keep it to a minimum, and use only what is absolutely essential and makes a clear contribution to the effectiveness of the work … i.e. when you have **no other choice**.*

- Feel free to ask questions: but only ask good questions. Dumb questions indicate a dumb actor or a misunderstanding of the role. Ask only what you need to know to make it work.

- Do not wear your technique on your sleeve. Do not demonstrate in any way your process. Do that out in the hall.

- Don't memorize. Use the script. But only for cues. Because you certainly should know the lines … the character's intentions … well enough so that you don't have your face buried in the text.

- For comedies: Don't improvise. Get the words right. It confuses the writers (who are very neurotic about their work). In comedy there is a high dependency on rhythm and phrasing. When you change things, even a word, the writers in the room will be distracted by thoughts like: "Did she leave that out because she didn't like it, or did she just forget it? Or what? Is it better her way?" etc., etc. Basically these mental distractions take them away from focusing on your performance.

- Make the scene work! (Mr Deckter repeated this emphatically three times.)

A few added personal observations

Each producer has his own way of conducting auditions, but in my experience when you audition for a comedic role, here's how the process will likely unfold. You will be called in for a preliminary reading and in that reading you should be prepared for two unexpected possibilities. (I know I wasn't.) The first is, the casting person who reads with you off-screen often will read quite well! This can be surprisingly disconcerting because in the back of your mind you may be distracted by thoughts like: "Gee, this guy's pretty good. Maybe they ought to cast him in my part." Good producers know, in contrast to drama, if they don't support the auditioning actor with a decent off-screen reader, they really won't be able to truly evaluate the comedic capacities of the actor. The second unexpected wrinkle is – particularly for television sitcoms – in many instances someone in the room will laugh at almost every line you say! You will say "Good morning," and someone will laugh very infectiously and you will be thinking to yourself, "Why is that person laughing? That wasn't funny." Some producers must feel that this weirdness will encourage the actor to loosen up and be even better. (It never worked with me. More importantly, for television sitcoms it serves to establish the rhythm of the laugh track, identifying whether the actor can sustain an impulse through the pause caused by the audience's reaction.

Okay, so you read well for the casting director and they call you back. In this second reading you are going to be "paired up" to audition with another actor, a stranger to you. The producers need to see how the two of you interrelate. This is another instance where Twenty-Year Friend is so important. This audition will either be on-camera, or live in front of the producers or the network "suits." You will often be given a rehearsal space and a bit of time to work with the other actor before going in.

So where do we start?

There's no formula. Trying to define how to make something funny is like trying to define how to make something beautiful. The only way to deal with comedy is to put it on its feet and work through it. By way of example, I studied at Harvey Lembeck's comedy improv workshop on the Paramount lot every Wednesday night for several years. (I was terrible at it.) Harvey's son, Michael, who eventually found great success as a comedy director (*Everybody Loves Raymond*, *Friends*, among many others) actively assisted his father. Several years ago I read an article in the *Los Angeles Times* Calendar section featuring him. He said:

> *I HAD BEEN TEACHING COMEDY IMPROV FOR YEARS.*
> *I FINALLY GOT MY FIRST DIRECTING GIG.*
> *I PREPARED LIKE MAD. BUT BY NOON THE FIRST*
> *DAY OF REHEARSALS I HAD ALREADY BEEN ASKED*
> *30 QUESTIONS I DIDN'T KNOW THE ANSWER TO.*
>
> … Michael Lembeck

When you pick up a script and read through it, very often what's funny is not so obvious. The tendency is to throw up your hands and conclude the writing is no good. But our job as actors is to make it work. So, no matter what, always keep in mind as you read a script:

> *SOMEWHERE, SOMEONE THINKS IT'S FUNNY.*
>
> … Ed Deckter

According to Shakespeare

> *TRAGEDY IS WHEN EVERYTHING STARTS OUT HAPPILY*
> *BUT ENDS UP A MESS.*
> *COMEDY IS WHEN EVERYTHING STARTS OUT A MESS*
> *BUT ENDS UP HAPPILY.*

Therefore, make sure you grasp the "mess" that embroils your character to start with. There must be something wrong, something extreme in the eyes of the character; a looming crisis; an impossible situation. In comedy there is no mystery. The audience knows what the problem is all along. The fun lies in seeing how the characters try to solve their problems and ultimately triumph, if only in some sma way, despite the complications their human foibles bring into play.

What's "funny" will often be found in one of two areas:

- the complications a character gets tangled in from misrepresenting himself
- a character having a point of view or behavior that is "not normal" or inappropriate to the circumstances.

Look for clues in the situation

Look for the comedy in the *situation*. Tell yourself the story. Define the circumstances. Identify the full implications of the circumstances and how they are complicated by the contrasting nature of the principal characters involved. You need to perceive what the "mess" is in the situation so that it can end up happily.

> *EVERYTHING IN LIFE IS A COMEDY,*
> *EXCEPT WHEN IT IS HAPPENING TO YOU.*
>
> ... Will Rogers

By way of example, I had a very talented student some years ago who came into the classroom the day before Parents' Weekend looking absolutely gray. I was setting up for class. We were by ourselves. When I asked her what was the matter she said, "Nothing." I said "Come on, something serious is obviously wrong." I urged her to unload her burden. She relented and told me her situation:

She explained that her father was a minister in a very prominent urban church far away back home on the east coast and that her mother was a high-profile participator in many of its charities and humanitarian events. They were very upstanding, proper people. Righteous civic fixtures. She went on to explain that she had been living with John, her boyfriend, off campus for the last three years. (knew this student, and he was a terrific guy.) "Okay, and?" I urged

She knew that her parents would have died, absolutely died!, if they found out she was living "in sin" with John. Sooooo … she had been sending home fake rent receipts, telephone bills, and forged utility checks for the last three years to make her parents think she had her own apartment. "Hummm," I said, and waited. She continued that John's parents, whom she absolutely loved, were coming to campus for Parents' Weekend … but John, she said, had been acting very strangely. "What do you mean, strange?" I asked. "Well," she said, "he's been making such a big deal out of where to have dinner, which is not at all his style … I have a feeling he is going to ask me to marry him." "That's wonderful … Isn't it?" I said. "Yes," she said, "of course … it would be … except … I just got a phone call from my parents. Surprise, surprise. They just arrived in town for Parents' Weekend."

Oh-oh. Now, that's a comedy.

Everything is starting out a mess. And wouldn't we just love to be a fly on the wall and see how she manages all this! (By the way, it all did end up happily. She was forgiven and they lived happily ever after.) It is instructive to note that she herself was very distraught when I talked with her. And I mean *gray*! The stakes for her couldn't have been higher.

Therefore:

Look for high personal stakes

Involving pride, humiliation, greed, etc … the classic human foibles of the seven deadly sins. As I said before, the audience knows what the situation is. The comedy lies in seeing how the characters maneuver to put things right. This sequence of unsuccessful efforts will cause the protagonist, when none of the maneuvering works – which it never does – to realize or come to terms with some personal shortcoming which, when put aside, clears the way for a happy resolution.

Something keeps the characters in the room

A strong force, a strong need or value. Ask yourself why the characters doesn't just walk out. This need, motive, or force, which keeps the character in the room, and therefore forces the character to deal with the difficult situation, is often germane to the circumstances ... and is often pivotal to discovering the comedy (the "mess") of the situation.

Look for contrasts not conflict

This is huge. It is critically important and yields good results. Did you ever notice how, with all the great comedy teams, there is a clear contrast between the two members? One is tall and thin, the other short and fat. One whimpers all the time, the other is feisty and assertive. One is a dingbat, the other is debonair. One talks non-stop, the other is mute. One has always got a wild scheme, the other is cynically skeptical. It goes on and on. *Contrast.*

Therefore:

Establish contrast between the characters' behavior or perceptions of the situation indicated by the writing:

E.g. If the script suggests one character is anxious, look to create the other as confident. If the writing indicates one is cautious, for the other perhaps choose bravado. If one thinks they should hurry, cause the other to dally. If one thinks things are dangerous, create the other to be devil-may-care, etc.

They don't have to be opposite points of view, but they do need to be in clear contrast with one another.

Play the contrasts between their perceived realities. Keep their approaches to solutions separate, or keep the characters perspectives separate.

You will see, if both characters have the same point of view, nothing comedic can develop.

Take a look at Jack Nicholson, Helen Hunt, Greg Kinnear, and Cuba Gooding in the James L. Brooks-directed 1997 comedy *As Good As It Gets.* Their work is genius, a virtual textbook on these concepts.

Look for contrast between the character's own behavior and what would be considered "normal" under the circumstances.

For example:

An insurance adjuster arrives at the crash site with a chipper "Good morning!!!"

The pastor finishes his dark sermon, solemnly leaves the pulpit, then celebrates his work by dancing a jig.

The brain surgeon looks over his patient, rubbing his hands together as if hungrily anticipating a thick juicy steak.

Jason Alexander, in describing his *Seinfeld* audition scene paired up with Jerry Seinfeld, chose to pull a handkerchief from his pocket and wave it in a semaphore fashion, as he said the lines (hysterically), "Women send signals, Jerry! They send signals!"

Look for a sudden contrast in the rhythm of the character's own speech, or a sudden switch to a contrasting point of view.

Good sitcom writing offers this opportunity abundantly. This is called a "Switch" or a "Drop" or a "Ladder." This is hard to describe, but you would recognize it immediately if someone demonstrated it for you. An example might be a sequence of sentences the character escalates with ever-intensifying hysteria ... until the last one, which switches then suddenly to a tone of total nonchalance. Or the character might express that something is totally repulsive! Revolting! Horrible! Then drops suddenly to comment on it cheerily with a self-satisfied smile.

(Horrified) "You mean he's going bald!"

Then: (chuckling) "How bald?"

In the end, all is forgiven

So don't let your character do anything that is clearly unforgivable.

Nobody dies, nobody fights to the death, and nobody tries to destroy anyone else ... if anything, you barely *touch* the other character ... and then, true to comedic contrast, they end up in a full body cast.

Avoid anger meant to punish

Anger meant to punish is not a comedic choice. Since comedy thrives on contrast (and therefore often seems to contain conflict), the characters will be at odds with one another. Otherwise we will have no comedy. But this can easily get off track and lead to an argument. Yes, people argue. In comedy people can indeed disagree vehemently on how to solve a mutual problem, but the minute one begins to degrade or excoriate or insult or punish the other, and the other retorts in kind, the argument will escalate to a fight ... and the comedy goes out the window.

A much better choice is incredulity. Look it up. It means to find the other's behavior or point of view to be so bizarre or offbeat as to be unbelievable.

You can scream, "You hit him with a frozen swordfish!" in order to degrade and hurt the other person. Or you can express dismay so as to communicate incredulously: "I can't believe you did that!"

The latter is a comedic choice.

Rehearse at full volume. Use emphatic body and facial gestures to communicate

Comedy almost always requires the actors to be *"larger than life."* It is a form chock full of high-energy, high-stakes situations involving *very theatrical characters*. At least one of the characters will have a problem, and will be desperate for a solution. Desperate! Especially for three-camera work, the characters are very physically and emotionally expressive. *When they talk, their bodies are much involved*. They gesticulate; they swagger; they slump; they guffaw; they squint; they use their bodies to express themselves! You will need to bring this "larger than life" capacity to the work. Stella Adler used to call this full volume *"the sound of truth."* It demands that you know why the character is talking, what he wants and how he is going to try to get it. When you first read this way at home, you will feel naked or incomplete … stupid even. Every line that makes you feel that way is a red flag signaling that the section needs more work. But you had better rehearse it that way in private, because the chances are very good that this is the energy you will be met with by the other cast members on the set.

Compare George Clooney's subdued physical manner in the serious drama *Michael Clayton* (2007) to his broadly physical comedic expressions in the Cohen Brothers' 2000 comedy *Oh Brother, Where Art Thou?*

Exercise: Your voice needs to be out "in front"

To understand what I mean by this, try the following: Hum so that your lips tingle. Then, keeping your voice in the same place, say an "M" word … "money" or "mother" or "monument." Develop the "m" word into a complete sentence. Go back to humming occasionally to check for the tingle, to check that your voice has not slipped back in your head or throat.

You will observe that this is actually where our voice is when we talk in real life. That is why Stella called it "the sound of truth." The high energy of many comedies requires this. Make no mistake, many good comedic ideas can be developed by mumbling to yourself, but eventually they will likely need to be projected "out front."

Pick up your cues. No dead air

In the sitcom form particularly, many problems are solved simply by quickening the pace.

This does not mean, "talk faster." It means there is little space between when "she" finishes talking and when "he" begins ... much like the actor's work on the stage.

In a melodrama there can be value in pausing to "think," or to pause over what has just been realized. But in situation comedy this does not work. The comedic form focuses on the overt, perceivable behavior, responses, points of view, and actions of the characters as revealed in their words, not on their interior thought processes. "Thinking" works in comedy only insofar as the "thinking" is incorporated into how the lines are delivered.

Communicate what you want to be perceived by the other character

In situation comedy pretty much nobody is innocent. They are maneuvering to get something they want, or make a point, or make a certain impression on the other. For example in life, when a past lover asks how you are and you respond "Great!" are you *really* great? Not likely ... but you want him or her to think you are by how you answer. That's what I mean by maneuvering.

We do this all the time in real life. In fact, the honesty or "connectedness" or the "coming from your center" that is appropriately emphasized in introductory acting workshops leads some actors to believe that their characters are telling the truth all the time. They aren't, any more than we ourselves are.

Think back on the last time when you successfully deceived someone … called in sick, or made up an excuse for canceling a date, pretended to be asleep, or pretended that you were *not* asleep, etc. The deception was actually an exercise in communication. Recognize how carefully and specifically you crafted your behavior and tone of voice. To be successful you had to be a consummate actor, a consummate communicator. In order to deceive, your focus was on communicating a perceivable point of view to the other. It had nothing to do with your true feelings or emotions. In fact, you were lying. It had only to do with what you wanted the other person to conclude was true.

Situation comedy puts a premium on this type of human behavior – of false bravado, putting on airs, feigned innocence, etc. This is the realm of sitcom acting.

Energy

As I said, in life we communicate by making our implied points of view perceptible to the other person. What we call the "energy" of the actor's performance is not so much a matter of volume, but rather a function of how specific the character's point of view is, and how emphatically they want to communicate it. "Larger than life" comes out of this effort to insure your character is communicating emphatically what they want the other person to infer. It usually implies a greater involvement of body and gesture in the expression.

Defining the character

Communication is a function of intention. Ask yourself, what is your intention when you say something? What specifically are you trying to *do* with your words? Encourage? Mock? Beg? Cajole? What? Consult the thesaurus for juicy synonyms. What do you want the other person to conclude is true about you or your point of view? Then be great at communicating it.

In past chapters we have defined "character" as what the individual does in a given circumstance. All sentences are verbs. They are actions, because all sentences are said in an effort to do something or affect something.

Exercise: Biggest building in the world

To understand what I am getting at, your line is: "It's the biggest building in the world." Say it out loud to another person (or to the lampshade across the room). By what you invest in this line:

Communicate (to the lampshade) this fact is a simple plain fact.

Convince the lampshade that this fact is indeed true.

Communicate this fact is true and any fool would know it.

Communicate this fact is true and comes as a surprise to you.

Communicate this fact is depressing to you.

Communicate this fact means danger to you.

Communicate this fact is boring to you.

Communicate this fact is impressive to you.

Communicate this fact is ironic.

Communicate this fact is hilarious to you.

Communicate you could care less.

The first intention above is called *Statement of Fact*. Statement of fact can be very powerful in drama but it rarely works in comedy. In comedy, an added point of view or intention has to be included, perceivable not only through voice but also through body and gesture. Your choice of which, combined with the other guidelines discussed in this chapter, defines, in fact, the nature of the "character."

Monologue approach

The esteemed teacher and coach Peter Flood offers another approach to exploring and defining a comedic character. He suggests writing out all your lines – only yours – in the same sequence as they are written in the scene, but now in the form of an unbroken, non-punctuated monologue. Rehearse and explore possibilities using this technique.

Summary

Preparation for comedic roles

- Look for clues in the situation. It starts out a mess and ends up happily.
- Create high personal stakes. Look to humankind's foibles.
- Communicate what you want to be perceived by the other character.
- Look for contrasts not conflict.
  - Establish contrasts between the various characters' apparent behavior or perceptions of the situation as indicated by the writing.
  - Look for contrast between the character's own behavior and what would be considered "normal" under the circumstances.
  - Look for a sudden contrast in the rhythm of the character's own speech, or a sudden switch to a contrasting point of view.

- In the end, all is forgiven, so don't do anything that is clearly unforgivable.
- Avoid anger meant to punish. Use incredulity instead.
- Rehearse at full volume. Characters are more theatrical, physically expressive.
- Pick up your cues. No dead air. Rehearse at full volume.
- In situation comedy pretty much nobody is innocent. They are all maneuvering for something.
- Defining the character: all sentences are actions, said in an effort to affect something. Ask yourself: What am I trying to do (communicate) under the circumstances? Be wary of statement of fact.

CHAPTER 15

Evil be now my good

… Satan

AUDITIONING FOR THE VILLAIN

Neither a story nor a hero can be more compelling than the antagonist. The villain sets the story in motion and dictates the tone of the tale. It is the actions and reactions of the antagonist that both begin and end the story. Faced with a blank piece of paper, a screenwriter cannot begin to shape a story until he identifies the villain and the world in which he operates. There is real honor in bringing the villain to life and significant opportunities for those who can play these roles.

Any experienced actor will tell you that playing the villain is downright fun. Naturally, the approaches discussed in Chapter 13, "Creating the character" hold sway here as well. The challenge lies in finding an authentic "key" to the character.

The purpose of this chapter is to lay out some guidelines, perspectives, and hints which will help you create a process for developing such characters. These ideas will tell you where to look. We will examine the character traits all villains have in common; identify three basic types of villain; and, finally, suggest some exercises associated with each type which will help get you started in developing and auditioning for villainous characters.

Let's start with The Random House Dictionary of the English Language.

Antagonist: One who is opposed to or strives against another; opponent; adversary. The adversary of the hero or of the protagonist of a drama.

Villain: A character in a play or novel who constitutes an important evil agency in the plot.

Evil: morally wrong; immoral; wicked; harmful; injurious

You cannot be a good villain unless you are a good screen actor. Aspiring to master the dynamics of the villain enriches an actor's capacity to be a better on-camera performer no matter what the role. Villains have very active minds. Their schemes require them to be observant and keenly perceptive as to the behavior of the other characters around them. They are driven by the strong subtext of their agenda. They have reasons for what they do that are known only to them. They are clever; unpredictable; compelling; contradictory; impassioned; and have a wicked sense of humor. In other words, the camera loves them.

Character traits

Good screen villains have a number of important dynamics in common which lead to the behavior we call "evil." They are individuals who are driven (within the context of the story) by a strong sense of various combinations of the following:

Independent ... they don't care what happens to any one else, only themselves.

Entitled ... they are owed something. They *deserve* what they want.

Iconoclastic ... they have no problem breaking the rules or the institutions that are in play, which they frame cynically as agents of hypocrisy or injustice.

Creative ... they are very intelligent, ingenious ... much smarter than the rest of us.

All-knowing ... they see through everything, even what the other person is thinking.

Strong sense of humor (irony/sarcasm) ... they have contempt for the values of the protagonist. Everyone else is a chump, or a fool, or a pest, indulged only as a means to an end.

These are the dynamics actors must bring to their villains. Pay close attention to them as you contemplate your choices for the character. Accomplished actors look for every opportunity, within the boundaries of what the writer gives them, to bring them to bear. That's what makes playing the villain so much fun: an actor gets to manifest these dynamics under the shelter the screenplay affords him. Basically, you get permission to be "bad." As the villain, you will have total power over what transpires in the story ... at least until the protagonist figures you out and catches up with you in the final act.

Three types

Excluding high school bullies and sorority bitches, villainous characters break down into three broad overlapping categories: those we would call "psychos"; those driven by some dark inclination to create chaos; and those who get caught up in an illicit scheme to get something. Keep in mind that the six character traits listed above are always in play in each of these types.

The first type ...

... are those with no empathy, satisfying a psychopathic need, usually a sexual release ... Jeffrey Dahmer-type characters, like those found in the films *8mm* (1999), the current television series *Dexter*, and *The Silence of the Lambs* (1991).

ONE OF THE MOST CONSISTENT FINDINGS ABOUT THE
BIOLOGY OF VIOLENCE IS THAT SADISTS AND COLD-BLOODED
KILLERS SHOW VIRTUALLY NO RESPONSE TO STRESS –
NO RACING HEART, NO SWEATING, NO ADRENALINE RUSH.

... *Newsweek*, May 21, 2001

In this case the key to the character does not lie in emotions. No method acting here. No effective memory. These characters don't "feel." Their heart rate never goes above 70 even as they wage their hideous mayhem. They enjoy delivering hurt or pain and do so without conscious remorse. Their confessions are very matter-of-fact. Other than a sadistic payoff, don't look for an emotional point of view that drives them to hurt others. There is no confusion or anxiety, no anger or revenge operating here. (Jeffrey Dahmer killed 17 men and boys, seeking sexual release by torturing and dismembering them. He has been examined under a microscope for years and still no one can explain the inner twist that drove him to do what he did.) These are the folks who, in real life, seemed so nice and normal to their neighbors.

I SPENT 18 YEARS WORKING WITH PEOPLE WHO
EVERYONE WOULD CALL EVIL – CHILD MOLESTERS,
MURDERERS – AND WITH FEW EXCEPTIONS I WAS
ALWAYS STRUCK BY THEIR ORDINARINESS.

... Michael Flynn, Psychologist, York College

As I write this, right here in this morning's *LA Times*, July 8, 2010, page 13, is an account of the arrest of a serial killer the police call the "Grim Sleeper." He has allegedly killed over a dozen women. His neighbor said this about him:

"A very good man. His daughter just graduated from college, I believe ... He's a good mechanic, worked out of his garage. I've been here since 1976 – that's how long I've known him. I'm not pretty shocked. I'm all the way shocked."

For the actor

Whatever the writer says these psycho characters do, they just do. These characters do bizarre things very matter-of-factly. They simply pull the trigger, put on a pair of high heels, and coolly sit down to a dinner of roast thigh. The only emotional intensity in the performances will come as a result of their (possible) physical struggle to kidnap or overcome their prey. For the actor, the nub of the portrayal will not lie in tapping into their motivations, it will lie in *the cunning processes by which they lure their prey, and conceal their deeds.*

To uncover the key to this type of villain – given that he or she appears to others to be perfectly normal – perhaps the following order of thought will help. Let's take a hypothetical: where in your imagination might you find pleasure in a villain's sadism? Preposterous? I know you are not a sadist. That's not the point. But where would it be for you if the circumstances were just so? For example if a beautiful masochist fell in love with you, and you with her or him, you might be willing to comply with their desires, if you were both compliant and if it were within the private boundaries of your own intimacy and it brought no real harm to either of you. Wouldn't you? Sure you might; you can imagine that. But, not being a sadist, what, in doing so, would you be satisfying in yourself: the need to please? Or the need to belong or be included? Or the need to be perfect? Or the need to find your true self in love? Or the need to be the hero? Or the expert? Or the need to control? Or to be intensely desired? See what I am getting at? The key here is to answer this question specifically, accurately … and most of all privately. Never tell, it will lose its power.

Explore yourself candidly. Find a parallel that energizes both you and the villain you are creating. Very importantly, it must be a point of view that you can appreciate, with utter conviction, as appropriate and honorable, given the circumstances.

Explore this question: As the villain, in serving yourself, how are you serving your victim? Yes you are killing them, but how does their sacrifice make their life better? How does it bring meaning to their life? (Many of the women the Grim Sleeper killed were prostitutes: women who, in his own words, "were no good." What internal logic does this point of view imply?)

Returning to the sadist/masochist example, once you have found your personal connection to the act of allowing yourself to deliver pain to another compliant human being, the next step is to assume and behave towards certain characters in the script – perhaps even the protagonist himself – as if they are actually closet masochists. (No matter that they would deny it. The villain knows what they are "hiding" and sees the clues everywhere.) The reality becomes: your character is there to show them the way to their true and fullest expression of self.

The next step is to filter everything the character sees and does through this point of view. It must be present and intensely active, if not apparent to the audience, *in all the villain's scenes*. The character is aware of these stirrings all the time, a secret calling pressing upon him, though he keeps them hidden. They color and influence every choice he makes. He is using his very best tools, his most cunning cover-ups – operating through the character traits outlined at the beginning of this chapter – to go undetected as he gets what he wants. All his schemes will work, up until the point where the protagonist finally figures it out and gets in his way.

This is, of course, a random hypothetical. Each script and character will have its own set of specifics. Do your research.

Remember, in our auditions we are always trying to *create a reality* … and in order to do that our characters must always be adjusting, proactively, to the ever-changing circumstances they are confronted with, as they pursue their covert agenda.

The second type …

… consists of those characters who are driven by some dark inclination to create chaos … Sacco and Vanzetti-type characters like those found in *The Dark Knight* (2008) and *Funny Games* (2007) ... all on a whim, really.

The key to portraying these folks is their incredible intelligence, which reveals itself in their ever-present dark sense of humor. (Heath Ledger's Joker is the quintessence of this type.) A good deal of their power lies in their cynical and uncanny analysis of those around them. They have a keen sense of the hypocrisy in the world. They are amused by its conventions and view as baseless the self-righteousness of the "good" people. They mock others' efforts to understand them. Ultimately there is nothing to understand. They toy with their adversary's interpretations of the "truth." They are entertained by the question, "How many legs can you pull off an insect before it can no longer walk?"

> *AS ANCIENT AS MYTH AND STORY IS THE EVIL*
> *FIGURE WHO HIDES BEHIND A FRIENDLY FACE.*
> ... Shanti Fader

Within the scope of a story, these folks make compelling and fascinating characters precisely because they defy our efforts to understand them. They are extremely creative, and very perceptive. They know what others are thinking and make tantalizing fun of their efforts to create a just or reasonable world. The key is in their dark sense of humor.

After all, why does Satan do what he does? He simply doesn't want to be told what to do. He resents it, like a rebellious child who doesn't want to go to bed. If Satan were to face his arch-enemy, God, he would snicker and ask, "Why should I do what *you* say? What makes *you* the boss of me?" He devotes himself to demonstrating the arbitrary and vain nature of the "goodness" of God's creations by destroying whatever amuses him to choose.

For the actor

Look to the fun of playing mind games, of being an unpredictable cipher, amused by one's own internal contradictions and the pathetic "decency" of others.

Exercise: The Evil Shadow

Add a section to your character portfolio in which you identified your Shadow Self (Chapter 13, page 203). Recall a time when you were evil, when you did something "bad" ... pushed your sister down the stairs, lied to your parents, inflicted pain, betrayed a juicy confidence, threw an ice ball and clobbered someone just for the impulsive pleasure of it. Imagine what you must have looked like at that moment. In the library's treasury of great photographers, search for eight or ten photographs that depict various shades of this side of yourself: Look for images of darker characters who, just like you at the time, harbored resentment towards those around them or didn't care about anyone but themselves. This is called your "Evil Shadow."

Just as with your Shadow Self, rehearse your scenes while looking into the eyes of your Evil Shadow portrait. See what this unveils in you. Keeping in mind the villain's character traits listed at the beginning of this chapter, explore both the impulses and the physical adjustments ... in voice, movement, and gesture ... the Evil Shadow inspires in you. Especially, remember the cynical sense of humor your character covertly has towards those around him and the contempt he holds for their so-called "decency."

The next step in using the Evil Shadow portrait is derived from the "mask" exercise developed at Juilliard years ago. In the mask exercise, actors are given a mask, a false face, to contemplate for an extended period of time. They are then allowed to put it on and experience what happens to their behavior.

In the same spirit, allow yourself to have conversations with other people ... scene partners, strangers, authority figures ... while in your mind superimposing the image of the Evil Shadow portrait onto the face of the other person as you talk with them. It is as if you see both the other person's face and the face of the Evil Shadow portrait at the same time. Keep the Evil Shadow image foremost in your mind. The change in you will be slight, but specific. (Much like the "big as the room" adjustment described on page 44.) This capacity will create an obliquely active mind and sense of power which is found in this second type of villainous character.

- Speak through your Evil Shadow. Explore the scene as you keep looking into the eyes of your Evil Shadow portrait.
- Mentally superimpose the image of the Evil Shadow onto the face of someone as you talk with them.

The third type ...

... are those who get caught up in a scheme to get something ... money, power, revenge, love ... like those villains found in *The Manchurian Candidate* (2004); *The Usual Suspects* (1995); *A Perfect Murder* (1998); *The Bone Collector* (1999).

These stories involve the villain's own reckoning with an issue, an injury, or a desire. To play these villains effectively, the actor must embody a vivid emotional point of view fortified by a moral justification for their deeds.

Especially if you are reading for the "villain," no matter how hideous or insidious his actions, it is essential to establish a value or issue that you have in common with the character. Otherwise you are going to be playing "cardboard cutout bad." When instructors say: "Don't judge the character," I find that impossible. Characters do "bad" things that I think they shouldn't do. But remember, there is a difference between the issue that stirs in a person, and the action the person ultimately resorts to. Basically the critical difference between law-abiding pedestrians and the "villain" is that the villain goes ahead and allows himself to wreak havoc. We innocents merely go home and stew about it.

> *EVILDOERS FEEL MORALLY JUSTIFIED IN*
> *COMMITTING THEIR CRIMES.*
>
> ... Richard Moran, Mount Holyoke College

We all have done "bad" things on occasion. But whenever I did a "bad" thing, later, looking back on it, I felt I had a good reason at the time.

Some years ago the nation was shocked by a woman named Susan Smith, a divorced mother of two little boys, living in a small Texas town, who fell in love with the town's richest bachelor. To make herself more attractive to him, she locked her sons in the family car and backed it into a lake, drowning them. Newsweek magazine, May 21, 2001, reported this is what she said about her deed: "I loved my children with all my heart. My children deserved to have the best, and now they will."

> *EVIL BE NOW MY GOOD*
>
> ... Satan, *Paradise Lost*

She did it for them.

The challenge in this work is *not* to interpret intellectually why a character does something. (Leave this to the writer and to the audience.) Such analysis leads actors to demonstrating, by way of characterization, what is "bad" or "demented" about the character. It calls to the fore the tendency to judge the villain as "wrong," and reduces the actor to dreaming up phony behavior, cardboard cutout versions of a "bad" person.

Playing "bad" is just as empty as playing "happy."

The villain has his nature, his reasons, his predilections, and his circumstances. The truth is, the only difference between the villain and ourselves is: the villain goes ahead and crosses a line we do not allow ourselves to cross. We "healthy" folks, if only briefly, harbor intense emotions of, for instance, revenge or jealousy, but that is as far as we allow it to go. The villain acts upon them! As actors, the villainous deeds – those deeds that are actually *illegal* – the murder, the fire, the physical assault – will not cause an acting problem. As an actor you will simply follow through and do what the script says. It won't be difficult. The actor's problem lies in the embodiment of the intense motivations and the management of those motivations throughout the body of the story ... rather than the resulting cruel deeds of mayhem themselves.

Let me quote the opening three paragraphs of an article by Denise Martin about actor Michael Emerson and his role on the hit television series *Lost* (2004–10). Emerson played a captivating villain over the run of the show.

> It is difficult to keep track of all the spiraling story lines in *Lost*, but this much the viewers know about the enigmatic Benjamin Linus: as a young man, he gassed father to death along with the rest of the Dharma initiative, and as a father himself, taunted a mercenary into shooting his daughter in the head.
>
> Heartless? Definitely. But a psychopath? Michael Emerson doesn't think so.
>
> "I think of Ben as a man whose mission and responsibilities are so grave that he cannot allow himself much humanity," says Emerson ... "He's cold because any trace of warmth makes him vulnerable to his enemies, who we know are powerful and formidable. He's one man against an army of monsters."
>
>   ... "Lost World," by Denise Martin,
> *LA Times*, Sept. 11, 2008, page S9

I want to make note of one other thought here, if a little randomly. Many stories contain the notion that there is a similarity between the villain and the protagonist. Many writers will allow the villain, when confronting the hero, to comment on what they have in common. The villain will see the two of them as the same, wanting the same things, the only difference being how they go about getting it.

FOR THE ACTOR, TO UNDERSTAND IS TO EXPERIENCE.

… Stella Adler

The work lies, once again, in discovering the connection between the "premise" of the character … his emotional point of view … and a value that you yourself have in parallel with the villain.

When auditioning for this third type of villain, at least one of the scenes – typically positioned toward the end of the screenplay – will require a high degree of emotional intensity. More often than not, the producer's audition schedule will not allow much preparation time to develop it. Therefore, personally, I don't try to find the specific psychology or issue that drives the character as scripted. When I do that I always end up faking the emotion I think the character would have. Rather, I try to recognize an issue that resonates emotionally already in myself, born of an injury or injustice I already suffer, and then I express and address that injustice using the text and actions of the written scene.

Much like the technique of superimposing the Evil Shadow portrait onto the face of your scene partner, this approach also relies on superimposing one element onto another … in this case, your own emotional issue onto the situation and dialogue of the character.

More often than not, working this way in preparation for an audition, I find I can very actively focus my intention and emotional orientation as I enter the room. I won't be faking anything because the scene will be giving me the opportunity to confront with integrity a very vital injury or issue from my own life, through the circumstances of the character as written.

Two "free write" exercises

The two exercises I describe below are structured to help you identify the personal issue to use. I call them **"Injury/Issue/Desire"** and its variation, **"Revenge."** They require that you express a personal experience as a "free write," on paper, as you speak the words you are writing out loud. Let me explain.

A "free write" is not an essay. It is not for someone else to read. It has no grammatical requirements. It can be done with pencil in hand or at the computer. It is an unedited outpouring of whatever words come into your head. It requires that you *express* yourself, rather than explain or describe, as if for the benefit of someone else.

The two exercises require that you free-write your responses to the questions they pose. But, very importantly, they require that you talk out loud, *speak the words as you write them*. This is critical. The aim is to rekindle the experience of confronting a given person from your own life. Find a private place to work. Keep at it. Whatever it takes.

For the free write, you will need to look to your own life. Look into your own private heart. The aim is to get in touch with your own "hot button issue." We all have them. As irrational as it may seem, trust what comes into your mind first. Focus not on "why" but rather on "what." And rather than explaining it, express it in the exercises outlined below.

Look to, for instance, your own sense of frustration over never getting what you want; or the infuriation when a person has contempt for you; or of your infuriation over abandonment; or of the intense importance of your living a romantic life rather than an ordinary one; or of not being understood; or of being wrongly judged. Look to the conclusions you drew from an unresolved injury, or injustice, or dream, or loss, from your own life.

Ask yourself when was the last time you got hysterically angry? What were the circumstances? What injustice or irony in the situation infuriated you? What made you "right" and them "wrong?" In other words, what was at issue?

It is important that you recognize that your upset is justified by a value or precept that you consider, within the equation of your own personality, to be valiant, honorable, and that would be totally and vehemently defendable in a public forum. Try to see the villain, in light of this value, as a would-be hero who stands for something.

Understand that this issue is what you have in parallel with the emotional state of the antagonist. It is a puzzle-solving process. Like being a detective. The screenplay, then, allows you to personally express or come to a reckoning with this issue through the words and actions of the character. When you find this connection you will speak authentically for the character.

A couple of years ago a student of mine, James Snyder, who is now doing quite well professionally, called from his car one afternoon in the middle of the term with great excitement. He said, "I just realized what you have been trying to tell me … that the 'talk to myself' rant and the dialogue of the character are the *same* … it's not like it, or sort of it, or kind of it … it is, in fact, *exactly* it! That is what the character is trying to say! They are the same. I get it now!"

That's right. That's how it works. The two of you are addressing the same issue. You are using different words to say the exact same thing, coming from the exact same place. Again: once you find it, never tell. It will lose its power.

Here are two exercises that may get you on the right road.

Injury/issue/desire free-write

Do this:

We all talk to ourselves. Sometimes it's about nothing, sometimes it is very much about something indeed.

1. Recall the most recent time when you were talking to yourself in an involved and animated manner. In your fantasy, who were you talking to? Think about the circumstances that triggered this imaginary "confrontation." What were you trying to accomplish in the "conversation?" What injustice were you addressing? Did you want to punish the other? Why? To make them understand something? What? Excoriate them? Destroy them? Humiliate them? Make them atone? Persuade them? Make them see the light? Make them feel guilty? Shake them until they understood? What? How and for what purpose? Stick with this. This may require you to focus on dynamics that are uncomfortable to face. Examine the event as carefully as you can.

2. Re-express this confrontation out loud, in a first person, as you "free-write" on paper. It should read like a tape recording of you talking to the person who injured you. Keep working until you rekindle the energy of the original episode. Do not edit this work. You might say some sentences over and over.

3. Then formulate as best you can what "issue" or "principle" or "premise" or "moral point of view" justifies your emotion and the actions or words you commanded in your fantasy. State it clearly. For example:

> "I trusted you! You betrayed me!" or
> "You humiliated me!" or
> "Is that how you treat someone you love!?" or
> "I was lonely, I needed help!" or
> "Say what you do and do what you say!" or
> "You got everything, I got nothing!" or
> "That's not fair!" etc.

4. Describe what you would like to do to the person to put things back balance.

Again: seek a clear expression of the injury, the issue, and your resulting desire, i.e. What they did to you, why it was wrong, and what you want to have happen.

After you have explored the expressions of your free write thoroughly … and rekindled your emotional connection to the injury, issue and desire therein … go to the scene you are working on and you will see that your own personal point of view can justify and motivate the actions of the character. Superimpose your issue on the character. In this regard you two are identical.

Ask yourself as you rehearse, when the scene is over, as you have played it, is your character's fantasy complete and satisfied? Or is there something more you'd like to chew on, or twist the knife a little further? If there is more you'd like to say, another point you'd like to score, find where in the text you might be able to do this.

Revenge free-write

What do you stand for? What is beyond what you are willing to tolerate? Think about a time when you wanted revenge. Someone did you wrong and you stewed about it. Think back and describe the incident(s) that represented a betrayal or transgression. Write this description out. Use aliases if you must. Then fantasize revenge. Free-write your fantasy.

1. Identify the relationship and what is fair for a person to expect from it.
2. Injury: what was the transgression? How did they violate you? Were you humiliated? Falsely accused? Abused? Set up? Betrayed? Cheated? Lied to? Conned? Insulted? Underestimated? Held in contempt? Manipulated? What?

3. Issue: what was wrong about what they did? Why would you be morally right to extract revenge?
4. Desire: fantasize the perfect revenge. How would you engineer/ design it?
5. Now see how the villain operates, using the circumstances of your personal revenge, applied to the circumstances in the script.

One further note

Look to the sentences in the dialogue which, right from the get go, you have known exactly how to say, or have had a clear connection to. Explore what that sentence implies to you personally and seek to recognize what's underneath the phrase that makes it so easy for you to connect to. You often will find the source of a substantial personal issue or injury that correlates directly from it, to you, to the scene.

Summary

Preparation for the role of the villain

Character traits

- Good screen villains are individuals who are driven (within the context of the story) by a strong sense of various combinations of the following:
    - Independent … they don't care what happens to anyone else.
    - Entitled … they are owed something. They deserve what they want.
    - Iconoclastic … they have no problem breaking the rules or the institutions that are in play, which they frame cynically as agents of hypocrisy or injustice.

- Creative ... they are very intelligent, ingenious ... much smarter than the rest of us.
- All-knowing ... they see through everything, even what the other person is thinking.
- Strong sense of humor (irony/sarcasm) ... they have contempt for the values of the protagonist. Everyone else is a chump, or a fool, or a pest, indulged only as a means to an end.

- **The first type** are those with no empathy, satisfying a psychopathic need, usually a sexual release. For the actor, the nub of the portrayal will lie in the cunning processes by which they lure their prey, and conceal their deeds.

- **The second type** consists of those characters who are driven by some dark inclination to create chaos ... all on a whim, really. The key to portraying these folks is their incredible intelligence and uncanny perceptions, revealed in their ever-present dark sense of humor.

  - "Evil Shadow" exercise

- **The third type** consists of those who get caught up in a scheme to get something ... money, power, revenge, love, etc. These stories involve the villain's own reckoning with an issue, an injury, or a desire. To play these villains effectively, the actor must embody a vivid emotional point of view fortified by a moral justification for their deeds.

  - Injury/issue/desire free write

CHAPTER 16

Lights! Camera! ... *then* Action

SECRETS TO CREATING A WINNING "VIRTUAL" AUDITION

The newest wrinkle in the evolution of on-camera auditioning is the nascent but growing practice of requiring an audition DVD. Known as a "virtual audition," this is not to be confused with what is called the actor's "reel," which is a composite sampling of the actor's past work. The requested video-recording audition tape is specific to the script in question and is meant to be sent to the casting office as a qualifying preliminary to a personal appearance. Actors presently are on their own here, often scrambling to find friends and equipment to record – self-produce, really – the requested scenes.

Obviously, excellent acting is a must. But not so obvious is the problem that producers, like any audience, cannot identify good acting through the fog of poor production quality. It is important that actors know certain basics about camera, lighting and sound technology so that even modest equipment has a chance to yield competitive results. This chapter enumerates the technical variables an actor should consider in the event of having to self-record such a video.

Technical and aesthetic variables

We live in a digital world. The technology is ever-changing. In this chapter I am addressing the critical basic concepts that apply to all video situations no matter what the equipment, with the understanding that however you choose to record your audition, it must eventually be configured to a format that can be transmitted or emailed over the internet.

Technical and aesthetic parameters can enhance or diminish the impact of on-camera performances.

Our goal is to determine the technical and aesthetic variables which:

- create a simple, un-distracting composition that focuses our attention on the actor
- highlight the actor's face while illuminating the eyes
- enable clearly audible sound quality.

The overall rule here is to treat this opportunity in exactly the same way you would if you were reading in person.

In the face of an audition opportunity, you are going to feel rushed and nervous about your acting choices. That's natural. But if you want to be competitive you will need to look after the factors I am discussing here. Be warned that thinking you can tape your audition sitting in front of a webcam would be a mistake … the results will look terrible. The smart thing would be to get the following worked out – as far as equipment and location and someone to help – ahead of time, before you are under the pressure to scurry and put an actual audition on tape.

Here's what you'll need:

- A quiet place with good light, having a plain background, and enough room to work.
- The camera should be of a type with the means of converting your work to a form transmittable over the internet.

Framing

Be aware that television is commonly called a "close-up medium," meaning it is the tighter shots that tell the story best on the small screen. The casting director will be watching your takes on a monitor, not a movie screen. So this is the composition that best accommodates the purposes of a virtual audition.

Referring to the list of terms below, for most virtual auditions the framing should be **medium to medium close-up**. It is this composition that features a clear view of your face and eyes, while also capturing the essence of expressive body movements or gestures. Because it is a tighter shot it has the added benefit of diminishing the importance of being in a specific location.

Some terms:

Long shot:	The whole body, including the environment
Medium long shot:	From the knees up
Medium shot:	From the waist up (best for stage play auditions)
Medium close-up:	From the thorax up (mid chest)
Close-up:	From the clavicle up (shoulders)
Extreme close-up:	Exclusively the whole face or part of the face only

Follow the "1/3" convention: meaning the eyes of the subject should be about one-third of the way down from the top of the frame.

The best framing for comedy? Probably a little wider **medium shot** to make room for a broader physical expression.

Camera position

The position of the camera affects the impression the character makes on the viewer.

The most "invisible" or neutral – and therefore, for on-camera auditions, the best – choice is to position the lens height at the actor's eye level. If the camera is positioned below eye level and is therefore "looking up" to the character, the effect is to make the character look stronger, more ominous, or imposing. If the camera is positioned above eye level, the effect is to "look down" on the character. This angle tends to humble the character, diminish him.

Sound

Perhaps surprisingly, sound quality is the most important of all the factors we are discussing. If the sound is not good, none of the rest matters … not even your acting.

Good sound quality will be influenced by two factors: the proximity of the microphone to the actor, and the nature of the location where you are taping.

Choose a location or room that minimizes distracting audio factors. Lots of hard surfaces, like those in a bare hallway, can cause an echo-y effect that makes a person sound like they are standing in a chamber. And of course you don't want incidental outside background noises intruding into your work. In a professional sound recording studio, heavy soundproof doors, as well as thickly carpeted floors, walls and ceilings, eliminate these problems. Understandably, that extreme is not going to be possible, but you want to consider these factors when selecting a site to videotape your audition.

Did you ever notice that when you are talking to someone on a cell phone you can tell whether they are outside or in a lavatory or hallway? The sound you hear is affected by the nature of the environment. It is a fact – if a bit esoteric – that every room has a unique sound that is affected even by the number of people standing quietly in the room. Professional sound engineers call this factor the "room tone."

The best choice is a well-carpeted room, well-draped, with a minimum of hard surfaces or any extraneous background noise. A plain, solid-colored, sound-absorbent drape or curtain makes a good backdrop for both audio and aesthetic reasons (see "Background" below).

Sound and picture

The other critical audio factor is how close the microphone is to the actor. The closer the better. But for typical amateur set-ups, the microphone will be attached to the camera body. This means that when positioning the camera, you need to be mindful of the sound quality, which will diminish the further the actor is from the camera/ microphone. While it is best to have the microphone as close to the actor as possible, putting the camera too close can not only be distracting for the actor, but also cause a less than complimentary distortion, a "fisheye" broadening of the face. So, experiment with this, juggling both the visual and audio factors to see what works best with the equipment you have.

One other note: The person you are reading with will be off-screen, standing next to the camera. Their sound level will be affected by where they stand relative to the microphone. You need to experiment with where they stand to make sure they are recorded loud enough to be heard, but not so loud that they drown you out.

The background

Choose a setting that offers a plain or nondescript background. Position yourself as far from the background as the situation allows. Being away from the wall or whatever is in the background will draw our undivided attention to you. It will solve the problem of being upstaged by the movement of your own wall shadow behind you. It reduces the perceptibility of distracting background details.

Because of the audio considerations mentioned above, a thick plain-colored drape is a good choice for a backdrop. But it may just as well be one that suits the scripted setting while not distracting the viewer. Remember the subject is you, not it.

There should be nothing moving in the background, nothing to arouse a viewer's curiosity or draw attention even for an instant away from you. If you choose to sit by a window, utilizing its soft indirect light, fine ... or stand near a darkened doorway, fine. But no flowery drapes or distracting posters or any items of curiosity should be in view.

Unless it enhances the scene, you will want to avoid such visual language as "being cornered" or "up against a wall." Avoid unfiltered windows; open doors; any distracting movement in the background.

Color is contrast

Try to pick a background that affords a contrast between the color of whatever is behind you and your skin tone. If you are lighter skinned, try to arrange a set-up, if possible, so that the background is darker or less illuminated than your face. This will draw our attention to you. If you are of a darker skin color, look for a background whose color enhances your face as the focus of our attention.

Lighting

The most complimentary light is "soft." Therefore look for lighting that is diffused, filtered, ambient, or indirect.

Avoid harsh, direct light. From where you stand in front of the camera, if you can see a bare bulb or the direct light from the sun, it is likely that your lighting is harsh and uncomplimentary. If it makes you squint, change it. If it creates strong shadows across your face, change it. If it is situated too directly overhead and therefore shrouds your eyes in shadow, change it.

The simplest solution is often the best ... which means using the light that is in the room naturally; the indirect light that comes through a window or skylight; then perhaps augmenting this light with artificial lighting.

Today's video cameras are effective under surprisingly low light levels. Lower light levels are generally more complimentary and definitely cooler.

Whether or not you use artificial light or work with what is available naturally in the room, it is helpful to understand that classically, all light can be broken down into three sources: "key," "fill" and "back."

Key light

The key light is the main source of illumination. It is what gives depth and modeling to the contours of your face. It has a directionality to it ... somewhat like the sun shining down on you, or that of a single lamp in a darkened room, or of the daylight coming from the only window in a room.

This light comes from a position off-screen to one side or the other of the camera – usually above eye level at the two or ten o'clock position – according to how it best compliments your face. A key light source placed directly out front and too high can make your face look flat like a "mug shot." Placing it too low – like a flashlight under your chin – will make you look like you are in a horror movie.

If you need to use an artificial key light, with today's cameras the best choice is for the light to be of low intensity ... enough to light your face but without spilling over and illuminating the background. Angling the key more to one side or the other so that it lights your face but does not fall on the background helps to enhance the contrast between you and the background.

Fill light

No matter what the source or where it is positioned relative to your face, the key light will often, by definition, cast shadows over the contours of your face. That's what gives depth and distinction to your features. Sometimes it is necessary to soften these shadows – to fill them in. In this case a second light is sometimes used, called the "fill." The fill is a very "soft," frontal light of less intensity than the key – which means it is positioned on the opposite side of the camera from the key and closer to the camera than the key.

Back light

Any light coming from off screen and *behind* the subject is called a "back" light. When all three light sources are working in harmony, the back light highlights the back of the shoulders and the back of the head. It creates a "halo" effect and serves to enhance the subject by separating them visually from the background.

For comedy, "flat" lighting is best – meaning light that illuminates your face and the background evenly with few shadows. More dramatic lighting entails shadows in the background, a darkened ceiling, and more "modeling" of your face.

Note: Don't lose sight of the fact that for scruffy characters you want the technical effects of your DVD to be a little nasty. For the more glamorous or romantic roles, the quality of the lighting should be more refined.

Wardrobe

Re-read the wardrobe chapter and follow its guidelines as to what to wear when reading for a specific character. No costumes. Make sure your wardrobe not only suggests that you would be perfect for the part, but also draws the viewer's attention to your face rather than to some aspect of your garment. Avoid tee-shirts that have a message or distracting graphics. Avoid striped clothing that can set up distracting interference patterns; or jewelry that dangles too much. Avoid fabrics that rustle too much.

Taping sequence

In essence, when you are taping a virtual audition, you are making a little movie. Make a good one.

The slate – meaning you, identifying who you are, in medium close-up – is going to be super-critical. Most virtual auditions are nixed before ever getting past the slate. So how you first appear is critical … and how you present this shot is also critical. To my taste, I don't like a face to suddenly pop in front of me, abruptly appearing on the screen. I like the actor to enter an initially empty frame to slate. It is a judgment call as to which speaks best for the character: either slating "brightly" as if to a good friend; or with attitude.

Suggestions

1. Fade in on the empty (abstract) background. Your name (title card) superimposed.
2. Name (title card) fades out.
3. You enter, pause slightly then slate directly to camera in medium to medium close-up.

At this point you can either start the scene or experiment with the following option.

- After your slate, camera fades to black.
- Fades back up on empty background.
- Subject re-enters from the same direction starting the scene in medium close-up.

    Option: Scene is played with other character off-screen.

    Option: Scene is delivered to camera as if the camera were the other person.

Option: It is sometime possible to re-fashion the scene as if it were a monologue.

Note: If the scene calls for the subject to be talking to two people … make the spatial separation clear, i.e. put "them" far enough apart so we can tell clearly whom you are addressing.

To finish:

It is always most effective, if it can be remotely justified, to exit the frame at the end of the scene. In what direction? This is a judgment call. Use your instinct. It depends on what the scene implies. If the scene substantiates the status quo, exit in the direction you came in from. If the scene implies the character is moving on in life, exit to the opposite direction.

I prefer characters to enter from the left side of the frame, i.e. from "camera left" (as the camera sees it.) If the character is moving on to perform a subsequent scene, exit camera right and re-enter from the left for the second scene. This implies a progression of story. Re-entering the frame from the side you left from makes it seem as if you are re-entering frame to add a second thought.

If you choose to deliver your scene to camera: either exit frame or, if this cannot be justified, look back at who is looking at you … as camera fades out.

Title card

Perhaps your 8 × 10

The importance of having a reel

Because of the overwhelming number of submissions that often result from requests for virtual auditions (sometimes over 1000!) casting agents have procedures for cutting down on the numbers. Many filter out from consideration any audition that does not have a "reel" attached, or at least some supporting video. The submissions with video attached are automatically filtered to the top.

Creating a reel

Your reel should contain only excellent acting, with the best work first. It should be not much more than about two minutes long, shorter if you are short on quality material. It typically should:

1. Start with music fading in over black.
2. Fade in your name over the black screen with the music continuing under.
3. Fade up and dissolve a series of three of your best 8 10 photos. Music continuing under.
4. With the music still playing under, begin an MOS (scenes without dialogue) series of short "looks," each lasting for only three seconds or so, clips of you from film roles you have played.
   The aim is to give the viewer a sense of your "energy" or "quality," what you look like in various situations, each just a short look of you in motion ... e.g. you turning to camera and smiling; you kissing the girl; pointing a gun; celebrating; commanding the troops; standing at the altar; laughing; angry; tossing a bouquet; running out of a room; shouting ... whatever captures the impression you would like to make. Just a little montage series of your best moments on film. Don't be repetitive. Less is more. You understand, this is all unfolding with the music continuing still under.
5. After, say, ten seconds or so of these "looks" you will fade out both the picture and the music.
6. Fade up to your best dialogue scenes. Superimpose for a moment the film's titles with your name if you have them. This sequence of your best scenes should be edited to *feature you*. Use fades, freeze frames, whatever it takes to enhance your best moments. Do not be tempted to tell a story, or to establish a clear context,

which usually means your scene partner will have to be too much included. Show only your best work.

If you don't have scenes of yourself from a film or TV project, create and videotape a monologue. But excellent acting only. Use music, stills, streaming clips, videos, YouTube, some rough some smooth, some dark some light ... whatever you can edit together to create an enticing suggestion of your capacities.

If you are totally without any catalogue of material, I suggest you get an acting friend and a good-quality video camera and go out on a series of Saturdays and film each other in a variety of photographically interesting situations. Don't confuse this with posing or modeling. Real moments only. These snippets would be used with a music accompaniment, to enhance an excellently delivered monologue.

7. End with a label of your name and how you can be easily reached, over black or over a freeze frame that captures you well.

Summary

Viewers reflexively attribute the impressions created by these technical elements to the individual they are watching on the screen.

Camera

- Avoid webcam
- Lens positioned at eye level
- Medium close-up framing
- Camera proximity takes sound quality into effect.

Sound

- If the sound is not clearly audible, nothing else matters.
- Choose a quiet site with no chamber-like echo or distracting off-screen sounds.

- Keep the microphone as close as possible to the actor without being intrusive.
- Balance your audio level with that of your off-screen actor.
- Avoid wardrobe fabrics that rustle.

Background

- Position the subject as far from the background as possible.
- Strive to have the background abstract and/or out of focus, containing no distracting objects or details, including your own shadow.
- Be aware of visual metaphors, e.g. "up against the wall," "backed into a corner."
- Look to create a contrast between your skin tone and the color of the background.

Lighting

- Avoid overhead fluorescent lights.
- Employ light sources that are indirect, soft, filtered, natural.
- Your face should be the most brightly-lit object on the screen.
- Make sure your eyes are clearly visible.
- Avoid harsh facial shadows. Use a fill light to soften if necessary.
- If artificial light is needed, use lower-wattage light sources. Try to keep light off the background.
- Use a back light to highlight the actor if desired.
- Flat, open, uniform light for comedy; darker shadows, pools of light, for drama.

CHAPTER 17

Overall summary and a few choice perspectives

From their desk behind the camera, then, this is what they are looking for in the actor:

1. An eagerness to audition … a sense that the actor has something he is excited to perform or communicate. This quality is evident the instant the actor walks into the room.
2. A professional, experienced demeanor. The actor comes in, commands the space, responds to what he finds in the room, and does what he has to do to "be in the room."
3. A wardrobe detail that enhances the effect of the character in the scene. Wardrobe is more important than a novice might think.
4. The sound of truth, rather than a general presentation of words unconnected to specific purpose, merely imitating the sound of reality.
5. Specificity … the very perceivable phenomenon of an actor talking to a specific person for a specific reason. This implies a specific purpose and specific interpretation of the scene.
6. A sense of place. The actor conveys that the scene is unfolding in a specific place, and that the place, the environment, influences or affects, however subtly, the character's behavior or the unfolding of the event.
7. Thoughtful execution. The events of the scene are thoughtfully adapted to the physical constraints of the audition situation.

8. The character behaves intelligently, resourcefully, and with humor. The character's behavior is appropriate to the circumstances of the scene.
9. The character avoids anger that seeks to punish or destroy, or that comes too easily or goes on too long.
10. The scene is an event. Something transpires.
11. A confident exit.
12. None of the above matters if they are moved or entertained or swept away.

A casting director's good advice

Years ago I was cast as the guest lead in the premier episode for a new series called *Remington Steele*. This is the series that made Pierce Brosnan a star. During a lull in shooting, which was going well, I had a conversation with the casting director, Rubin Cannon, a man who was very supportive of my career. I made an off-handed comment about how frustrating it was for actors, since so often casting decisions seem to have nothing to do with acting ability, but rather the color of your hair or how tall you are. (An actor typically calls his/her agent after a reading that went well only to find out "they went with the blond," for instance.) Rubin set me straight with a very helpful perspective. He said, "Joe, you have to understand, I am paid a lot of money to bring in perhaps 20 actors for a role, all of whom I know to be well suited for the part. Of those 20, eight are going to give great readings and will be called back to read for the producers. Of those eight, all of whom are right for the part, four are going to give Emmy award-winning performances right there in the office. So who are we going to choose? Any of the four would be a great choice, so the producers have the luxury of making their decision based on what seem to be very superficial criteria."

Try not to get discouraged. Frustration is the enemy. Keep studying. Keep plugging. Do your job: read great each and every time.

Thoughts about the shoot itself

Because this book is about auditioning for the camera, I have limited my comments to that. But let me say this: if you observe and practice what I suggest in this book, you will be fairly well prepared for what you find on the set when you get your first job. Yes, there are added considerations that you will deal with on the set. My experience is that they are looking for the actor who makes it work and when they find it – meaning you – they will help you do well when it comes to the shoot. They will treat you like a professional. They are not going to mother you. They are not going to worry about your self-esteem. They are not going to congratulate you for doing what you are being very well paid to do. They won't keep any secrets. It's not a test or a booby trap meant to prove you are no good or too inexperienced. So trust them. If no one is saying anything to you, just keep doing what you're doing, because they would change it if it weren't working.

The best job description I ever heard for the director is: he helps everyone. The medium of film requires a massive collaboration among many artisans with many skills. Each person has been hired because of the specific capabilities that he or she has. You could say that the art of producing is to hire the right combination of personnel with the right combination of talents to create the effect envisioned for the project. Except in rare instances, once the shooting starts, no one is learning as they go. Time is too expensive. The issues and the choices have pretty much been settled during pre-production. The director has been consulted as to the choices that needed to be made about a myriad of issues.

What I'm getting at is that there's not a whole lot of talk on a movie set. The actor is expected to show up prepared. You not only know your lines, but you are to have specific ideas about how the scene will go, anticipating various possibilities: ideas that will work, choices that you're prepared to actualize right then and there. Without a lot of talk about it! Talk can go till midnight.

The actors will gather on the set and rehearse the scene. Do the idea you like best. Just do it. If no one says anything, it's "in." If changes need to be made, you and your coach should have envisioned those possibilities and prepared for them. This shouldn't scare you. Remember, you auditioned successfully, probably twice, counting the callback, sometimes three times just to make sure. Your auditions served in essence as a communication between you and the director as to what he can expect you to bring to the role. That implies that your ideas about the role are valid. You demonstrated them in your audition. He wouldn't have hired you if you two weren't on the same page. So if you have options for him to choose from, be prepared to *show* him the choices, rather than discuss them. A person could get fired for over-indulging some "arty-farty" idea that took valuable time away from the shoot. Until you're a big important star, the time for experimentation is in your rehearsals at home, or on the phone with the director before the shooting begins.

Final comment

YOU CAN HAVE GREAT ART OR PERFECT ART.
... Jascha Heifetz, violinist

Many years ago, as the story goes, the great violinist Jascha Heifetz was recording a concerto with the New York Philharmonic Orchestra. After the recording session was over it was discovered that Mr Heifetz's violin somehow got out of tune during the third movement of the concerto. The record producer urged the maestro to put his instrument in tune and re-record the third movement. Mr Heifetz declined. "But we have it all set up!" said the producer. "All the musicians are here. Everything is in place. All we have to do is re-do the third movement. It won't take 20 minutes." But the great violinist declined yet again, saying, "You can either have great art or perfect art."

Trust your rehearsal. Go in there and get what it is the character wants. Be in the place and deal with the problem in real time. You don't get the part because you say the lines right. You will get the part because you had the guts to go in there and deal in real time with a problem that means something to you personally for a reason that is important, that supports the story and "makes it work." Go for it.

Remember the anecdote I told you about the casting director, Jennifer Part, who stopped me on the steps over at Screen Gems? She said:

> *She never saw me give a bad audition, and that was not a compliment.*

What she was trying to tell me was: you've got to go out on a limb. You're probably not going to get the part unless it means something to you and unless you have a strong point of view. And when it does, you are going to find that you will have to take chances in order to express accurately what that meaning is. And when you are willing to do that, sometimes you are going to be way wrong … but we are artists, we are brave, it goes with the territory, and that's what makes it worth doing.

End

That's all I've got. I hope it helps. You'll see, it turns out salvation is nowhere else but in the work. Break a leg.

Bibliography

Bruder *et al.* (1986) *A Practical Handbook for the Actor*. New York, N.Y., USA, Vintage Books

Caine, Michael (1990) *Acting in Film*. New York, N.Y., USA, Applause Books

Field, Syd (1994) *Screenplay*. New York, N.Y., USA, Dell Publishing

Goldman, William (1983) *Adventures in the Screen Trade*. New York, N.Y., USA, Warner Books

Hagen, Uta (1973) *Respect for Acting*. New York, N.Y., USA, Macmillan

Kissel, Howard (2000) *Stella Adler, The Art of Acting*. New York, N.Y., USA, Applause Books

Linson, Art (1993) *A Pound of Flesh*. New York, N.Y., USA, Grove Press

Mehrabian, A. (1981) *Silent messages: Implicit communication of emotions and attitudes*. Belmont, CA., Wadsworth (currently distributed by Albert Mehrabian, am@kaaj.com)

Meisner, S. and Longwell, D. (1987) *Sanford Meisner on Acting*. New York, N.Y., USA, Vintage Books

Moss, Larry (2005) *The Intent to Live*. New York, N.Y., USA, Bantam Books

Nelson, Shawn (1994) *The Impersonal Actor* (Audiotapes). Box 17706, Beverly Hills, Ca., 90210, USA

See, Joan (1993) *Acting in Commercials*. New York, N.Y., USA, Backstage Books

Shurtleff, Michael (1978) *Audition*. New York, N.Y., USA, Bantam Books

Truby's Writer's Studio (1998). Audiotaped Lectures

Weston, Judith (1996) *Directing Actors*. Studio City, Ca., USA, Michael Wiese Productions

Index

acting, defined, 172
Acting in Commercials (See), 6, 72, 168
acting workshops, 167
action sentences, 18, 24
active looking exercise, 47–8
activities, 101; of characters, 74–8; engrossment in, showing, 51–2, 70–1
actor types, 92–3
Adler, Stella, 79, 99, 101, 137, 144, 156, 160, 168, 171, 204, 236
agents: on-camera interviews, 8–9, 15; meetings with, 4–5, 13, 51–4; monologues for, 55–8; reciprocal nature of relationship, 54–5
Ailes, Roger, 22–3
Alexander, Jason, 217
Altman, Robert, 63
anger meant to punish, avoiding, 218
antagonists, 129, 132, 133, 134, 226
Arnoldi, Charles, 128
As Good as It Gets, 119, 217
attitude, 193

Audition (Shurtleff), 68
auditions, on-camera, 9, 83–104; going first, avoiding, 87–8; introduction of camera to audition process, 3–4; nerves, dealing with, 33–8; pairs, auditioning in, 104–8, 113; planning and communicating proposed activities, 86–7, 90–3; questions, asking, 89–90; reading with someone, 84, 94; setup, 83–4; slating to camera, 14, 94, 102–3, 106–7; strategies, 87–100; villain role *see* villain, auditioning for; wardrobe selection, 137–45; and writers, 115–16; *see also* entering audition room
authenticity, 22–3

back light, 250
background, 247–8, 255
Bass, Ronald, 122
Beatles, The, 10
Beatty, Warren, 9

behavior, 9, 15–16, 21, 50, 217
behavior studies, 6
Bening, Annette, 9
Beretta, 141
Berle, Milton, 208
Bible, 29
big as the room exercise, 44
biggest building exercise, 222–3
Blackmore, Robert, 119, 128
Blake, Robert, 141
body language, 43, 79, 219;
    emotional relationships,
    communicating, 5–6, 15, 18, 21,
    24, 53
Bogdanovitch, Peter, 68
Bone Collector, The, 233
Bonnie and Clyde, 122
Brando, Marlon, 173, 192
Bridges, Jeff, 68
Brooks, James L., 217
Brosnan, Pierce, 257
Bull Durham (film), 160

Caan, James, 97
Caine, Michael, 6
callbacks, 108–12, 113, 143
camera angle, 85
camera frame, establishing size of,
    93–4
camera position, 246, 254
Cannell, Stephen, 16
casting directors, 13, 14, 15, 16, 100,
    212, 257; in audition office, 83,
    84; monologues for, 55–8;
    videotaping of meetings with,
    4–5; *see also* auditions,
    on-camera; interviews, on-
    camera
casting office, calling ahead to, 90
chairs, 53
character portfolio, creating, 201–2
characters, 76, 127, 216; actions of,
    74–8, 191–3; creating, 183–98;

defining of, 222–3; identifying
    nerves of, 36–7, 39; identifying
    "problem," 190–1; issues, 196–8;
    meaning of "character," 183;
    relationships, 194–5;
    underestimating, 187–90
Charlie's Angels, 144
chase scenes, 150
Chekhov, Anton, 140, 193
circumstances, 170, 177; character
    creation, 194–8; physical, 195–6
clichés, 139
Clooney, George, 219
Close, Glenn, 153
close-ups, 85–6, 95, 147; medium,
    91, 93–4, 245
clothing *see* wardrobe selection
color, as contrast, 248
comedy, 245; clues in situation,
    looking for, 214, 220;
    communication skills, 220–1,
    222; contrasts, 216–18; vs.
    drama, 56; guidelines for,
    208–24; preparation for comedic
    roles, 223–4; stand-up, 20; vs.
    tragedy, 213
commercials, 143–4
communication: comedy, 220–1,
    222; of emotional relationships
    see emotional relationships,
    communicating
concentration, 78–81, 175
contemporary choices, monologues,
    56
contingencies, 90–1, 92–3
contrasts, 216–18, 248
conversing with the camera, 41–2,
    45, 47, 61; monologues,
    delivering, 57–8
Cool Hand Luke, 122
Cory, Jeff, 168, 184
Costner, Kevin, 160
costume, vs. wardrobe, 138

Country Music Awards (2008), 28
Cruise, Tom, 122, 124, 146
Cukor, George, 95
Cummings, Robert, 209
cutting, 150

Dahmer, Jeffrey, 227, 228
Damnation Alley, 10
Dark Knight, The, 231
day players, 129–30
De Niro, Robert, 142
deadpan expression, avoiding, 47
decency, 232
deception, 221
Deckter, Ed, 88, 209–11, 213
declarative sentences, 12
demonstration choices, 81
Devil Wears Prada, The, 179, 196
Dewhurst, Colleen, 184
Dexter, 227
dialogue scenes, 150
Directing Actors (Weston), 168
directors, 110–12
Douglas, Kirk, 26–7, 28, 29, 31
Douglas, Michael, 115
drama, structure of, 114–36;
    first act, 120, 122–3, 128–30,
    131; second act, 120–1, 124–5,
    130–2, 133, 135; third act, 122,
    126, 133–4; general, 119–20
dramatic roles, preparation for,
    203–4
dress rehearsals, 137
"dumb" questions, 90, 211

Ed Sullivan Show, The, 174
8mm, 227
Eliot, T.S., 168
Emerson, Michael, 235
Emerson, Ralph Waldo, 3, 14, 15
emotional relationships,
    communicating: to agent, 53; on
    camera, 5–6, 15–16, 18, 19, 21

ending of responses, 46–8
entering audition room, 67–82;
    activities, being engrossed in,
    70–1; concentration, 78–81; and
    decision-makers, 67–70; only
    after being called, 88; presence,
    on-camera, 72–3; *see also*
    auditions, on-camera; entry
    verbs
entry verbs, 73–4, 76, 78, 85, 89,
    191; selection of, 75, 77,
    79–80
Epstein, Brian, 10
era, 178
events, scenes as, 118
evil, 226
Evil Shadow portrayal, 232–3, 236
exit frames, 102
expressiveness, body, 42–4
eye contact, 44–5, 57; with camera,
    49–50
eye movement, 151
eyes, use in photography, 61

Fader, Shanti, 231
Fatal Attraction, 153
Fenton, Mike, 10
Feury, Peggy, 79, 141, 168, 170, 173,
    184
fidgeting, 44
Field, Syd, 116
fill light, 250
film acting, 146–7
film effectiveness, 117–18
first act, 120, 122–3, 128–30, 131
Flood, Peter, 168, 223
Flynn, Michael, 228
Foote, Horton, 156, 161
Ford, Harrison, 127
Forrest Gump, 191
four-foot circle, imaginary, 107,
    108
framing, 245

Free Association Technique, 5, 13–22; exercise, 17
Funny Games, 231

gazing, 151–2
general meetings, 4
Genesis, 29
genre, 178
gestures, 42, 43, 219; emotional relationships, communicating, 5–6, 15, 18, 21, 24, 53
Godfather I, 192–3
Godfather II, 122
Golino, Valeria, 122
good cause, being nervous on behalf of, 33
Gooding, Cuba, 217
greetings, 88
"Grim Sleeper," 228

Hagan, Uta, 72
hand-shaking, avoiding, 88
Hanks, Tom, 191
Harris, Thomas, 158, 162
Hawn, Goldie, 106
headshots, 58–63
Heifetz, Jascha, 259
Hitchcock, Alfred, 209
Hoffman, Dustin, 122, 124, 155–6, 173, 184
Hopkins, Anthony, 184
humour, use of, 52, 53, 231; nerves, dealing with, 28, 32, 33–5, 38, 39
Hunt, Helen, 217

I Can Get It for You Wholesale, 68
ideas, focusing on, 38
impact/impression, creating, 9, 15, 21, 52, 68–9
Impersonal Actor, The (Nelson), 74, 168
incredulity, 218

"Injury/Issue/Desire" (free write exercise), 237–8, 239–40
Intent to Live, The (Moss), 168, 171
internet, 59, 63
interviews, on-camera, 9, 16–17, 23, 40–50; ending of responses, 46–8; expressiveness, body, 42–4; eye contact, 44–5; format, 21; introduction of camera to interview process, 3–4, 5; nerves, dealing with *see* nervousness; relationship with camera, establishing, 48–50; thinking, conveying, 45–6
It Should Happen to You, 95

Jurassic Park, 150

key light, 249
Kinnear, Greg, 217

Last Picture Show, The, 68, 71
lead, reading for, 134–5
leaving happily, 48, 103
Ledger, Heath, 231
Lee, James, 134
Lembeck, Harvey, 213
Lembeck, Michael, 213
Lemmon, Jack, 95
Lenny (film), 173
Levinson, Barry, 122
lighting, 248–50, 255
lines, forgetting, 97
Linson, Art, 54
listening, 161–2
Live on Sunset Strip (stand-up performance), 27
looking: direction of character's gaze, 148, 150–2; in headshots, 61
Lorde, Audre, 33
Lost, 235
love scenes, 132, 136, 151, 204–7
lover metaphor, for camera, 6

magic, making, 35

making believe, 172

Manchurian Candidate, The, 233

Marathon Man, 173

Martin, Dean, 8

Martin, Denise, 235

mask exercise, 232–3

material, choice of, 57

McCain, John, 42

meaning, 20

medium close-up, 91, 93–4, 245

meetings: with agents or casting directors, 4–5, 13, 51–4; of lovers, 205–7

Mehrabian, Albert, 15

Meisner, Sandy, 172, 185

melodramas, 209, 220

memorization, vs. performance, 96–8

"mental verbs," working with, 73, 80

Michael Clayton, 119, 219

"middle distance," 153–4

mindreader, camera as, 4, 5, 6, 25–6, 46

modeling, 60

Molen, Gerald R., 122

moment: imperfection of, acknowledging, 30; public speaking, 38; reality of, commenting on with humor, 33–5, 39, 52, 53

monologues, 55–8, 223, 254

Moonlighting, 71

Moran, Richard, 234

Morrow, Barry, 122

Moss, Larry, 168, 171

motion, and change, 149–53

movements, 149–50

negative comments, avoiding, 48, 112

Negro, Mary Joan, 197

Nelson, Shawn, 74, 153–4, 168, 188

nervousness, 25–39, 58; acknowledging, 26–8, 30, 31–5; on-camera auditions, 33–8; examples from well-known performers, 26–9; humour, use of, 28, 32, 33–5, 39; personal strategy, developing, 29–33; verbalizing how physically manifesting, 28, 31–2, 34, 35, 39

news reporters, 47

Nicholson, Jack, 184, 217

Nicklaus, Jack, 37

Obama, Barack, 42

O'Donnell, Rosie, 28, 31

Oh Brother, Where Art Thou? 219

Old Man, 156–7, 161

Olivier, Laurence, 173, 174–5

on-camera entry *see* entering audition room

opening scenes, 127

O'Reilly, Bill, 28

"over" playing, 95–6, 147

page numbers, 117, 118–19, 128–34

pairs, auditioning in, 104–8, 112, 113; entering in relationship, 105–7

pantomime, avoiding, 102

Part, Jennifer, 169, 170, 260

passion, for characters, 170, 171

Penn, Sean, 32, 138, 173

Perfect Murder, A, 233

performance: audition as, 83; energy of, 221; vs. memorization, 96–8

personifying the camera, 40–2

photography, 59–60

physical perfection, assumption of, 199–200

picture and sound, 247

place, 155–63; "hospital" example, 157, 159–60, 162; metaphor of, 155, 158–62

planning, in auditions, 86–7, 90–1;
and contingencies, 92–3
Plato, 71, 80
plot, 178
poetry, 20
politicians, 6
position, changing, 43, 53
"post slate," 103
posture, 42
Practical Handbook for the Actor,
148
preconceptions, dealing with,
198–203
preliminary meetings, 4
preparation, 167; for comedic roles,
223–4; for dramatic roles, 203–4
presence, on-camera, 72–3
primates, 29
proactive choices, vs. reactive,
186–7
producers, 212
professional milieu, 178
profile, locking in, 108
prompts, 97
props, 98–100, 101
protagonists, 116, 120, 129–35, 180
Pryor, Richard, 27, 28, 29, 31
psychos, 227, 229
public speaking, 15, 31

questions: asking, 15, 89–90;
"dumb," 90, 211; responding to,
14, 16–17, 19, 23–4
Quinn, Anthony, 36

Raiders of the Lost Ark, 127
Rain Man, 122–6
reactions, 146, 147, 149
receptionists, importance of, 52–3
Red Dragon, The (Harris), 158
reels, 243, 252–4
rehearsals, 92, 96, 111, 152, 207
Reinhold, Judge, 209

relationship with camera,
establishing, 48–50
relaxation, 29
Remington Steele, 257
research, 194
"Revenge" (free write exercise),
237–8, 240–1
Richards, Michael, 189
Rocky I, 122
Rogers, Will, 214
romantic scenes, 132, 136, 151,
204–7
Russell, Kurt, 106

sadism, 229, 230
Satan, 231, 234
scenes: breaking down, 181–2;
centering in screenplay, 132–3;
ending, 102; identifying worth of,
37; opening, 127; pairs,
auditioning in, 107–8; physical
actions at beginning of, 191–3;
preparation, 207; story analysis,
179–82
screenplay, 118; scene dead center
in, 132–3; structure, 119–20;
well-written, 126, 178, 209
Screenplay (Field), 116
screenwriting and screenwriters,
20–2, 116–17
script, 102, 149; in hand, 96, 97, 98;
as prop, 100–1
Seagull, The (Chekhov), 193
second act, 120–1, 124–5, 130–2,
133, 135
secret, entering with, 76
See, Joan, 6, 72, 168
Seinfeld, 189, 217
self-deprecating humor, 32, 33–4
self-honesty, 200–3
self-promotion, 58–9
setting, 178
Shadow Self, 203, 232

Shepherd, Cybill, 71
shoots, 258–9
Shurtleff, Michael, 68
sides, 178
Silence of the Lambs, 227
Silent Messages (Mehrabian), 15
simpatico issue, 14, 60, 61
single, the, 85–6
situation comedy, 217, 220, 221
slating to camera, 14, 94, 102–3,
    106–7
Smight, Jack, 10
Smith, Susan, 234
snapshot images, 17, 18
Snyder, James, 238
soap operas, 143
soliloquies, 56, 174
Solkoski, Melvin, 144
sound, 246–7, 254–5
speech, 146–7, 148
Spielberg, Stephen, 150
stage acting, vs. film acting, 146, 147
stage fright *see* nervousness
Stanislavski, Konstantin, 156
stereotypes, 139
story analysis, 177–80
Streetcar Named Desire, A, 173
Streets of San Francisco, 115
Streisand, Barbra, 68
Stutz, Phi, 203
subtext, 146
success, 167
super objective of character, 179
supporting characters, 117, 129,
    131–2, 133, 135, 136, 180

talent, 172
talk shows, 32, 71
taping sequence, 251–2
television, 245
ten-minute rule, 11, 13
tenses, use of, 18
Thalberg, Irving, 20, 21

thinking/thoughts, conveying, 16, 19,
    45–6, 72, 153; in films, 147–8
third act, 122, 126, 133–4
Thompson, Emma, 76
Thornton, Billy Bob, 72
tone of voice *see* vocal tone
Tootsie, 118
Tracy, Spencer, 4
tragedy, vs. comedy, 213
Truby, John, 116
true nature, conveying on camera, 6,
    25–6
Truffaut on Hitchcock, 209
truth, 30, 156; being yourself on
    camera, 4, 5, 8
Tunnel, 151
25% rule, 144
20/20, 26
Twenty-Year Friend technique, 5,
    7–13, 212; auditioning in pairs,
    104, 107, 110; exercise, 11–12;
    meetings with agents, 52, 53, 54
two shot, 85–6, 107

"under" playing, 95–6, 147
Usual Suspects, The, 233

verbs, 93; *see also* entry verbs
videotaping, 55, 108, 243; on-
    camera auditions/interviews, 45,
    68, 84; meetings with agents/
    casting directors, 4–5
villain, auditioning for, 117, 133, 135,
    225–42; first type, 227–30, 242;
    second type, 230–3, 242; third
    type, 233–6, 242; character
    traits, 226–7, 241–2; "free write"
    exercises, 237–8; ordinariness of
    villain, 228; preparation for role,
    241–2
violence, biology of, 228
"virtual" auditions, 243–54; shoots,
    258–9; taping sequence, 251–2;

technical and aesthetic variables, 244–51
vocal tone, 5–6, 15, 18, 21, 24, 53; entering audition room, 79–80
voice projection, 94–6, 219–20; *see also* tone of voice

waiting rooms, 51
Walters, Barbara, 26–7
wardrobe selection, 52, 89, 109, 137–45, 198; headshots, 61–3; "virtual" auditions, 250–1

Welles, Orson, 71
Weston, Judith, 168
Whal, Yale, 51
wide shot, 85
writer's block, 16
Wyeth, Andrew, 168–9

Zane, Lora, 172
zooming in, 106–7